What Readers Are Saying About
Deploying Rails

Deploying Rails will help you transform your deployment process from brittle chaos into something organized, understandable, and repeatable.

➤ **Trek Glowacki**
   Independent developer

Covering such a wide range of useful topics such as deployment, configuration management, and monitoring, in addition to using industry-standard tools following professionally founded best practices, makes this book an indispensable resource for any Rails developer.

➤ **Mitchell Hashimoto**
   Lead developer, Vagrant

Targeted for the developer, *Deploying Rails* presents, in a clear and easily understandable manner, a bevy of some of the less intuitive techniques it has taken me years to assemble as a professional. If you build Rails apps and have ever asked, "Where/how do I deploy this?" this book is for you.

➤ **James Retterer**
   Senior software engineer, Getty Images

Deploying Rails

Automate, Deploy, Scale, Maintain, and Sleep at Night

Anthony Burns

Tom Copeland

The Pragmatic Bookshelf

Dallas, Texas • Raleigh, North Carolina

Many of the designations used by manufacturers and sellers to distinguish their products are claimed as trademarks. Where those designations appear in this book, and The Pragmatic Programmers, LLC was aware of a trademark claim, the designations have been printed in initial capital letters or in all capitals. The Pragmatic Starter Kit, The Pragmatic Programmer, Pragmatic Programming, Pragmatic Bookshelf, PragProg and the linking g device are trademarks of The Pragmatic Programmers, LLC.

Every precaution was taken in the preparation of this book. However, the publisher assumes no responsibility for errors or omissions, or for damages that may result from the use of information (including program listings) contained herein.

Our Pragmatic courses, workshops, and other products can help you and your team create better software and have more fun. For more information, as well as the latest Pragmatic titles, please visit us at *http://pragprog.com*.

The team that produced this book includes:

Brian Hogan (editor)
Potomac Indexing, LLC (indexer)
Kim Wimpsett (copyeditor)
David Kelly (typesetter)
Janet Furlow (producer)
Juliet Benda (rights)
Ellie Callahan (support)

Printed in the United States of America.
ISBN-13: 978-1-93435-695-1
Printed on acid-free paper.
Book version: P01—July, 2012

Contents

Preface ix

Acknowledgments xv

1. Introduction 1
   1.1 Where Do We Host Our Rails Application?   1
   1.2 Building Effective Teams with DevOps   5
   1.3 Learning with MassiveApp   7

2. Getting Started with Vagrant 9
   2.1 Installing VirtualBox and Vagrant   10
   2.2 Configuring Networks and Multiple Virtual Machines   18
   2.3 Running Multiple VMs   21
   2.4 Where to Go Next   24
   2.5 Conclusion   25
   2.6 For Future Reference   25

3. Rails on Puppet 27
   3.1 Understanding Puppet   27
   3.2 Setting Up Puppet   28
   3.3 Installing Apache with Puppet   33
   3.4 Configuring MySQL with Puppet   44
   3.5 Creating the MassiveApp Rails Directory Tree   47
   3.6 Writing a Passenger Module   50
   3.7 Managing Multiple Hosts with Puppet   54
   3.8 Updating the Base Box   55
   3.9 Where to Go Next   56
   3.10 Conclusion   58
   3.11 For Future Reference   59

4.	**Basic Capistrano**		**61**
	4.1	Setting Up Capistrano	62
	4.2	Making It Work	65
	4.3	Setting Up the Deploy	68
	4.4	Pushing a Release	69
	4.5	Exploring Roles, Tasks, and Hooks	76
	4.6	Conclusion	80
5.	**Advanced Capistrano**		**81**
	5.1	Deploying Faster by Creating Symlinks in Bulk	81
	5.2	Uploading and Downloading Files	83
	5.3	Restricting Tasks with Roles	85
	5.4	Deploying to Multiple Environments with Multistage	87
	5.5	Capturing and Streaming Remote Command Output	88
	5.6	Running Commands with the Capistrano Shell	90
	5.7	Conclusion	93
6.	**Monitoring with Nagios**		**95**
	6.1	A MassiveApp to Monitor	96
	6.2	Writing a Nagios Puppet Module	98
	6.3	Monitoring Concepts in Nagios	105
	6.4	Monitoring Local Resources	106
	6.5	Monitoring Services	110
	6.6	Monitoring Applications	121
	6.7	Where to Go Next	125
	6.8	Conclusion	126
	6.9	For Future Reference	127
7.	**Collecting Metrics with Ganglia**		**129**
	7.1	Setting Up a Metrics VM	130
	7.2	Writing a Ganglia Puppet Module	131
	7.3	Using Ganglia Plugins	140
	7.4	Gathering Metrics with a Custom Gmetric Plugin	143
	7.5	Producing Metrics with Ruby	146
	7.6	Where to Go Next	148
	7.7	Conclusion	149
	7.8	For Future Reference	150
8.	**Maintaining the Application**		**153**
	8.1	Managing Logs	153
	8.2	Archiving Application Data	158

	8.3	Organizing Backups and Configuring MySQL Failover	160
	8.4	Making Downtime Better	169
9.		**Running Rubies with RVM**	**173**
	9.1	Installing RVM	174
	9.2	Serving Applications with Passenger Standalone	177
	9.3	Using Systemwide RVM	180
	9.4	Watching Passenger Standalone with Monit	182
	9.5	Contrasting Gemsets and Bundler	184
	9.6	Conclusion	184
10.		**Special Topics**	**185**
	10.1	Managing Crontab with Whenever	185
	10.2	Backing Up Everything	188
	10.3	Using Ruby Enterprise Edition	193
	10.4	Securing sshd	196
	10.5	Conclusion	197
A1.		**A Capistrano Case Study**	**199**
	A1.1	Requires and Variables	199
	A1.2	Hooks and Tasks	201
A2.		**Running on Unicorn and nginx**	**205**
	A2.1	Installing and Configuring nginx	206
	A2.2	Running MassiveApp on Unicorn	208
	A2.3	Deploying to nginx and Unicorn	209
	A2.4	Where to Go Next	210
		Bibliography	**213**
		Index	**215**

Preface

Ruby on Rails has taken the web application development world by storm. Those of us who have been writing web apps for a few years remember the good ol' days when the leading contenders for web programming languages were PHP and Java, with Perl, Smalltalk, and even C++ as fringe choices. Either PHP or Java could get the job done, but millions of lines of legacy code attest to the difficulty of using either of those languages to deliver solid web applications that are easy to evolve.

But Ruby on Rails changed all that. Now thousands of developers around the world are writing and delivering high-quality web applications on a regular basis. Lots of people are programming in Ruby. And there are plenty of books, screencasts, and tutorials for almost every aspect of bringing a Rails application into being.

We say "almost every aspect" because there's one crucial area in which Rails applications are not necessarily a joy; that area is deployment. The most elegant Rails application can be crippled by runtime environment issues that make adding new servers an adventure, unexpected downtime a regularity, scaling a difficult task, and frustration a constant. Good tools do exist for deploying, running, monitoring, and measuring Rails applications, but pulling them together into a coherent whole is no small effort.

In a sense, we as Rails developers are spoiled. Since Rails has such excellent conventions and practices, we expect deploying and running a Rails application to be a similarly smooth and easy path. And while there are a few standard components for which most Rails developers will reach when rolling out a new application, there are still plenty of choices to make and decisions that can affect an application's stability.

And that's why we've written this book. After several years of full-time consulting for companies that were writing and fielding Rails applications, we've learned a few things about running busy Rails applications in production environments. Throughout this book we'll explore various aspects of deploying

Rails applications, and we'll review and apply the practices and tools that helped us keep our consulting clients happy by making their Rails applications reliable, predictable, and, generally speaking, successful. When you finish reading this book, you'll have a firm grasp on what's needed to deploy your application and keep it running. You'll also pick up valuable techniques and principles for constructing a production environment that watches for impending problems and alerts you before things go wrong.

Who Should Read This Book?

This book is for Rails developers who, while comfortable with coding in Ruby and using Rails conventions and best practices, may be less sure of how to get a completed Rails application deployed and running on a server. Just as you learned the Rails conventions for structuring an application's code using REST and MVC, you'll now learn how to keep your application faithfully serving hits, how to know when your application needs more capacity, and how to add new resources in a repeatable and efficient manner so you can get back to adding features and fixing bugs.

This book is also for system administrators who are running a Rails application in production for the first time or for those who have a Rails application or two up and running but would like to improve the runtime environment. You probably already have solid monitoring and metrics systems; this book will help you monitor and measure the important parts of your Rails applications. In addition, you may be familiar with Puppet, the open source system provisioning tool. If so, by the end of this book you'll have a firm grasp on using Puppet, and you'll have a solid set of Puppet manifests. Even if you're already using Puppet, you may pick up a trick or two from the manifests that we've compiled.

Finally, this book is for project managers who are overseeing a project where the primary deliverable is a Rails application that performs some business functionality. You can use the major sections in this book as a checklist. There's a chapter on monitoring; what kind of monitoring is being done on your application, and what kind of situations might occur where would you like to trigger some sort of alert? There's a chapter on metrics; what kind of charts and graphs would best tell you how the application is meeting the business's needs? If your application has some basic story for each chapter in this book, you'll know that you're covering the fundamentals of a solid Rails application environment.

What Is in the Book?

This book is centered around an example social networking application called MassiveApp. While MassiveApp may not have taken the world by storm just yet, we're confident that it's going to be a winner, and we want to build a great environment in which MassiveApp can grow and flourish. This book will take us through that journey.

We'll start with Chapter 2, *Getting Started with Vagrant*, on page 9, where we'll learn how to set up our own virtual server with Vagrant, an open source tool that makes it easy to configure and manage VirtualBox virtual machines.

In Chapter 3, *Rails on Puppet*, on page 27, we'll get an introduction to what's arguably the most popular open source server provisioning tool, Puppet. We'll learn about Puppet's goals, organization, built-in capabilities, and syntax, and we'll build Puppet manifests for the various components of MassiveApp including Apache, MySQL, and the MassiveApp Rails directory tree and supporting files. This chapter will provide you with a solid grasp of the Puppet knowledge that you'll be able to build on in later chapters and, more importantly, in your applications.

In Chapter 4, *Basic Capistrano*, on page 61, we'll explore the premier Rails deployment utility, Capistrano. We'll build a deployment file for MassiveApp, and we'll describe how Capistrano features such as hooks, roles, and custom tasks can make Capistrano a linchpin in your Rails development strategy.

Chapter 5, *Advanced Capistrano*, on page 81 is a deeper dive into more advanced Capistrano topics. We'll make deployments faster, we'll use the Capistrano multistage extension to ease deploying to multiple environments, we'll explore roles in greater depth, and we'll look at capturing output from remote commands. Along the way we'll explain more of the intricacies of Capistrano variables and roles. This chapter will get you even further down the road to Capistrano mastery.

In Chapter 6, *Monitoring with Nagios*, on page 95, we'll look at monitoring principles and how they apply to Rails applications. We'll build a Nagios Puppet module that monitors system, service, and application-level thresholds. We'll build a custom Nagios check that monitors Passenger memory process size, and we'll build a custom Nagios check that's specifically for checking aspects of MassiveApp's data model.

Chapter 7, *Collecting Metrics with Ganglia*, on page 129 will cover the nuts and bolts of gathering metrics around a Rails application, both from an infrastructure level and an application level. We'll install and configure Ganglia, and we'll explore the Ganglia plugin ecosystem. Then we'll write a new Ganglia metric collection plugin for collecting MassiveApp user activity.

Chapter 8, *Maintaining the Application*, on page 153 discusses the ongoing care and feeding of a production Rails application. We'll talk about performing backups, recovering from hardware failures, managing log files, and handling downtime...both scheduled and unscheduled. This chapter is devoted to items that might not arise during the first few days an application is deployed but will definitely come up as the application weathers the storms of user activity.

Chapter 9, *Running Rubies with RVM*, on page 173 covers the Ruby enVironment Manager (RVM). RVM is becoming more and more common as a Rails development tool, and it has its uses in the Rails deployment arena as well. We'll cover a few common use cases for RVM as well as some tricky issues that arise because of how RVM modifies a program's execution environment.

Chapter 10, *Special Topics*, on page 185 discusses a few topics that don't fit nicely into any of the previous chapters but are nonetheless interesting parts of the Rails deployment ecosystem. We'll sweep through the Rails technology stack starting at the application level and proceeding downward to the operating system, hitting on various interesting ideas as we go. You don't need to use these tools and techniques in every Rails deployment, but they're good items to be familiar with.

Finally, we'll wrap up with a few short appendixes. The first will cover a line-by-line review of a Capistrano deployment file, and the second will discuss deploying MassiveApp to an alternative technology stack consisting of nginx and Unicorn.

How to Read This Book

If you're new to Rails deployment, you can read most of this book straight through. The exception would be Chapter 5, *Advanced Capistrano*, on page 81, which you can come back to once you've gotten your application deployed and have used the basic Capistrano functionality for a while.

If you're an advanced Rails developer, you may be more interested in the system administration sections of this book. You can get a working knowledge of Puppet by reading Chapter 3, *Rails on Puppet*, on page 27, and you may pick up some useful monitoring and metrics tips from those chapters. Chapter 8, *Maintaining the Application*, on page 153 is also worth a read to ensure you have your bases covered with applications that you've already deployed.

If you're a system administrator, you may want to read the Rails-specific parts of Chapter 6, *Monitoring with Nagios*, on page 95 and Chapter 7, *Collecting Metrics with Ganglia*, on page 129 to see how to hook monitoring and metrics tools up to a Rails application. You might also be interested in Chapter 8, *Maintaining the Application*, on page 153 to see a few solutions to problems that come up with a typical Rails application. If you have a number of Rails applications running on a single server, you will also be interested in Chapter 9, *Running Rubies with RVM*, on page 173 to see how to isolate those applications' runtime environments.

Throughout this book we'll have short "For Future Reference" sections that summarize the configuration files and scripts presented in the chapter. You can use these as quick-reference guides for using the tools that were discussed; they'll contain the final product without all the explanations.

Tools and Online Resources

Throughout the book we'll be building a set of configuration files. Since we want to keep track of changes to those files, we're storing them in a revision control system, and since Git is a popular revision control system, we're using that. Git's home page[1] contains a variety of documentation options, and you'll find some excellent practical exercises on http://gitready.com/. You'll want to have Git installed to get the most out of the examples.

This book has a companion website[2] where we post articles and interviews and anything else that we think would be interesting to folks who are deploying Rails applications. You can also follow us on Twitter at http://twitter.com/deployingrails/.

The code examples in this book are organized by chapter and then by subject. For example, the chapter on Vagrant includes a sample Vagrantfile for running multiple virtual machines, and the path to the file is shown as vagrant/multiple_vms/Vagrantfile. In this case, all that chapter's code examples are located in the vagrant directory, and this particular file is located in a multiple_vms subdirectory to differentiate it from other example files with the same name. As another example, the chapter on monitoring shows the path to an example file as monitoring/nagios_cfg_host_and_service/modules/nagios/files/conf.d/hosts/app.cfg. In this case, all the examples are in the monitoring directory, nagios_cfg_host_and_service is a subdirectory that provides some structure to the various examples in that

---

1.   http://git-scm.com/
2.   http://deployingrails.com/

chapter, and modules/nagios/files/conf.d/hosts/app.cfg is the path to where the file would actually be located in a Puppet repository. If you're in doubt as to where a particular file would go, you can follow this convention. If it still seems unclear, you can look in the book's repositories on GitHub that we discuss in more detail in Section 1.3, *Learning with MassiveApp*, on page 7.

Acknowledgments

This book pulls together our interactions with so many people that it's hard to list everyone who's helped it come into being. Nonetheless, we'd like to recognize certain individuals in particular.

We'd like to thank the technical reviewers for their efforts. After we reread this text for the fiftieth time, our reviewers read it with fresh eyes and found issues, made pithy suggestions, and provided encouraging feedback. Alex Aguilar, Andy Glover, James Retterer, Jared Richardson, Jeff Holland, Matt Margolis, Mike Weber, Srdjan Pejic, and Trek Glowacki, thank you! Many readers provided feedback, discussions, and errata throughout the beta period; our thanks go out to them (especially Fabrizio Soppelsa, John Norman, Michael James, and Michael Wood) for nailing down many typos and missing pieces and helping us explore many informative avenues.

Many thanks to the professionals at the Pragmatic Bookshelf. From the initial discussions with Dave Thomas and Andy Hunt to the onboarding process with Susannah Pfalzer, we've been impressed with how dedicated, responsive, and experienced everyone has been. A particular thank-you goes to Brian Hogan, our technical editor, for his tireless shepherding of this book from a few sketchy chapter outlines to the finished product. Brian, you've provided feedback when we needed it, suggestions when we didn't know we needed them, and the occasional firm nudge when we were floundering. Thanks for all your time, effort, and encouragement!

This is a tools book; each chapter discusses at least one and usually several open source projects. The authors of these tools have made our lives better, and this book possible, by their long-term efforts. So, a hearty thank-you to Mitchell Hashimoto for Vagrant, Luke Kanies for Puppet, Yukihiro Matsumoto for Ruby, David Heinemeier Hansson for Ruby on Rails, Matt Massie for Ganglia, Ethan Galstad for Nagios, and all the other leaders of the projects we use in this book.

Anthony Burns

Foremost, I'd like to thank my loving wife, Ellie, for putting up with all the long nights spent locked in my office. For my part in this book, I could not have done it without the knowledge and experience of Tom Copeland to back me up every step of the way. I would also like to thank my wonderful parents, Anne and Tim, as well as Chad Fowler, Mark Gardner, Rich Kilmer, and the rest of the folks formerly from InfoEther for opening all of the doors for me that enabled me to help write this book. And lastly, without the shared motivations of my good friend Joshua Kurer, I would never have made it out to the East Coast to begin the journey that led me here today.

Tom Copeland

Thanks to my coauthor, Tony Burns, for his willingness to dive into new technologies and do them right. Using Vagrant for this book's many exercises was an excellent idea and was entirely his doing.

Thanks to Chris Joyce, who got me started by publishing my first two books under the umbrella of Centennial Books. The next breakfast is on me!

Finally, a very special thanks to my wife, Alina, and all our children for allowing me the many hours that I poured into this project and, better still, for supporting and encouraging me throughout.

## CHAPTER 1

Introduction

A great Rails application needs a great place to live. We have a variety of choices for hosting Rails applications, and in this chapter we'll take a quick survey of that landscape.

Much of this book is about techniques and tools. Before diving in, though, let's make some more strategic moves. One choice that we need to make is deciding where and how to host our application. We also want to think philosophically about how we'll approach our deployment environment. Since the place where we're deploying to affects how much we need to think about deployment technology, we'll cover that first.

1.1 Where Do We Host Our Rails Application?

Alternatives for deploying a Rails application generally break down into either using shared hosting, via Heroku, or rolling your own environment at some level. Let's take a look at those options.

Shared Hosting

One option for hosting a Rails application is to rent resources in a shared hosting environment. A shared hosting environment means that your application is running on the same server as many other applications. The advantage of shared hosting is cost; the price is usually quite good. There's also a quick ramp-up time; you can have an application deployed and fielding requests within a few minutes of signing up for an account and configuring your domain name. There's no need for any capital investment (no writing big checks for hardware), and any future server failures are someone else's problem.

The downsides are considerable, though. Shared hosting, as the name implies, means that the resources that are hosting the application are, well, *shared*. The costs may be low for a seemingly large amount of resources, such as disk space and bandwidth. However, once you start to use resources, the server your application is hosted on can often encounter bottlenecks. When another user's application on the same server has a usage spike, your own application may respond more slowly or even lock up and stop responding, and there isn't much you can do about it. Therefore, you can expect considerable variation in application performance depending on what else is happening in the vicinity of your application's server. This can make performance issues come and go randomly; a page that normally takes 100 milliseconds to load can suddenly spike to a load time of two to three seconds with no code changes. The support and response time is usually a bit rough since just a few operations engineers will be stretched between many applications. Finally, although hardware issues are indeed someone else's problem, that someone else will also schedule server and network downtime as needed. Those downtime windows may not match up with your plans.

That said, shared hosting does still have a place. It's a good way to get started for an application that's not too busy, and the initial costs are reasonable. If you're using shared hosting, you can skip ahead to the Capistrano-related chapters in this book.

Heroku

Heroku is a popular Rails hosting provider. It deserves a dedicated discussion simply because the Heroku team has taken great pains to ensure that deploying a Rails application to Heroku is virtually painless. Once you have an account in Heroku's system, deploying a Rails application is as simple as pushing code to a particular Git remote. Heroku takes care of configuring and managing your entire infrastructure. Even when an application needs to scale, Heroku continues to fit the bill since it handles the usual required tasks such as configuring a load balancer. For a small application or a team with limited system administration expertise, Heroku is an excellent choice.

The hands-off nature of deploying on Heroku does have its drawbacks. One downside is that, like with shared hosting, the cost rapidly increases as your application's usage grows. Heroku's prices are reasonable given the excellent quality of the service, but this is nonetheless something to consider. Another downside is the lack of flexibility. Heroku has a defined set of tools that your application can use; for example, your application must run atop the PostgreSQL relational database rather than using MySQL.

There are other limitations, some of which can be worked around using Heroku's "add-ons," but generally speaking, by outsourcing your hosting to Heroku, you're choosing to give up some flexibility in exchange for having someone else worry about maintaining your application environment. There are some practical issues, such as the lack of access to logs, and finally, some businesses may have security requirements or concerns that prevent them from putting their data and source code on servers they don't own. For those use cases, Heroku is out of the question.

Like shared hosting, Heroku may be the right choice for some. We choose not to focus on this deployment option in this book since the Heroku website has a large collection of up-to-date documentation devoted to that topic.

Rolling Your Own Environment

For those who have quickly growing applications and want more control, we come to the other option. You can build out your own environment. Rolling your own application's environment means that you're the system manager. You're responsible for configuring the servers and installing the software that will be running the application. There's some flexibility in these terms; what we're addressing here is primarily the ability to do your own operating system administration. Let's look at a few of the possibilities that setting up your own environment encompasses.

In the Cloud

When creating your own environment, one option is to use a cloud-based virtual private server (VPS) service such as Amazon's Elastic Computing Cloud or the Rackspace Cloud. VPSs have rapidly become one of the most popular options for deploying web applications. With a VPS, you don't have a physical server, but you will have a dedicated virtual machine (VM) that needs to be configured. You won't have to worry about stocking spare parts, you won't have any capital expenditures, and any downtime issues will be handled by your hosting provider. On the downside, you are using a VM, so performance issues can pop up unexpectedly. Disk input/output performance is something to consider with a VM, especially with data-centric applications. Costs may also increase dramatically as the application resource needs grow. But you do have full control over the software above the operating system layer; if you want to run the latest beta of MySQL or deploy an Erlang component, that's a decision you're free to make.

Managed VMs with Engine Yard

Engine Yard's platform-as-a-service offer lies somewhere between deploying to Heroku and running your own virtual server. Engine Yard provides a layer atop Amazon's cloud offerings so that you have an automatically built set of virtual servers configured (via Chef) with a variety of tools and services. If needed, you can customize the Chef recipes used to build those servers, modify the deployment scripts, and even ssh directly into the instances. Engine Yard also provides support for troubleshooting application problems. The usual caveats apply; outsourcing to a platform implies some loss of flexibility and some increase in cost, but it's another point on the deployment spectrum.

Dedicated Hosting

Getting closer to the metal, another option is to host your application on a dedicated machine with a provider like Rackspace or SoftLayer. With that choice, you can be sure you have physical hardware dedicated to your application. This option eliminates a whole class of performance irregularities. The up-front cost will be higher since you may need to sign a longer-term contract, but you also may need fewer servers since there's no virtualization layer to slow things down. You'll also need to keep track of your server age and upgrade hardware once every few years, but you'll find that your account representative at your server provider will be happy to prompt you to do that. There's still no need to stock spare parts since your provider takes care of the servers, and your provider will also handle the repair of and recovery from hardware failures such as bad disk drives, burned-out power supplies, and so on.

As with a cloud-based VPS solution, you'll be responsible for all system administration above the basic operation system installation and the network configuration level. You'll have more flexibility with your network setup, though, since your provider can physically group your machines on a dedicated switch or router; that usually won't be an option for a cloud VM solution.

Colocation and Building Your Own Servers

A still lower-level option is to buy physical servers from a reseller (or build them from components) and host them either in a colocation facility or in a space that you own and operate. An example of this might be the server room in your building. This gives you much more control over hardware and networking but will also require that your team handles hardware failures and troubleshoots networking issues. Some will find this requirement a good motivation for building better fault tolerance into their application's architecture. The capital cost of buying the servers and power control systems and the operational cost of hiring staff for your datacenter are considerations, and there's always the fear of over or under-provisioning your capacity. But if you need more control than hosting with a provider, this is the way to go.

A Good Mix

We feel that a combination of physical servers at a server provider and some cloud servers provides a good mix of performance and price. The physical servers give you a solid base of operations, while the cloud VMs let you bring on temporary capacity as needed.

This book is targeted for those who are rolling their own environment in some regard, whether the environment is all in the cloud, all on dedicated servers, or a mix of the two. And if that's your situation, you may already be familiar with the term *DevOps*, which we'll discuss next.

1.2 Building Effective Teams with DevOps

While Ruby on Rails is sweeping through the web development world, a similar change is taking place in the system administration and operations world under the name DevOps. This term was coined by Patrick Debois to describe "an emerging set of principles, methods, and practices for communication, collaboration, and integration between software development (application/software engineering) and IT operations (systems administration/infrastructure) professionals."[1] In other words, software systems tend to run more smoothly when the people who are writing the code and the people who are running the servers are all working together.

This idea may seem either a truism or an impossible dream depending on your background. In some organizations, software is tossed over the wall from development to operations, and after a few disastrous releases, the operations team learns to despise the developers, demand meticulous documentation for each release, and require the ability to roll back a release at the first sign of trouble. In other organizations, developers are expected to understand some system administration basics, and operations team members are expected to do enough programming so that a backtrace isn't complete gibberish. Finally, in the ideal DevOps world, developers and operations teams share expertise, consult each other regularly, plan new features together, and generally work side by side to keep the technical side of the company moving forward and responding to the needs of the business.

---

1. http://en.wikipedia.org/wiki/DevOps

One of the primary practical outcomes of the DevOps movement is a commitment to automation. Let's see what that means for those of us who are developing and deploying Rails applications.

Automation Means Removing Busywork

Automation means that we're identifying tasks that we do manually on a regular basis and then getting a computer to do those tasks instead. Rather than querying a database once a day to see how many users we have, we write a script that queries the database and sends us an email with the current user count. When we have four application servers to configure, we don't type in all the package installation commands and edit all the configuration files on each server. Instead, we write scripts so that once we have one server perfectly configured, we can apply that same configuration to the other servers in no more time than it takes for the packages to be downloaded and installed. Rather than checking a web page occasionally to see whether an application is still responding, we write a script to connect to the application and send an email if the page load time exceeds some threshold.

Busywork doesn't mean that the work being done is simple. That iptables configuration may be the result of hours of skillful tuning and tweaking. It turns into busywork only when we have to type the same series of commands each time we have to roll it out to a new server. We want repeatability; we want to be able to roll a change out to dozens of servers in a few seconds with no fear of making typos or forgetting a step on each server. We'd also like to have records showing that we did roll it out to all the servers at a particular time, and we'd like to know that if need be, we can undo that change easily.

Automation Is a Continuum

Automation is like leveling up; we start small and try to keep improving. A shell script that uses curl to check a website is better than hitting the site manually, and a monitoring system that sends an email when a problem occurs and another when it's fixed is better still. Having a wiki[2] with a list of notes on how to build out a new mail server is an improvement over having no notes and trying to remember what we did last time, and having a system that can build a mail server with no manual intervention is even better. The idea is to make progress toward automation bit by bit; then we can look around after six months of steady progress and be surprised at how far we've come.

---

2.   http://en.wikipedia.org/wiki/Wiki

We want to automate problems as they manifest themselves. If we have one server and our user base tops out at five people, creating a hands-off server build process may not be our biggest bang for the buck. But if those five users are constantly asking for the status of their nightly batch jobs, building a dashboard that lets them see that information without our intervention may be the automation we need to add. This is the "Dev" in DevOps; writing code to solve problems is an available option.

So, we're not saying that everything must be automated. There's a point at which the time invested in automating rarely performed or particularly delicate tasks is no longer being repaid; as the saying goes, "Why do in an hour what you can automate in six months?" But having a goal of automating as much as possible is the right mind-set.

Automation: Attitude, Not Tools

Notice that in this automation discussion we haven't mentioned any software package names. That's not because we're averse to using existing solutions to automate tasks but instead that the automation itself, rather than the particular technological means, is the focus. There are good tools and bad tools, and in later chapters we'll recommend some tools that we use and like. But any automation is better than none.

Since we're talking about attitude and emotions, let's not neglect the fact that automation can simply make us happier. There's nothing more tedious than coming to work and knowing that you have to perform a repetitive, error-prone task for hours on end. If we can take the time to turn that process into a script that does the job in ten minutes, we can then focus on making other parts of the environment better.

That's the philosophical background. To apply all of these principles in the rest of this book, we'll need an application that we can deploy to the servers that we'll be configuring. Fortunately, we have such an application; read on to learn about MassiveApp.

1.3 Learning with MassiveApp

MassiveApp, as befits its name, is a social networking application that we expect to be wildly successful just as soon as we can get the word out to all the popular blogs and start-up news sites. The primary innovation that MassiveApp brings is the ability to share URLs with other people; we think it's really going to take off. If not, we'll add it to our résumé as a growing experience. In the meantime, we've built ourselves a fine application, and we want to deploy it into a solid environment.

For the purposes of illustrating the tools and practices in this book, we're fortunate that MassiveApp is also a fairly conventional Rails 3.2 application. It uses MySQL as its data store, implements some auditing requirements, and has several tables (accounts, shares, and bookmarks) that we expect to grow at a great rate. It's a small application (as you can see in its Git repository[3]), but we still want to start off with the right infrastructure pieces in place.

Since we're building a Rails deployment environment, we also have a companion repository that contains all our system configuration and Puppet scripts. This is located on GitHub as well.[4] It has not only the finished configuration but also Git branches that we can use to build each chapter's configuration from scratch.

Let's set up those directories. First we'll create a deployingrails directory and move into it.

```
$ mkdir ~/deployingrails
$ cd ~/deployingrails
```

Now we can clone both repositories.

```
$ git clone git://github.com/deployingrails/massiveapp.git
Cloning into 'massiveapp'...
remote: Counting objects: 237, done.
remote: Compressing objects: 100% (176/176), done.
remote: Total 237 (delta 93), reused 189 (delta 45)
Receiving objects: 100% (237/237), 42.97 KiB, done.
Resolving deltas: 100% (93/93), done.
$ git clone git://github.com/deployingrails/massiveapp_ops.git
«very similar output»
```

We'll be creating quite a few subdirectories in the deployingrails directory as we work to get MassiveApp deployed.

We've established some of the underlying principles of deployment and DevOps. Let's move on to seeing how we can set up the first thing needed for successful deployments: our working environment. In the next chapter, we'll explore two useful utilities that will let us practice our deployments and server configuration without ever leaving the comfort of our laptop.

---

3. https://github.com/deployingrails/massiveapp
4. https://github.com/deployingrails/massiveapp_ops

## CHAPTER 2

Getting Started with Vagrant

In the previous chapter, we discussed choosing a hosting location and decided that rolling our own environment would be a good way to go. That being the case, knowing how to construct a home for MassiveApp is now at the top of our priority list. We don't want to leap right into building out our actual production environment, though. Instead, we'd like to practice our build-out procedure first. Also, since MassiveApp will run on several computers in production, it would be handy to run it on several computers in a practice environment as well.

You may well have a couple of computers scattered about your basement, all whirring away happily. But these computers probably already have assigned roles, and rebuilding them just for the sake of running this book's exercises is not a good use of your time. At work, you may have access to an entire farm of servers, but perhaps you don't want to use those as a test bed; even simple experiments can be a little nerve-racking since an errant network configuration can result in getting locked out of a machine.

Another possibility is to fire up a few server instances in the cloud. By *cloud* we mean any of a number of virtual machine providers, like Amazon's Elastic Computing Cloud (EC2), the Rackspace Cloud, Slicehost, Bytemark, and so forth. The downside of using these cloud providers is that you'll be charged for the time you use. Worse yet, suppose you start up an instance and forget about it. Over the course of a week or two, it could burn five, even ten, dollars of your hard-earned money! And we don't want to be responsible for suggesting that. There's also the need for a good network connection when working with cloud servers, and even a fast connection might not be enough to handle large file transfers effectively. Finally, you (or your employee) may have concerns about putting your company's code and data onto servers over which you have no physical control.

Instead, we'll explore two tools: VirtualBox[1] and Vagrant.[2] These will let us run VM instances on our computer. To quote from the Vagrant website, Vagrant is "a tool for building and distributing virtualized development environments." It lets you manage virtual machines using Oracle's VirtualBox and gives you the ability to experiment freely with a variety of operating systems without fear of damaging a "real" server.

Setting up these tools and configuring a few virtual machines will take a little time, so there is an initial investment here. But using these tools will allow us to set up a local copy of our production environment that we'll use to develop our system configuration and test MassiveApp's deployment. And as MassiveApp grows and we want to add more services, we'll have a safe and convenient environment in which to try new systems.

2.1   Installing VirtualBox and Vagrant

First we need to install both Vagrant and VirtualBox.

Installing VirtualBox

Vagrant is primarily a driver for VirtualBox virtual machines, so VirtualBox is the first thing we'll need to find and install. VirtualBox is an open source project and is licensed under the General Public License (GPL) version 2, which means that the source code is available for our perusal and we don't have to worry too much about it disappearing. More importantly for our immediate purposes, installers are available for Windows, Linux, Macintosh, and Solaris hosts on the VirtualBox website.[3] There's also an excellent installation guide for a variety of operating systems on the site.[4] Armed with those resources, we can download and run the installer to get going. We'll want to be sure to grab version 4.1 or newer, because current releases of Vagrant depend on having a recent VirtualBox in place.

Now that VirtualBox is installed, we can run it and poke around a bit; it's an extremely useful tool by itself. In the VirtualBox interface, there are options to create virtual machines and configure them to use a certain amount of memory, to have a specific network configuration, to communicate with serial and USB ports, and so on. But now we'll see a better way to manage our VirtualBox VMs.

---

1.   http://virtualbox.org
2.   http://vagrantup.com
3.   http://www.virtualbox.org/wiki/Downloads
4.   http://www.virtualbox.org/manual/ch04.html

Installing Vagrant

The next step is to install Vagrant on our computer. The Vagrant developers have thoughtfully provided installers for a variety of systems, so let's go to the download page.[5] There we can grab the latest release (1.0.2 as of this writing) and install it. This is the preferred method of installation, but if you need to, you can also fall back to installing Vagrant as a plain old RubyGem.

Once we've installed Vagrant, we can verify that all is well by running the command-line tool, aptly named vagrant, with no arguments. We'll see a burst of helpful information.

```
$ vagrant
Usage: vagrant [-v] [-h] command [<args>]

    -v, --version                  Print the version and exit.
    -h, --help                     Print this help.

Available subcommands:
     box
     destroy
     halt
     init
     package
     provision
     reload
     resume
     ssh
     ssh-config
     status
     suspend
     up
«and more»
```

We can also get more information on any command by running vagrant with the command name and the -h option.

```
$ vagrant box -h
Usage: vagrant box <command> [<args>]

Available subcommands:
     add
     list
     remove
     repackage
```

---

5. http://downloads.vagrantup.com/

Now that Vagrant is installed, we'll use it to create a new VM on which to hone our Rails application deployment skills.

Creating a Virtual Machine with Vagrant

Vagrant has built-in support for creating Ubuntu 10.04 virtual machines, and we've found Ubuntu to be a solid and well-maintained distribution. Therefore, we'll use that operating system for our first VM. The initial step is to add the VM definition; in Vagrant parlance, that's a *box*, and we can add one with the vagrant box add command. Running this command will download a large file (the Ubuntu 10.04 64-bit image, for example, is 380MB), so wait to run it until you're on a fast network, or be prepared for a long break.

```
$ vagrant box add lucid64 http://files.vagrantup.com/lucid64.box
[vagrant] Downloading with Vagrant::Downloaders::HTTP...
[vagrant] Downloading box: http://files.vagrantup.com/lucid64.box
«a nice progress bar»
```

The name "lucid64" is derived from the Ubuntu release naming scheme. "lucid" refers to Ubuntu's 10.04 release name of Lucid Lynx, and "64" refers to the 64-bit installation rather than the 32-bit image. We could give this box any name (for example, vagrant box add my_ubuntu http://files.vagrantup.com/lucid64.box would name the box my_ubuntu), but we find that it's easier to keep track of boxes if they have names related to the distribution.

Ubuntu is a popular distribution, but it's definitely not the only option. A variety of other boxes are available in the unofficial Vagrant box index.[6]

Once the box is downloaded, we can create our first virtual machine. Let's get into the deployingrails directory that we created in Section 1.3, *Learning with MassiveApp*, on page 7.

```
$ cd ~/deployingrails/
$ mkdir first_box
$ cd first_box
```

Now we'll run Vagrant's init command to create a new Vagrant configuration file, which is appropriately named Vagrantfile.

```
$ vagrant init
A `Vagrantfile` has been placed in this directory. You are now
ready to `vagrant up` your first virtual environment! Please read
the comments in the Vagrantfile as well as documentation on
`vagrantup.com` for more information on using Vagrant.
```

---

6. http://vagrantbox.es

Where Am I?

One of the tricky bits about using virtual machines and showing scripting examples is displaying the location where the script is running. We're going to use a shell prompt convention to make it clear where each command should be run.

If we use a plain shell prompt (for example, $), that will indicate that a command should be run on the host, in other words, on your laptop or desktop machine.

If a command is to be run inside a virtual machine guest, we'll use a shell prompt with the name of the VM (for example, vm $). In some situations, we'll have more than one VM running at once; for those cases, we'll use a prompt with an appropriate VM guest name such as nagios $ or app $.

Let's open Vagrantfile in a text editor such as TextMate or perhaps Vim. Don't worry about preserving the contents; we can always generate a new file with another vagrant init. We'll change the file to contain the following bit of Ruby code, which sets our first VM's box to be the one we just downloaded. Since we named that box lucid64, we need to use the same name here.

introduction/Vagrantfile
```
Vagrant::Config.run do |config|
  config.vm.box = "lucid64"
end
```

That's the bare minimum to get a VM running. We'll save the file and then start our new VM by running vagrant up in our first_box directory.

```
$ vagrant up
[default] Importing base box 'lucid64'...
[default] Matching MAC address for NAT networking...
[default] Clearing any previously set forwarded ports...
[default] Forwarding ports...
[default] -- 22 => 2222 (adapter 1)
[default] Creating shared folders metadata...
[default] Clearing any previously set network interfaces...
[default] Booting VM...
[default] Waiting for VM to boot. This can take a few minutes.
[default] VM booted and ready for use!
[default] Mounting shared folders...
[default] -- v-root: /vagrant
```

Despite the warning that "This can take a few minutes," this entire process took just around a minute on a moderately powered laptop. And at the end of that startup interval, we can connect into our new VM using ssh.

```
$ vagrant ssh
Last login: Wed Aug 11 17:51:58 2010
vm $
```

VirtualBox Guest Additions

When firing up a new VirtualBox instance, you may get a warning about the "guest additions" not matching the installed version of VirtualBox. The guest additions make working with a VM easier; for example, they allow you to change the guest window size. They are included with VirtualBox as an ISO image within the installation package, so to install the latest version, you can connect into your VM and run these commands:

```
vm $ sudo apt-get install dkms -y
vm $ sudo /dev/cdrom/VBoxLinuxAdditions-x86.run
```

If you're running Mac OS X and you're not able to find the ISO image, look in the Applications directory and copy it over if it's there; then mount, install, and restart the guest.

```
$ cd ~/deployingrails/first_box/
$ cp /Applications/VirtualBox.app/Contents/MacOS/VBoxGuestAdditions.iso .
$ vagrant ssh
vm $ mkdir vbox
vm $ sudo mount -o loop /vagrant/VBoxGuestAdditions.iso vbox/
vm $ sudo vbox/VBoxLinuxAdditions.run
Verifying archive integrity... All good.
Uncompressing VirtualBox 4.1.12 Guest Additions for Linux.........
«and more output»
vm $ exit
$ vagrant reload
```

Alternatively, you can download the guest additions from the VirtualBox site.

```
vm $ mkdir vbox
vm $ wget --continue --output-document \
  vbox/VBoxGuestAdditions_4.1.12.iso\
   http://download.virtualbox.org/virtualbox/4.1.12/VBoxGuestAdditions_4.1.12.iso
vm $ sudo mount -o loop vbox/VBoxGuestAdditions_4.1.12.iso vbox/
«continue as above»
```

This is all the more reason to build a base box; you won't want to have to fiddle with this too often.

Take a moment to poke around. You'll find that you have a fully functional Linux host that can access the network, mount drives, stop and start services, and do all the usual things that you'd do with a server.

When we create a VM using Vagrant, under the covers Vagrant is invoking the appropriate VirtualBox APIs to drive the creation of the VM. This results in a new subdirectory of ~/VirtualBox VMs/ with the virtual machine image, some log files, and various other bits that VirtualBox uses to keep track of VMs. We can delete the Vagrantfile and the VM will still exist, or we can delete the VM (whether in the VirtualBox user interface or with Vagrant) and the Vagrantfile will still exist. We've found it's most convenient to treat the Vagrantfile and the VM as being connected, though; that way, we can completely manage the VM with Vagrant.

Working with a Vagrant Instance

We can manage this VM using Vagrant as well. As we saw in the vagrant command output in *Installing Vagrant*, on page 11, we can suspend the virtual machine, resume it, halt it, or outright destroy it. And since creating new instances is straightforward, there's no reason to keep an instance around if we're not using it.

We connected into the VM without typing a password. This seems mysterious, but remember the "Forwarding ports" message that was printed when we ran vagrant up? That was reporting that Vagrant had successfully forwarded port 2222 on our host computer to port 22 on the virtual machine. To show that there's nothing too mysterious going on, we can bypass Vagrant's vagrant ssh port-forwarding whizziness and ssh into the virtual machine. We're adding several ssh options (StrictHostKeyChecking and UserKnownHostsFile) that vagrant ssh adds by default, and we can enter vagrant when prompted for a password.

```
$ ssh -p 2222 \
  -o StrictHostKeyChecking=no -o UserKnownHostsFile=/dev/null vagrant@localhost
Warning: Permanently added '[localhost]:2222' (RSA) to the list of known hosts.
vagrant@localhost's password:
Last login: Thu Feb  2 00:01:58 2012 from 10.0.2.2
vm $
```

Vagrant includes a "not so private" private key that lets vagrant ssh connect without a password. We can use this outside of Vagrant by referencing it with the -i option.

```
$ ssh -p 2222 \
  -o StrictHostKeyChecking=no -o UserKnownHostsFile=/dev/null \
  -i ~/.vagrant.d/insecure_private_key vagrant@localhost
Warning: Permanently added '[localhost]:2222' (RSA) to the list of known hosts.
Last login: Thu Feb  2 00:03:34 2012 from 10.0.2.2
vm $
```

The Vagrant site refers to this as an "insecure" key pair, and since it's distributed with Vagrant, we don't recommend using it for anything else. But it does help avoid typing in a password when logging in. We'll use this forwarded port and this insecure private key extensively in our Capistrano exercises.

Now we have a way of creating VMs locally and connecting to them using ssh. We're getting closer to being able to deploy MassiveApp, but first let's work with Vagrant so that our newly created virtual machines will have all the tools we'll need to run MassiveApp.

Building a Custom Base Box

We used the stock Ubuntu 10.04 64-bit base box to build our first virtual machine. Going forward, though, we'll want the latest version of Ruby to be installed on our virtual machines. So, now we'll take that base box, customize it by installing Ruby 1.9.3, and then build a new base box from which we'll create other VMs throughout this book. By creating our own customized base box, we'll save a few steps when creating new VMs; for example, we won't have to download and compile Ruby 1.9.3 each time.

Let's create a new virtual machine using the same Vagrantfile as before. First we'll destroy the old one just to make sure we're starting fresh; we'll use the force option so that we're not prompted for confirmation.

```
$ cd ~/deployingrails/first_box
$ vagrant destroy --force
[default] Forcing shutdown of VM...
[default] Destroying VM and associated drives...
```

This time we have a basic Vagrantfile in that directory, so we don't even need to run vagrant init. For this VM we won't have to download the base box, so creating it will take only a minute or so. We'll execute vagrant up to get the VM created and running.

```
$ vagrant up
$ vagrant ssh
vm $
```

Our VM is started and we're connected to it, so let's use the Ubuntu package manager, apt-get, to fetch the latest Ubuntu packages and install some development libraries. Having these in place will let us compile Ruby from source and install Passenger.

```
vm $ sudo apt-get update -y
vm $ sudo apt-get install build-essential zlib1g-dev libssl-dev libreadline-dev \
     git-core curl libyaml-dev libcurl4-dev libsqlite3-dev apache2-dev -y
```

Now we'll remove the Ruby installation that came with the lucid64 base box.

```
vm $ sudo rm -rf /opt/vagrant_ruby
```

Next we'll download Ruby 1.9.3 using curl. The --remote-name flag tells curl to save the file on the local machine with the same filename as the server provides.

```
vm $ curl --remote-name http://ftp.ruby-lang.org/pub/ruby/1.9/ruby-1.9.3-p194.tar.gz
```

Now we can uncompress the file, move into the expanded directory, and compile the code.

```
vm $ tar zxf ruby-1.9.3-p194.tar.gz
vm $ cd ruby-1.9.3-p194/
vm $ ./configure
«lots of output»
vm $ make
«and more output»
vm $ sudo make install
«still more output»
```

We'll verify that Ruby is installed by running a quick version check.

```
vm $ ruby -v
ruby 1.9.3p194 (2012-04-20 revision 35410) [x86_64-linux]
```

Next we'll verify the default gems are in place.

```
vm $ gem list

*** LOCAL GEMS ***

bigdecimal (1.1.0)
io-console (0.3)
json (1.5.4)
minitest (2.5.1)
rake (0.9.2.2)
rdoc (3.9.4)
```

We've set up our VM the way we want it, so let's log out and package up this VM as a new base box.

```
vm $ exit
$ vagrant package
[vagrant] Attempting graceful shutdown of linux...
[vagrant] Cleaning previously set shared folders...
[vagrant] Creating temporary directory for export...
[vagrant] Exporting VM...
[default] Compressing package to: [some path]/package.box
```

This created a package.box file in our current directory. We'll rename it and add it to our box list with the vagrant box add command.

```
$ vagrant box add lucid64_with_ruby193 package.box
[vagrant] Downloading with Vagrant::Downloaders::File...
[vagrant] Copying box to temporary location...
[vagrant] Extracting box...
[vagrant] Verifying box...
[vagrant] Cleaning up downloaded box...
```

Now we'll verify that Vagrant knows about our base box with the vagrant box list command.

```
$ vagrant box list
lucid32
lucid64
lucid64_with_ruby193
```

Our new box definition is there, so we're in good shape. Let's create a new directory on our host machine and create a Vagrantfile that references our new base box by passing the box name to vagrant init.

```
$ mkdir ~/deployingrails/vagrant_testbox
$ cd ~/deployingrails/vagrant_testbox
$ vagrant init lucid64_with_ruby193
A `Vagrantfile` has been placed in this directory. You are now
ready to `vagrant up` your first virtual environment! Please read
the comments in the Vagrantfile as well as documentation on
`vagrantup.com` for more information on using Vagrant.
```

Now we'll fire up our new VM, ssh in, and verify that Ruby is there.

```
$ vagrant up
«lots of output»
$ vagrant ssh
vm $ ruby -v
ruby 1.9.3p194 (2012-04-20 revision 35410) [x86_64-linux]
```

It looks like a success. We've taken the standard lucid64 base box, added some development libraries and the latest version of Ruby, and built a Vagrant base box so that other VMs we create will have our customizations already in place.

Installing a newer Ruby version isn't the only change we can make as part of a base box. A favorite .vimrc, .inputrc, or shell profile that always gets copied onto servers are all good candidates for building into a customized base box. Anything that prevents post-VM creation busywork is fair game.

Next we'll build another VM that uses other useful Vagrant configuration options.

2.2 Configuring Networks and Multiple Virtual Machines

Our previous Vagrantfile was pretty simple; we needed only one line to specify our custom base box. Let's build another VM and see what other customizations Vagrant has to offer. Here's our starter file:

vagrant/Vagrantfile
```
Vagrant::Config.run do |config|
  config.vm.box = "lucid64"
end
```

Setting VM Options

The Vagrantfile is written in Ruby; as with many other Ruby-based tools, Vagrant provides a simple *domain-specific language* (DSL) for configuring VMs. The outermost construct is the Vagrant::Config.run method call. This yields a Vagrant:: Config::Top object instance that we can use to set configuration information. We can set any VirtualBox option; we can get a comprehensive list of the available options by running the VirtualBox management utility.

```
$ VBoxManage --help | grep -A 10 modifyvm
VBoxManage modifyvm          <uuid|name>
  [--name <name>]
  [--ostype <ostype>]
  [--memory <memorysize in MB>]
«and more options»
```

Our example is setting the host name and the memory limit by calling config.vm.customize and passing in an array containing the command that we're invoking on the VirtualBox management utility, followed by the configuration items' names and values.

```
vagrant/with_options/Vagrantfile
config.vm.customize ["modifyvm", :id, "--name", "app", "--memory", "512"]
```

We've found that it's a good practice to specify the name and memory limit for all but the most trivial VMs. Most of the other items in the customize array we probably won't need to worry about since they're low-level things such as whether the VM supports 3D acceleration; VirtualBox will detect these values on its own. The VirtualBox documentation[7] is a good source of information on the settings for customizing a VM.

Setting Up the Network

Our VM will be much more useful if the host machine can access services running on the guest. Vagrant provides the ability to forward ports to the guest so we can (for example) browse to localhost:4567 and have those HTTP requests forwarded to port 80 on the guest. We can also set up a network for the VM that makes it accessible to the host via a statically assigned IP address. We can then assign an alias in the host's /etc/hosts file so we can access our VM by a domain name in a browser address bar, by ssh, or by other methods.

First let's add a setting, host_name, to specify the host name that Vagrant will assign to the VM. This will also be important later for Puppet, which will check the host name when determining which parts of our configuration to run.

---

7.   https://www.virtualbox.org/manual/UserManual.html

```
config.vm.host_name = "app"
```

We want to be able to connect into the VM with ssh, and we'd also like to browse into the VM once we get MassiveApp deployed there. Thus, we'll add several instances of another setting, forward_port. This setting specifies the port on the VM to forward requests to (port 80) and the port on the host to forward (port 4567). With this in place, browsing to port 4567 on the host machine will let us view whatever the VM is serving up on port 80. For forwarding the ssh port, we include the :auto option, which tells Vagrant that if the port isn't available, it should search for another available port. Whenever we add new forward_port directives, we need to restart the VM via vagrant reload. Let's add those directives.

```
config.vm.forward_port 22, 2222, :auto => true
config.vm.forward_port 80, 4567
```

The next setting, network, specifies that this VM will use a host-only network so that this VM won't appear as a device on the network at large. This setting also specifies the VM's IP address on the host-only network. We want to avoid using common router-assigned subnets such as 127.0.0.2 or 192.168.*, because they may clash with existing or future subnets that a router assigns. The Vagrant documentation recommends the 33.33.* subnet, and we've found that works well. Keep in mind that when multiple Vagrant VMs are running, they will be able to communicate as long as they are in the same subnet. So, a VM with the IP address 33.33.12.34 will be able to talk to one at 33.33.12.56 but not at 33.44.12.34. Let's add a network setting to our Vagrantfile.

```
config.vm.network :hostonly, "33.33.13.37"
```

Like with the port forwarding settings, changing the network requires a VM restart.

Sharing Folders

Vagrant provides access to the contents of a directory on the host system using share_folder directives. A share_folder setting specifies a descriptive label, the destination path of the directory on the VM, and the path to the source directory (relative to the Vagrantfile). We can have as many of these as we like and can even use shared folders to share application code between the host and the VM. As an example, let's share in the /tmp directory on the host under the path /hosttmp on the guest by adding a share_folder directive.

vagrant/with_options/Vagrantfile

```
config.vm.share_folder "hosttmp", "/hosttmp", "/tmp"
```

This greatly simplifies moving data back and forth between the VM and the host system, and we'll use this feature throughout our configuration exercises.

2.3 Running Multiple VMs

Vagrant enables us to run multiple guest VMs on a single host. This is handy for configuring database replication between servers, building software firewall rules, tweaking monitoring checks, or almost anything for which it's helpful to have more than one host for proper testing. Let's give it a try now; first we need a new directory to hold our new VM.

```
$ mkdir ~/deployingrails/multiple_vms
$ cd ~/deployingrails/multiple_vms
```

Now we'll need a Vagrantfile. The syntax to define two separate configurations within our main configuration is to call the define method for each with a different name.

```
Vagrant::Config.run do |config|
  config.vm.define :app do |app_config|
  end
  config.vm.define :db do |db_config|
  end
end
```

We'll want to set vm.name and a memory size for each VM.

```
Vagrant::Config.run do |config|
  config.vm.define :app do |app_config|
    app_config.vm.customize ["modifyvm", :id, "--name", "app", "--memory", "512"]
  end
  config.vm.define :db do |db_config|
    db_config.vm.customize ["modifyvm", :id, "--name", "db", "--memory", "512"]
  end
end
```

We'll use the same box name for each VM, but we don't need to forward port 80 to the db VM, and we need to assign each VM a separate IP address. Let's add these settings to complete our Vagrantfile.

vagrant/multiple_vms/Vagrantfile

```
Vagrant::Config.run do |config|
  config.vm.define :app do |app_config|
    app_config.vm.customize ["modifyvm", :id, "--name", "app", "--memory", "512"]
    app_config.vm.box = "lucid64_with_ruby193"
    app_config.vm.host_name = "app"
```

Instances Need Unique Names

If you attempt to start more than one VM with the same name (in other words, the same modifyvm --name value), you'll get an error along the lines of "VBoxManage: error: Could not rename the directory." The fix is to either choose a different instance name for the new VM or, if the old VM is a leftover from previous efforts, just destroy the old VM. Note that halting the old VM is not sufficient; it needs to be destroyed.

```
    app_config.vm.forward_port 22, 2222, :auto => true
    app_config.vm.forward_port 80, 4567
    app_config.vm.network :hostonly, "33.33.13.37"
  end
  config.vm.define :db do |db_config|
    db_config.vm.customize ["modifyvm", :id, "--name", "db", "--memory", "512"]
    db_config.vm.box = "lucid64_with_ruby193"
    db_config.vm.host_name = "db"
    db_config.vm.forward_port 22, 2222, :auto => true
    db_config.vm.network :hostonly, "33.33.13.38"
  end
end
```

Our VMs are defined, so we can start them both with vagrant up. The output for each VM is prefixed with the particular VM's name.

```
$ vagrant up
[app] Importing base box 'lucid64_with_ruby193'...
[app] Matching MAC address for NAT networking...
[app] Clearing any previously set forwarded ports...
[app] Forwarding ports...
[app] -- 22 => 2222 (adapter 1)
[app] -- 80 => 4567 (adapter 1)
[app] Creating shared folders metadata...
[app] Clearing any previously set network interfaces...
[app] Preparing network interfaces based on configuration...
[app] Running any VM customizations...
[app] Booting VM...
[app] Waiting for VM to boot. This can take a few minutes.
[app] VM booted and ready for use!
[app] Configuring and enabling network interfaces...
[app] Setting host name...
[app] Mounting shared folders...
[app] -- v-root: /vagrant
[db] Importing base box 'lucid64_with_ruby193'...
[db] Matching MAC address for NAT networking...
[db] Clearing any previously set forwarded ports...
[db] Fixed port collision for 22 => 2222. Now on port 2200.
[db] Fixed port collision for 22 => 2222. Now on port 2201.
[db] Forwarding ports...
[db] -- 22 => 2201 (adapter 1)
```

```
[db] Creating shared folders metadata...
[db] Clearing any previously set network interfaces...
[db] Preparing network interfaces based on configuration...
[db] Running any VM customizations...
[db] Booting VM...
[db] Waiting for VM to boot. This can take a few minutes.
[db] VM booted and ready for use!
[db] Configuring and enabling network interfaces...
[db] Setting host name...
[db] Mounting shared folders...
[db] -- v-root: /vagrant
```

We can connect into each VM using our usual vagrant ssh, but this time we'll also need to specify the VM name.

```
$ vagrant ssh app
Last login: Wed Dec 21 19:47:36 2011 from 10.0.2.2
app $ hostname
app
app $ exit
$ vagrant ssh db
Last login: Thu Dec 22 21:19:54 2011 from 10.0.2.2
db $ hostname
db
```

Generally, when we apply any Vagrant command to one VM in a multiple-VM cluster, we need to specify the VM name. For a few commands (for example, vagrant halt), this is optional, and we can act on all VMs by not specifying a host name.

To verify inter-VM communications, let's connect from db to app via ssh using the vagrant account and a password of vagrant.

```
db $ ssh 33.33.13.37
The authenticity of host '33.33.13.37 (33.33.13.37)' can't be established.
RSA key fingerprint is ed:d8:51:8c:ed:37:b3:37:2a:0f:28:1f:2f:1a:52:8a.
Are you sure you want to continue connecting (yes/no)? yes
Warning: Permanently added '33.33.13.37' (RSA) to the list of known hosts.
vagrant@33.33.13.37's password:
Last login: Thu Dec 22 21:19:41 2011 from 10.0.2.2
app $
```

Finally, we can shut down and destroy both VMs with vagrant destroy.

```
$ vagrant destroy --force
[db] Forcing shutdown of VM...
[db] Destroying VM and associated drives...
[app] Forcing shutdown of VM...
[app] Destroying VM and associated drives...
```

We used two VMs in this example, but Vagrant can handle as many VMs as you need up to the resource limits of your computer. So, that ten-node Hadoop cluster on your laptop is finally a reality.

2.4 Where to Go Next

We've covered a fair bit of Vagrant functionality in this chapter, but there are a few interesting areas that are worth exploring once you're comfortable with this chapter's contents: using Vagrant's bridged network capabilities and using the Vagrant Puppet provisioner.

Bridged Networking

We've discussed Vagrant's "host-only" network feature (which hides the VM from the host computer's network) in *Setting Up the Network*, on page 19. Another option is *bridged networking*, which causes the VM to be accessible by other devices on the network. When the VM boots, it gets an IP address from the network's DHCP server, so it's as visible as any other device on the network.

This is a straightforward feature, so there's not too much detail to learn, but it's worth experimenting with so that it's in your toolbox. For example, with bridged networking, a guest VM can serve up a wiki, an internal build tool, or a code analysis tool. Co-workers on the same network can browse in and manage the guest as needed, all without disturbing the host computer's ability to restart a web or database service. It's a great feature to be aware of.

The Puppet Provisioner

We'll spend the next chapter, and much of the rest of this book, discussing Puppet and its uses. But to glance ahead, Vagrant provides a *provisioning* feature whereby a guest can be entirely configured with Puppet manifests. With this feature, a guest can be built from a standard base box but on boot can be pointed to a Puppet repository. The guest then uses the resources defined in that Puppet repository to install packages, create directories, start services, or do anything else that needs to be done to make the guest useful. This means that, theoretically, in the time that it takes Puppet to install the packages, you could build a scaled-down production infrastructure mirror (app server, database server, Redis, memcached, Sphinx, and so on) by pointing a set of VMs to the same Puppet manifests that the production servers are using. It's a very powerful feature and can eliminate a lot of one-off server build guesswork.

2.5   Conclusion

In this chapter, we covered the following:

- Installing VirtualBox in order to create virtual machines
- Setting up Vagrant to automate the process of creating and managing VMs with VirtualBox
- Creating a customized Vagrant base box to make new box setup faster
- Examining a few of the features that Vagrant offers for configuring VMs

In the next chapter, we'll introduce Puppet, a system administration tool that will help us configure the virtual machines that we can now build quickly and safely. We'll learn the syntax of Puppet's DSL and get our Rails stack up and running along the way.

2.6   For Future Reference

Creating a VM

To create a new VM using Vagrant, simply run the following commands:

```
$ mkdir newdir && cd newdir
$ vagrant init lucid64 && vagrant up
```

Creating a Custom Base Box

To cut down on initial box setup, create a customized base box.

```
$ mkdir newdir && cd newdir $ vagrant init lucid64 && vagrant up
# Now 'vagrant ssh' and make your changes, then log out of the VM
$ vagrant package
$ vagrant box add your_new_base_box_name package.box
```

A Complete Vagrantfile

Here's a Vagrantfile that uses a custom base box, shares a folder, forwards an additional port, and uses a private host-only network:

```
vagrant/with_options/Vagrantfile
Vagrant::Config.run do |config|
  config.vm.customize ["modifyvm", :id, "--name", "app", "--memory", "512"]
  config.vm.box = "lucid64_with_ruby193"
  config.vm.host_name = "app"
  config.vm.forward_port 22, 2222, :auto => true
  config.vm.forward_port 80, 4567
  config.vm.network :hostonly, "33.33.13.37"
  config.vm.share_folder "hosttmp", "/hosttmp", "/tmp"
end
```

CHAPTER 3

Rails on Puppet

Now that we know how to create a virtual machine, we need to know how to configure it to run MassiveApp. We could start creating directories and installing packages manually, but that would be error-prone, and we'd need to repeat all those steps the next time we built out a server. Even if we put our build-out process on a wiki or in a text file, someone else looking at that documentation has no way of knowing whether it's the current configuration or even whether the notes were accurate to begin with. Besides, manually typing in commands is hardly in keeping with the DevOps philosophy. We need some automation instead.

One software package that enables automated server configuration is Puppet.[1] Puppet is both a language and a set of tools that allows us to configure our servers with the packages, services, and files that they need. Commercial support is available for Puppet, and also a variety of tutorials, conference presentations, and other learning materials are available online. It's a popular tool, it's been around for a few years, and we've found it to be effective, so it's our favorite server automation utility.

3.1 Understanding Puppet

Puppet automates server provisioning by formalizing a server's configuration into *manifests*. Puppet's manifests are text files that contain declarations written in Puppet's domain-specific language (DSL). When we've defined our configuration using this DSL, Puppet will ensure that the machine's files, packages, and services match the settings we've specified.

---

1.   http://puppetlabs.com

To use Puppet effectively, though, we still have to know how to configure a server; Puppet will just do what we tell it. If, for example, our Puppet manifests don't contain the appropriate declarations to start a service on system boot, Puppet won't ensure that the service is set up that way. In other words, system administration knowledge is still useful. The beauty of Puppet is that the knowledge we have about systems administration can be captured, formalized, and applied over and over. We get to continue doing the interesting parts of system administration, that is, understanding, architecting, and tuning services. Meanwhile, Puppet automates away the boring parts, such as editing configuration files and manually running package installation commands.

In this chapter, we'll install and configure Puppet and then write Puppet manifests that we can use to build out virtual machines on which to run MassiveApp. By the end of this chapter, not only will we have a server ready for receiving a MassiveApp deploy, but we'll also have the Puppet configuration necessary to quickly build out more servers. And we'll have gained the general Puppet knowledge needed to create additional Puppet manifests as we encounter other tools in later chapters.

3.2 Setting Up Puppet

We'll accumulate a variety of scripts, files, and Puppet manifests while developing a server's configuration. We also need a place to keep documentation on more complex operations procedures. That's a bunch of files and data, and we don't want to lose any of it. So, as with everything else when it comes to development, putting these things in version control is the first key step in creating a maintainable piece of our system.

We cloned this book's massiveapp_ops GitHub repository in Section 1.3, *Learning with MassiveApp*, on page 7, and if we list the branches in that repository, we see that it contains an empty branch.

```
$ cd ~/deployingrails/massiveapp_ops/
$ git branch -a
  empty
* master
  without_ganglia
  without_nagios
  remotes/origin/HEAD -> origin/master
  remotes/origin/empty
  remotes/origin/master
  remotes/origin/without_ganglia
  remotes/origin/without_nagios
```

Puppet Alternatives: Chef

Chef[a] is a popular alternative to Puppet. It's also open source, and it can be run on an in-house server the same as we're running Puppet. Alternatively, it's supported by OpsCode, which provides the same functionality in a software-as-a-service solution.

There is a variety of terminology and design differences, but generally Chef has the same primary focus as Puppet: automating the configuration of servers. We've found that Puppet has a larger community and supports configuring more service types, and we've used Puppet effectively on a variety of projects, so that's the tool we'll focus on in this book. However, all the same principles apply; automation is good, we need repeatability, and so on.

---

a. http://wiki.opscode.com/display/chef/Home

To work through this chapter's exercises from scratch, we can check out that empty branch.

```
$ git checkout --track origin/empty
Branch empty set up to track remote branch empty from origin.
Switched to a new branch 'empty'
```

We're working in an empty directory now, but it won't be empty for long. Let's configure the virtual machine on which we'll use Puppet. We want to use the lucid64_with_ruby193 base box that we built in *Building a Custom Base Box*, on page 16, so we'll create a new directory.

```
$ cd ~/deployingrails/
$ mkdir puppetvm
$ cd puppetvm
```

And we'll use the same Vagrantfile that we built out in Section 2.2, *Configuring Networks and Multiple Virtual Machines*, on page 18. This time, however, we'll add a share for our newly cloned (or created) Git repository.

puppetrails/puppetvm/Vagrantfile
```
Vagrant::Config.run do |config|
  config.vm.customize ["modifyvm", :id, "--name", "app", "--memory", "512"]
  config.vm.box = "lucid64_with_ruby193"
  config.vm.host_name = "app"
  config.vm.forward_port 22, 2222, :auto => true
  config.vm.network :hostonly, "33.33.13.37"
  config.vm.share_folder "puppet", "/etc/puppet", "../massiveapp_ops"
end
```

When we start the VM and ssh into it, we can see that it can access our Git repository via the shared folder.

Installing Puppet from a Package

As this book went to print, the preferred Puppet installation method changed from using the gem to using a system package (for example, a deb or an rpm). Installing via a gem still works fine, but if you find an up-to-date package for your operating system, it may get you up and running with Puppet with less hassle.

```
$ vagrant up
«lots of output»
$ vagrant ssh
app $ ls -l /etc/puppet/.git/
total 12
drwxr-xr-x 1 vagrant vagrant  68 2011-10-14 13:59 branches
-rw-r--r-- 1 vagrant vagrant 111 2011-10-14 13:59 config
-rw-r--r-- 1 vagrant vagrant  73 2011-10-14 13:59 description
«and more»
```

Puppet comes packaged as a RubyGem. As of this writing, the current stable release is in the 2.7.*x* branch and supports both Ruby 1.8 and 1.9. However, should you install Puppet with a system package manager, you will most likely install a release from the 0.25.*x* or 2.6.*x* branch. This is a major downside since those older versions are missing many features and bug fixes from more recent versions, and 0.25.*x* supports only Ruby 1.8. So, we always install the Puppet gem to ensure we have the latest code.

There are two steps to installing Puppet as a gem. First we need to create a user and group for Puppet to use. We won't need to log in as the puppet user, so we'll set the shell to /bin/false.

```
app $ sudo useradd --comment "Puppet" --no-create-home \
  --system --shell /bin/false puppet
```

Next we'll install the gem.

```
app $ sudo gem install puppet -v 2.7.12 --no-rdoc --no-ri
Successfully installed facter-1.6.5
Successfully installed puppet-2.7.12
2 gems installed
```

We prefer to specify a particular version number when installing Puppet; that way, we know what we're working with. A dependent gem, facter, was also installed. facter is the tool that Puppet uses to gather information about the system in order to populate variables and determine which parts of our configuration to run. Let's see some of the variables that Facter provides by running the facter command-line utility.

Puppet Version Numbers

Puppet release version numbers made a large jump at one point; the stable release went from 0.25.x to 2.6.0. That's not a typo; it increased by an order of magnitude! So, although 0.25 looks like a very old version, it's really not that far back. That said, the newer versions provide better functionality, and it's a good idea to favor them.

```
app $ facter
architecture => amd64
domain => home
facterversion => 1.6.5
《...》
hostname => app
id => vagrant
interfaces => eth0,eth1,lo
ipaddress => 10.0.2.15
ipaddress_eth0 => 10.0.2.15
ipaddress_eth1 => 33.33.13.37
《...》
macaddress => 08:00:27:1a:b2:ac
macaddress_eth0 => 08:00:27:1a:b2:ac
macaddress_eth1 => 08:00:27:93:de:88
《...》
puppetversion => 2.7.12
rubyversion => 1.9.3
```

We can see plenty of information about our VM, including the network interfaces, MAC addresses, host name, and versions of Puppet and Ruby. All those keys and values are available as *variables* in Puppet. For now, the important thing is that Puppet can access all sorts of useful information about the VM on which it's running.

Let's set up a minimal Puppet repository. We need a manifests subdirectory to hold our main Puppet configuration files.

```
app $ cd /etc/puppet
app $ mkdir manifests
```

And let's put a file named site.pp in that directory; adding the following contents ensures that Puppet can find the binaries for our Ruby and RubyGems installations:

puppetrails/initial/manifests/site.pp
```
Exec {
  path => "/usr/local/sbin:/usr/local/bin:/usr/sbin:/usr/bin:/sbin:/bin"
}
```

We want to commit this to our repository, but before we do a commit, we'll want to set up a Git username. If we don't set this up, the commits will have vagrant as the author, and we'd rather have an actual name attached.

```
app $ git config --global user.name "Your Name"
app $ git config --global user.email your.name@yourdomain.com
```

Now we'll add our current Puppet configuration to our Git repository.

```
app $ git add .
app $ git commit -m "Initial Puppet manifests"
[empty 7904e6f] Initial Puppet manifests
1 files changed, 3 insertions(+), 0 deletions(-)
create mode 100644 manifests/site.pp
```

Like Vagrant, Puppet has a command-line utility; it's appropriately named puppet. We can run this utility with a help option to see the available commands.

```
app $ puppet help
Usage: puppet <subcommand> [options] <action> [options]

Available subcommands, from Puppet Faces:
  ca                Local Puppet Certificate Authority management.
  catalog           Compile, save, view, and convert catalogs.
《...》
Available applications, soon to be ported to Faces:
  agent             The puppet agent daemon
  apply             Apply Puppet manifests locally
  cert              Manage certificates and requests
  describe          Display help about resource types
《...》
```

We can also get help for any of the Puppet subcommands; here's an example:

```
app $ puppet help apply
puppet-apply(8) -- Apply Puppet manifests locally
========

SYNOPSIS
--------
Applies a standalone Puppet manifest to the local system.
《and more》
```

We're ready to run Puppet for the first time. We're going to run puppet apply, which won't apply any actual changes since we haven't defined any. However, Puppet uses a number of directories to store system information, security certificates, and other internal files it needs to run, and we'll use sudo so that Puppet will have permission to create those directories.

```
app $ sudo puppet apply --verbose manifests/site.pp
```

> **Technology Choices**
>
> We've chosen Apache for the web server, Passenger for the application server, and MySQL for the database server running MassiveApp. Each one of these components is open source, has successfully run many applications, and has vast amounts of configuration and tuning information online. These are not necessarily the correct choices for every application, but defaulting to these will get an application off the ground and far down the road before they need to be reevaluated. It's a great place to start, and maybe even to finish.

When developing a Puppet configuration, it's helpful to pass the --verbose flag to Puppet so that it displays any extended information that might be available if an error happens. We'll see output like this from puppet apply:

```
info: Applying configuration version '1319427535'
info: Creating state file /var/lib/puppet/state/state.yaml
notice: Finished catalog run in 0.02 seconds
```

We'll also see a few lines of output like the following ones. This is because the Puppet developers are still bringing the codebase up-to-date for Ruby 1.9.3; these should go away in future Puppet releases.

```
Could not load confine test 'operatingsystem': cannot load such file \
  -- puppet/provider/confine/operatingsystem
```

We've successfully built a tiny Puppet repository and executed Puppet on our VM. Now we'll build out the VM with a standard Rails application stack. That is, we'll configure Apache, MySQL, and Passenger, and we'll put the Rails application directory tree into place. Along the way, we'll learn all about how Puppet helps us manage our VM's services and configuration.

3.3 Installing Apache with Puppet

A key part of MassiveApp's infrastructure is Apache, and we'll start our MassiveApp build-out by defining a Puppet manifest that installs and configures Apache. As a side benefit, this will lead us through a variety of Puppet language and usage details.

Building an Initial Apache Puppet Manifest

Currently we have this initial set of files in /etc/puppet, with our site.pp containing only a single exec declaration that places various directories on Puppet's execution path.

```
- /manifests
  |- /site.pp
```

We could easily install Apache with Ubuntu's package manager (that is, sudo apt-get install apache2 -y), but we want to write the corresponding Puppet directives to install it instead. To get Puppet to install Apache, we need to define a *resource* to tell Puppet about what needs to be installed. In this case, Puppet calls this resource type a *package*, so we need to use a package declaration. Let's add this into site.pp.

puppetrails/only_package/manifests/site.pp
```
Exec {
  path => "/usr/local/sbin:/usr/local/bin:/usr/sbin:/usr/bin:/sbin:/bin"
}
package {
  "apache2":
    ensure => present
}
```

This package declaration is a fine example of the Puppet DSL. There's a type declaration, package, followed by a block delimited by curly braces. That block contains a *title* for the instance of the type that we're configuring, apache2. That title is associated with various *parameters* that affect how Puppet will act on the type. In this case, we've declared an ensure parameter that's set to present. This declaration is our way to tell Puppet that it should ensure there is a package called apache2 installed on the system.

That's a short summary of the package resource type, but we can get many more details about this resource type via the puppet describe command.

```
app $ puppet describe package

package
=======
Manage packages.  There is a basic dichotomy in package
support right now:  Some package types (e.g., yum and apt) can
retrieve their own package files, while others (e.g., rpm and sun)
cannot.  For those package formats that cannot retrieve their own files,
«and many more details»
```

Whenever we discuss a new resource type, it's worth running puppet describe to see what the Puppet maintainers considered important enough to document in this summary.

We've been using the word *package*, but what exactly does that mean? In Ubuntu, the standard package manager is dpkg, and the packages are contained in .deb files. If our VM were running a Red Hat–based operating system, we'd use the Red Hat Package Manager (RPM), and the packages would be contained in .rpm files. Through the use of generic types (like package), Puppet provides an abstraction layer over these packaging system differences. In other words, we can write a single Puppet configuration file and use it to provision multiple servers running different operating systems.

With that background, let's get the apache2 package in place. To do this, we'll run the Puppet client.

```
app $ sudo puppet apply --verbose manifests/site.pp
info: Applying configuration version '1315534357'
notice: /Stage[main]//Package[apache2]/ensure: ensure changed 'purged' to 'present'
notice: Finished catalog run in 10.78 seconds
```

Now if we run dpkg, we can see that apache2 is installed.

```
app $ dpkg --list apache2
«some table headers»
ii   apache2   2.2.14-5ubuntu8.8   Apache HTTP Server metapackage
```

If we rerun Puppet, the apache2 package won't be reinstalled. Instead, Puppet will notice that it's already in place and consider that package declaration fulfilled.

```
app $ sudo puppet apply --verbose manifests/site.pp
info: Applying configuration version '1325010497'
notice: Finished catalog run in 0.03 seconds
```

This is the Puppet life cycle. We figure out what resources we need on our server, we build manifests that describe those resources, and we run the puppet client to put those resources in place.

Apache is installed and started, and the default Ubuntu package install scripts will ensure that it starts on boot, but what if someone carelessly modifies the system so that Apache isn't set to start automatically? We can guard against that possibility with another Puppet type, service, which helps us manage any kind of background process that we want to stay running. Let's add this to site.pp.

```
puppetrails/package_and_service/manifests/site.pp
Exec {
  path => "/usr/local/sbin:/usr/local/bin:/usr/sbin:/usr/bin:/sbin:/bin"
}
package {
  "apache2":
    ensure => present
}
service {
  "apache2":
    ensure => true,
    enable => true
}
```

Like the package declaration, the service resource declaration has a title of apache2 and an ensure parameter. Rather than setting ensure to present, though, we're setting it to true. For the service type, setting ensure to true tells Puppet to attempt to start the service if it's not running. We've also added an enable parameter with a value of true that ensures this service will start on boot. Thus, each time we run the Puppet client, Puppet will ensure that Apache is both running and set to start on boot. And as with package, we can get many more details on service by running puppet describe service.

We've seen the package and service Puppet types so far. We'll use a variety of other types over the course of this book, but for a full listing, go to the Puppet type reference documentation.[2] A quick scan of the types listed there will give you a feel for the depth of Puppet's resource support: cron jobs, files and directories, mailing lists, users, and more are in Puppet's built-in repertoire.

Managing a Configuration File with Puppet

Next let's see how to manage one of the Apache configuration files using Puppet. Under certain error conditions Apache will display the server administrator's email address to visitors. The value of this email address is controlled by the ServerAdmin setting. The default Apache configuration sets that email address to webmaster@localhost, but let's change that setting to vagrant@localhost. To do this, let's open /etc/apache2/apache2.conf and add this line to the end of the file:

```
ServerAdmin vagrant@localhost
```

So, now we've customized our Apache configuration. But what if we build out another server? We'll need to make the same change to Apache on that server. And although we might remember this change, if we have a dozen changes to six different services' configuration files, there's no way we'll remember them all. That's where Puppet comes in. We'll capture this configuration change and formalize it into our Puppet manifests, and Puppet will manage that for us. To get started, we'll add a file resource to site.pp.

puppetrails/with_file/manifests/site.pp
```
Exec {
  path => "/usr/local/sbin:/usr/local/bin:/usr/sbin:/usr/bin:/sbin:/bin"
}
package {
  "apache2":
    ensure => present
}
```

---

2.   http://docs.puppetlabs.com/references/stable/type.html

```
service {
  "apache2":
    ensure => true,
    enable => true
}
file {
  "/etc/apache2/apache2.conf":
    source => "puppet:///modules/apache2/apache2.conf",
    mode   => 644,
    owner  => root,
    group  => root
}
```

The format of the file resource is something we've seen before; we have a type
name containing a title and a set of parameters. In the case of the file resource,
the title is the full path to the file. The parameters are where we're seeing some
things for the first time. There are several permissions-related parameters;
owner and group tell Puppet who should own the file, and mode contains the
standard Unix file system permissions.

The source parameter is a little more involved. That parameter tells Puppet to
look in /etc/puppet/modules/apache2/files/ for the file that should be compared to
the default file located at /etc/apache2/apache2.conf. In other words, the authoritative configuration file is located in the Puppet directory, and we want to use
that to overwrite the corresponding file in /etc/apache2. Since we're telling Puppet
that there's a modules directory containing that authoritative configuration file,
we need to create that directory and copy the default apache2.conf there.

```
app $ mkdir -p modules/apache2/files/
app $ cp /etc/apache2/apache2.conf modules/apache2/files/
```

Now as an experiment, let's open /etc/apache2/apache2.conf and remove the
directive we just added (that is, the line starting with ServerAdmin). We can see
that Puppet knows that the file has been changed by running Puppet with
the --noop option; this flag tells Puppet to not actually make any changes. By
including the --show_diff options, we'll see the changes that would have happened
if we had run Puppet without the --noop option.

```
app $ sudo puppet apply --verbose --noop --show_diff manifests/site.pp
info: Applying configuration version '1319427848'
--- /etc/apache2/apache2.conf    2011-10-23 20:44:06.492314742 -0700
+++ /tmp/puppet-file20111023-3337-122xno1        2011-10-23 20:44:08.623293237 -0700
@@ -235,3 +235,4 @@
 # Include the virtual host configurations:
 Include /etc/apache2/sites-enabled/

+ServerName vagrant@localhost
notice: /Stage[main]//File[/etc/apache2/apache2.conf]/content: \
```

```
  current_value {md5}c835e0388e5b689bfdf96f237g9b25c8, \
  should be {md5}f2088e3a492feace180633822d4f4cb5 (noop)
notice: /etc/apache2/apache2.conf: Would have triggered 'refresh' from 1 events
notice: Class[Main]: Would have triggered 'refresh' from 1 events
notice: Stage[main]: Would have triggered 'refresh' from 1 events
notice: Finished catalog run in 0.13 seconds
```

We've verified that Puppet will make the change we want. To make that change happen, we'll run Puppet without the --noop flag.

```
app $ sudo puppet apply --verbose manifests/site.pp
info: Applying configuration version '1315801207'
info: FileBucket adding {md5}86aaee758e9f530be2ba5cc7a3a7d147
info: /Stage[main]//File[/etc/apache2/apache2.conf]:
  Filebucketed /etc/apache2/apache2.conf to puppet
  with sum 86aaee758e9f530be2ba5cc7a3a7d147
notice: /Stage[main]//File[/etc/apache2/apache2.conf]/content:
  content changed '{md5}86aaee758e9f530be2ba5cc7a3a7d147'
  to '{md5}89c3d8a72d0b760adc1c83f05dce88a3'
notice: Finished catalog run in 0.14 seconds
```

As we expected, Puppet overwrote the target file's contents with our changes. Let's commit our current Puppet repository contents to Git so that our Apache configuration file will have an audit trail.

```
app $ git add .
app $ git commit -m "Building out Apache resource declarations"
[empty cdaacec] Building out Apache resource declarations
2 files changed, 254 insertions(+), 0 deletions(-)
create mode 100644 modules/apache2/files/apache2.conf
```

Now we can install and configure a service using Puppet, and we know that each time we run Puppet, it will enforce our configuration file changes. This is already a vast improvement over manually installing and configuring packages, but we have more improvements to make. Next we'll look at making our Puppet repository cleaner and easier to understand.

Organizing Manifests with Modules

So far, we've seen how to create Puppet manifests to manage packages, services, and configuration files. We've used these to set up Apache, which is one of the basic components on which MassiveApp will run.

But more resources will become hard to manage in a single file; our site.pp is getting pretty cluttered already. It'd be better for us to structure our manifests so that we can find things easily and so that there are clear boundaries between the Puppet configuration for each part of MassiveApp's infrastructure.

Puppet's answer to this problem is to structure the manifests using *modules*. Modules allow us to organize our manifests into logical pieces, much as we do with modules in Ruby or packages in Java. We've already gotten started on a module structure for our Apache-related Puppet configuration by creating a modules/apache2/files directory holding our customized apache2.conf. To get further down this road, let's create a modules/apache2/manifests directory and copy the existing site.pp file into an init.pp file there.

```
app $ mkdir modules/apache2/manifests
app $ cp manifests/site.pp modules/apache2/manifests/init.pp
```

Our new Apache module's init.pp needs to declare a Puppet *class* as a container for the module's resources. Declaring a class is as simple as deleting the exec declaration and wrapping the remaining contents of init.pp inside a class declaration.

puppetrails/module_with_file/modules/apache2/manifests/init.pp
```
class apache2 {
  package {
    "apache2":
      ensure => present
  }
  service {
    "apache2":
      ensure => true,
      enable => true
  }
  file {
    "/etc/apache2/apache2.conf":
      source => "puppet:///modules/apache2/apache2.conf",
      mode   => 644,
      owner  => root,
      group  => root
  }
}
```

We can do some cleanup now by deleting all the Apache-related resources from manifests/site.pp, leaving us with only the exec resource.

puppetrails/initial/manifests/site.pp
```
Exec {
  path => "/usr/local/sbin:/usr/local/bin:/usr/sbin:/usr/bin:/sbin:/bin"
}
```

With that done, we have a functioning Puppet repository again. Let's make the same sort of change we did before to /etc/apache2/apache2.conf (delete the new ServerAdmin line) and then rerun Puppet to verify that everything is working.

```
app $ sudo puppet apply --verbose manifests/site.pp
info: Applying configuration version '1325012538'
notice: Finished catalog run in 0.02 seconds
```

Hm, not much happened. That's because we need to tell Puppet to include our Apache module in the manifests that will be applied when we run the Puppet client. To do that, we *include* the module in our manifests/site.pp file.

puppetrails/apache_include/manifests/site.pp
```
Exec {
  path => "/usr/local/sbin:/usr/local/bin:/usr/sbin:/usr/bin:/sbin:/bin"
}
include apache2
```

Now we can run Puppet and see our changes applied.

```
app $ sudo puppet apply --verbose manifests/site.pp
info: Applying configuration version '1315996920'
info: FileBucket adding {md5}81703bb9023de2287d490f01f7deb3d1
info: /Stage[main]/Apache/File[/etc/apache2/apache2.conf]:
  Filebucketed /etc/apache2/apache2.conf to puppet
  with sum 81703bb9023de2287d490f01f7deb3d1
notice: /Stage[main]/Apache/File[/etc/apache2/apache2.conf]/content:
  content changed '{md5}81703bb9023de2287d490f01f7deb3d1'
  to '{md5}89c3d8a72d0b760adc1c83f05dce88a3'
notice: Finished catalog run in 0.12 seconds
```

Our module is working; Puppet has overwritten the file, and we're back to our desired configuration.

We've seen Puppet modules in action now, so let's pause and review a few things about using them.

- A module lives in Puppet's modules directory.
- A module directory is named after the service or resource that it provides.
- A module needs an init.pp file containing its resource declarations in the modules/module_name/manifests directory.
- Our manifests/site.pp needs to include a module for Puppet to activate it.

Our directory structure with one module in place looks like this:

```
- /manifests
  |- /site.pp
- /modules
  |- /apache2
    |- /files
      | - /apache2.conf
    |- /manifests
      | - /init.pp
```

We'll see a lot more of modules in this and other chapters; they're a Puppet mainstay. Now let's continue our MassiveApp server build-out by adding more resources to our Apache module.

Restarting Apache on Configuration Changes

Our Puppet manifests install Apache and ensure the initial configuration is in place. We'll be making changes to the Apache configuration, though, and we'll need to restart Apache when that happens. The Puppet way to do this is to use the "package-service-file" configuration pattern. That is, we want Puppet to ensure that the Apache package is installed, ensure that the configuration file is present, and then ensure that the service is running with that file.

To enforce these dependencies, we'll use some new Puppet parameters in our existing resource declarations. First let's enhance our Apache package resource declaration by adding a before parameter that ensures the package is installed before our custom configuration file is copied in.

puppetrails/apache_package_file_service/modules/apache2/manifests/init.pp
```
package {
  "apache2":
    ensure => present,
    before => File["/etc/apache2/apache2.conf"]
}
```

The before parameter declares a Puppet *dependency*; without this dependency, Puppet can execute the resources in any sequence it sees fit. The right side of that declaration (that is, File["/etc/apache2/apache2.conf"]) is a reference to the resource on which we're depending. This can be any resource, and the text within the brackets is just the title of that resource.

We have one dependency in place. We really have two dependencies, though, since we don't want to start the Apache service until our customized configuration file is copied in, and we want to restart the service any time there is a change in the configuration file. So, let's use another Puppet service parameter, subscribe, so that the Puppet notifies the service when configuration changes happen.

puppetrails/apache_package_file_service/modules/apache2/manifests/init.pp
```
service {
  "apache2":
    ensure    => true,
    enable    => true,
    subscribe => File["/etc/apache2/apache2.conf"]
}
```

Now if we shut down Apache, remove the ServerAdmin directive that we put in /etc/apache2/apache2.conf, and rerun Puppet, the configuration file will be updated before the service is started.

```
app $ sudo puppet apply --verbose manifests/site.pp
info: Applying configuration version '1316316205'
info: FileBucket got a duplicate file {md5}81703bb9023de2287d490f01f7deb3d1
info: /Stage[main]/Apache/File[/etc/apache2/apache2.conf]:
  Filebucketed /etc/apache2/apache2.conf to puppet
  with sum 81703bb9023de2287d490f01f7deb3d1
notice: /Stage[main]/Apache/File[/etc/apache2/apache2.conf]/content:
  content changed '{md5}81703bb9023de2287d490f01f7deb3d1'
  to '{md5}89c3d8a72d0b760adc1c83f05dce88a3'
info: /etc/apache2/apache2.conf: Scheduling refresh of Service[apache2]
notice: /Stage[main]/Apache/Service[apache2]/ensure:
  ensure changed 'stopped' to 'running'
notice: /Stage[main]/Apache/Service[apache2]: Triggered 'refresh' from 1 events
notice: Finished catalog run in 1.24 seconds
```

The before and subscribe parameters are known as Puppet *metaparameters* and can be used with any resource type. We'll mention various other metaparameters as we continue to build out MassiveApp's Rails stack, and there's excellent documentation on all the metaparameters on the Puppet site.[3] We can also see a good overview of subscribe and other metaparameters using puppet describe with a --meta flag.

```
app $ puppet describe --meta service
«notes on service resource»
- **subscribe**
    References to one or more objects that this object depends on. This
    metaparameter creates a dependency relationship like **require,**
    and also causes the dependent object to be refreshed when the
    subscribed object is changed. For instance:
«notes on other metaparameters»
```

We'll also need a virtual host for Apache to serve up MassiveApp. We'll add another file to our files directory that contains the virtual host definition.

puppetrails/modules/apache2/files/massiveapp.conf
```
<VirtualHost *:80>
  ServerName massiveapp
  DocumentRoot "/var/massiveapp/current/public/"
  CustomLog /var/log/apache2/massiveapp-access_log combined
  ErrorLog /var/log/apache2/massiveapp-error_log
</VirtualHost>
```

---

3. http://docs.puppetlabs.com/references/stable/metaparameter.html

And we'll manage this file with Puppet by adding another file resource to modules/apache2/manifests/init.pp. Like the file resource for apache2.conf, this resource is also dependent on the Apache service resource and notifies Apache when it changes. Now our file resource block looks like this:

puppetrails/modules/apache2/manifests/init.pp
```
file {
  "/etc/apache2/apache2.conf":
    owner  => root,
    group  => root,
    mode   => 644,
    source => "puppet:///modules/apache2/apache2.conf";
  "/etc/apache2/sites-enabled/massiveapp.conf":
    source  => "puppet:///modules/apache2/massiveapp.conf",
    owner   => root,
    group   => root,
    notify  => Service["apache2"],
    require => Package["apache2"];
}
```

Another Puppet run, and we have our Apache configuration in place. We'll get an Apache warning about the MassiveApp DocumentRoot (/var/massiveapp/current) not existing, but we'll create that in the next chapter, and it's just a warning, so we'll let it slide for now.

Let's verify that Apache is actually working. First we'll need to forward a port to our guest; therefore, we'll exit the VM and modify our Vagrantfile so port 4567 will be forwarded.

puppetrails/puppetvm_with_port_80_forwarded/Vagrantfile
```
Vagrant::Config.run do |config|
  config.vm.customize ["modifyvm", :id, "--name", "app", "--memory", "512"]
  config.vm.box = "lucid64_with_ruby193"
  config.vm.host_name = "app"
  config.vm.forward_port 22, 2222, :auto => true
  config.vm.forward_port 80, 4567
  config.vm.network :hostonly, "33.33.13.37"
  config.vm.share_folder "puppet", "/etc/puppet", "../massiveapp_ops"
end
```

Since we're adding a new forwarded port, we need to reload the VM.

```
$ vagrant reload
[default] Attempting graceful shutdown of VM...
[default] Clearing any previously set forwarded ports...
[default] Forwarding ports...
[default] -- 22 => 2222 (adapter 1)
[default] -- 80 => 4567 (adapter 1)
«and more»
```

Once the VM comes up, we can open a web browser on the host, enter http://localhost:4567 in the address bar, and there's our basic Apache web page announcing "It works!"

Before moving on, let's get all our changes into our Git repository.

```
app $ git add .
app $ git commit -m "More Apache"
[master 7b96dd8] More Apache
 3 files changed, 261 insertions(+), 0 deletions(-)
«and more»
```

Next we'll continue building out our Rails stack by installing MySQL.

3.4 Configuring MySQL with Puppet

Now that we've configured one service with Puppet, configuring another is much easier. As far as Puppet is concerned, MySQL and Apache are more or less the same resource but with different package, file, and service names.

Let's build out a new module directory for MySQL. First we'll create the appropriate directories.

```
app $ mkdir -p modules/mysql/files modules/mysql/manifests
```

Now we'll build our modules/mysql/manifests/init.pp, and we'll populate that file with the same package-file-service pattern as we did with our Apache module.

puppetrails/mysql_pfs/modules/mysql/manifests/init.pp
```
class mysql {
  package {
    "mysql-server":
      ensure => installed,
      before => File["/etc/mysql/my.cnf"]
  }
  file {
    "/etc/mysql/my.cnf":
      owner  => root,
      group  => root,
      mode   => 644,
      source => "puppet:///modules/mysql/my.cnf"
  }
  service {
    "mysql":
      ensure    => running,
      subscribe => File["/etc/mysql/my.cnf"]
  }
}
```

In addition to these resources, we'll also add two exec resources; the exec resource type lets us run arbitrary commands if certain conditions aren't met. These will set the MySQL root password to root once the service is started and then create the massiveapp_production database. Each exec needs an unless variable since we don't want to reset the password and attempt to create the database each time we run Puppet.

```
puppetrails/modules/mysql/manifests/init.pp
class mysql {
  package {
    "mysql-server":
      ensure => installed,
      before => File["/etc/mysql/my.cnf"]
  }
  file {
    "/etc/mysql/my.cnf":
      owner  => root,
      group  => root,
      mode   => 644,
      source => "puppet:///modules/mysql/my.cnf"
  }
  service {
    "mysql":
      ensure    => running,
      subscribe => File["/etc/mysql/my.cnf"]
  }
  exec {
    "mysql_password":
      unless  => "mysqladmin -uroot -proot status",
      command => "mysqladmin -uroot password root",
      require => Service[mysql];
    "massiveapp_db":
      unless  => "mysql -uroot -proot massiveapp_production",
      command => "mysql -uroot -proot -e 'create database massiveapp_production'",
      require => Exec["mysql_password"]
  }
}
```

We're creating the database here using Puppet rather than using the built-in Rails Rake tasks (that is, db:create). Creating the database this way gives us some flexibility. For example, we might want to provision a new environment with the database and several MySQL user accounts already in place before we deploy MassiveApp. We also might want to tighten up security and disable database creation ability for the user that Rails uses to connect to MySQL. Using Puppet for this function gives us that option.

Even though we don't have any configuration changes to make to my.cnf at this point, we'll add the default MySQL configuration file contents to modules/mysql/files/my.cnf so that we're ready for any future additions. But wait; there's a bootstrapping problem here. That is, what does our desired my.cnf file look like, and how do we get it without installing the package with Puppet? What we'll do is install the package manually, grab the configuration file, and put it in our Puppet repository.

```
app $ sudo apt-get install mysql-server -y # and enter 'root' when prompted
app $ cp /etc/mysql/my.cnf modules/mysql/files/
```

This may seem a little like cheating; we're installing a package manually and then backfilling it with Puppet. But it's realistic, too. In the real world, we don't roll out new services without tuning configuration settings to fit our hardware and our usage needs. Installing the package and then using the service's default configuration file as a starting place is a good way to get a new service in place, and it allows us to record our configuration customizations in our repository.

We also need Puppet to load up our module, so we'll add it to our manifests/site.pp file.

puppetrails/mysql_apache_include/manifests/site.pp
```
Exec {
  path => "/usr/local/sbin:/usr/local/bin:/usr/sbin:/usr/bin:/sbin:/bin"
}
include apache2
include mysql
```

Now when we run Puppet, it ensures MySQL is installed, overwrites the default configuration file with our Puppet-controlled file, starts the MySQL service if it's not already running, and creates the massiveapp_production database.

```
app $ sudo puppet apply --verbose manifests/site.pp
info: Applying configuration version '1330308005'
notice: /Stage[main]/Mysql/Exec[massiveapp_db]/returns: executed successfully
notice: Finished catalog run in 0.26 seconds
```

And we can verify that MySQL has started and that our massiveapp_production database exists by accessing the MySQL console (see Figure 1, *Verify that MySQL has started*, on page 47).

As usual, let's commit our changes before moving on.

```
app $ git add .
app $ git commit -m "Support for MySQL"
```

We have our web and database services up and running. We've also learned about a few more Puppet capabilities, including the exec resource type and

```
app $ mysql -uroot -proot
Welcome to the MySQL monitor.  Commands end with ; or \g.
Your MySQL connection id is 47
Server version: 5.1.41-3ubuntu12.10 (Ubuntu)

Type 'help;' or '\h' for help. Type '\c' to clear the current input statement.

mysql> show databases;
+----------------------+
| Database             |
+----------------------+
| information_schema   |
| massiveapp_production |
| mysql                |
+----------------------+
3 rows in set (0.00 sec)

mysql>
```

Figure 1—Verify that MySQL has started

the unless parameter. Next we'll use Puppet to set up the directories where we'll deploy MassiveApp.

3.5 Creating the MassiveApp Rails Directory Tree

We have Apache and MySQL in place, and it's time to set up the directory tree to which we'll deploy MassiveApp. Let's start by creating a new module, massiveapp, with the usual directories.

```
app $ mkdir -p modules/massiveapp/files modules/massiveapp/manifests
```

To deploy MassiveApp, we need a directory that's owned by the user who's running the deployments, so our init.pp needs a file resource that creates the Rails subdirectories. Those who are familiar with the Capistrano deployment utility will notice that we're setting up a directory structure of the sort that Capistrano expects; we'll discuss that in much more depth in the next chapter.

We're also using a new syntax here; we're listing several directory titles in our type declaration. This prevents resource declaration duplication and results in Puppet applying the same parameters to all the directories. Here's our init.pp with our file resource declaration:

puppetrails/just_directories/modules/massiveapp/manifests/init.pp
```
class massiveapp {
  file {
    ["/var/massiveapp/",
```

```
      "/var/massiveapp/shared/",
      "/var/massiveapp/shared/config/"]:
      ensure => directory,
      owner  => vagrant,
      group  => vagrant,
      mode   => 775
  }
}
```

As usual, we'll include this module in our site.pp file.

puppetrails/with_massiveapp/manifests/site.pp
```
Exec {
  path => "/usr/local/sbin:/usr/local/bin:/usr/sbin:/usr/bin:/sbin:/bin"
}
include apache2
include massiveapp
include mysql
```

When we run Puppet, we get the expected directories.

```
app $ sudo puppet apply --verbose manifests/site.pp
info: Applying configuration version '1316435273'
notice: /Stage[main]/Massiveapp/File[/var/massiveapp/]/ensure: created
notice: /Stage[main]/Massiveapp/File[/var/massiveapp/shared/]/ensure: created
notice: /Stage[main]/Massiveapp/File[/var/massiveapp/shared/config/]/ensure: created
notice: Finished catalog run in 0.04 seconds
```

MassiveApp can't connect to MySQL without a database.yml file. We like to store our database.yml files on the server (and in Puppet) so that we don't need to keep our production database credentials in our application's Git repository. Storing it on the server also lets us change our database connection information (port, password, and so on) without needing to redeploy MassiveApp.

So, let's add a database.yml file to the config directory. This is a file resource but has different parameters than the earlier file resources, so we can't just combine it them. So, let's add a new file resource.

puppetrails/directories_and_db_yml/modules/massiveapp/manifests/init.pp
```
class massiveapp {
  file {
    ["/var/massiveapp/",
     "/var/massiveapp/shared/",
     "/var/massiveapp/shared/config/"]:
      ensure => directory,
      owner  => vagrant,
      group  => vagrant,
      mode   => 775
  }
  file {
    "/var/massiveapp/shared/config/database.yml":
```

```
        ensure  => present,
        owner   => vagrant,
        group   => vagrant,
        mode    => 600,
        source  => "puppet:///modules/massiveapp/database.yml"
    }
}
```

We need to put our database.yml file in our modules/massiveapp/files/ directory since
that's where we've set up Puppet to expect it.

puppetrails/modules/massiveapp/files/database.yml
```
production:
  adapter: mysql2
  encoding: utf8
  reconnect: true
  database: massiveapp_production
  username: root
  password: root
```

Now when we run Puppet, it copies our database.yml file into place.

```
app $ sudo puppet apply --verbose manifests/site.pp
info: Applying configuration version '1316517863'
notice:
 /Stage[main]/Massiveapp/File[/var/massiveapp/shared/config/database.yml]/ensure:
 defined content as '{md5}05754b51236f528cd82d55526c1e53c7'
notice: Finished catalog run in 0.07 seconds
```

We'll also need Bundler to be installed so that it's ready to install MassiveApp's
gems. Let's add a package declaration; this one uses the built-in Puppet provider
for RubyGems.

puppetrails/modules/massiveapp/manifests/init.pp
```
class massiveapp {
  file {
    ["/var/massiveapp/",
     "/var/massiveapp/shared/",
     "/var/massiveapp/shared/config/"]:
     ensure => directory,
     owner  => vagrant,
     group  => vagrant,
     mode   => 775
  }
  file {
    "/var/massiveapp/shared/config/database.yml":
     ensure  => present,
     owner   => vagrant,
     group   => vagrant,
     mode    => 600,
     source  => "puppet:///modules/massiveapp/database.yml"
```

```
  }
  package {
    "bundler":
      provider => gem
  }
}
```

When we run Puppet, it installs the gem as we'd expect.

```
app $ sudo puppet apply --verbose manifests/site.pp
info: Applying configuration version '1325588796'
notice: /Stage[main]/Massiveapp/Package[bundler]/ensure: created
notice: Finished catalog run in 2.27 seconds
```

With all those changes in place, we'll add this module to our Git repository as usual.

Creating a new module for MassiveApp seems a little odd since it's not a system-level package or service. But from a system administration perspective, the Rails directories, the configuration files and their permissions, and the Bundler RubyGem are nothing more than resources to be managed. And this module will become even more useful as cron jobs and new configuration files are added. A warning, though; we've found that application modules tend to become a dumping ground for all sorts of resources. Once one is established, it's worth reviewing the contents of it occasionally to see whether anything can be extracted into another module.

We've written Puppet manifests for our MassiveApp directory structure and our database connection configuration file. Let's set up Puppet manifests for Passenger, and we'll be ready to deploy MassiveApp.

3.6   Writing a Passenger Module

Passenger[4] is a Rails application server that makes it easy to run Rails applications under Apache. We like Passenger because it's reasonably easy to install, and once in place, it manages a pool of application instances so that we don't have to manage ports and process IDs. It even handles restarting an application instance after a certain number of requests.

Setting up Passenger consists of installing the Passenger RubyGem, building and installing the Passenger shared object library that will be loaded into Apache, and including several directives in our Apache configuration. Let's start by creating a new Puppet module for Passenger.

---

4.   http://modrails.com/

```
app $ mkdir -p modules/passenger/files modules/passenger/manifests
```

For our module's init.pp, we'll use another exec resource with a Puppet unless parameter that checks to see whether the gem is already installed by looking for the gem directory. We also don't want to install Passenger before Apache is in place, so we use a require parameter.

puppetrails/just_gem/modules/passenger/manifests/init.pp
```
class passenger {
  exec {
    "/usr/local/bin/gem install passenger -v=3.0.11":
      user    => root,
      group   => root,
      alias   => "install_passenger",
      require => Package["apache2"],
      unless  => "ls /usr/local/lib/ruby/gems/1.9.1/gems/passenger-3.0.11/"
  }
}
```

We can compile the Passenger Apache module with another exec resource, and we'll add a before parameter to our initial exec resource to reference that one. Now our init.pp file looks like this:

puppetrails/just_gem_and_module/modules/passenger/manifests/init.pp
```
class passenger {
  exec {
    "/usr/local/bin/gem install passenger -v=3.0.11":
      user    => root,
      group   => root,
      alias   => "install_passenger",
      before  => Exec["passenger_apache_module"],
      unless  => "ls /usr/local/lib/ruby/gems/1.9.1/gems/passenger-3.0.11/"
  }
  exec {
    "/usr/local/bin/passenger-install-apache2-module --auto":
      user    => root,
      group   => root,
      path    => "/bin:/usr/bin:/usr/local/apache2/bin/",
      alias   => "passenger_apache_module",
      unless  => "ls /usr/local/lib/ruby/gems/1.9.1/gems/\
passenger-3.0.11/ext/apache2/mod_passenger.so"
  }
}
```

Passenger has a number of configuration settings that are declared as Apache directives. Here's our configuration file; we'll put this in our Passenger module's file directory in modules/passenger/files/passenger.conf.

Why 1.9.1?

In this require parameter, we're checking the /usr/local/lib/ruby/gems/1.9.1/ directory tree. But we installed Ruby 1.9.3; what gives?

We can find the answer in the Ruby 1.9.2 release notes.[a] From that page, "This version is a 'library compatible version.' Ruby 1.9.2 is almost 1.9.1 compatible, so the library is installed in the 1.9.1 directory." It seems the same also applies to Ruby 1.9.3.

---

a.   http://www.ruby-lang.org/en/news/2010/08/18/ruby-1-9.2-released/#label-6

puppetrails/modules/passenger/files/passenger.conf

```
LoadModule passenger_module \
  /usr/local/lib/ruby/gems/1.9.1/gems/passenger-3.0.11/ext/apache2/mod_passenger.so
PassengerRoot /usr/local/lib/ruby/gems/1.9.1/gems/passenger-3.0.11
PassengerRuby /usr/local/bin/ruby
PassengerUseGlobalQueue on
PassengerMaxPoolSize 5
PassengerPoolIdleTime 900
PassengerMaxRequests 10000
```

These Passenger settings are documented in great detail on the Passenger website. Here are a few highlights, though:

- PassengerUseGlobalQueue <true or false> enables Passenger to hold pending HTTP requests in a queue and wait until an application instance is available. This prevents one or two slow requests from tying up subsequent requests.

- PassengerMaxPoolSize <n> helps cap Passenger resource usage. If a server is getting too many requests, Passenger will reject the request rather than spinning up application instances until it runs out of memory. This helps the server recover more quickly.

- PassengerPoolIdleTime <n> tells Passenger to shut down unused application instances after the indicated interval. When the site gets busy, Passenger starts more application instances to serve the traffic, and PassengerPoolIdleTime will let Passenger shut down the instances after the request spike passes and the instances are idle for a while.

- PassengerMaxRequests <n> provides memory leak recovery. With this setting in place, Passenger will restart an application instance after it has served the indicated number of requests. This continual recycling of instances helps keep memory leaks from becoming an issue. If this is set too low, Passenger will spend unneeded resources restarting application instances, so it's good to monitor an application's memory usage over time to help set this value correctly.

Let's add a file resource that copies the Passenger configuration file into place, and we'll complete the package-file-service pattern by adding another before parameter to our first exec resource. Now we have this init.pp file:

```
puppetrails/modules/passenger/manifests/init.pp
class passenger {

  exec {
    "/usr/local/bin/gem install passenger -v=3.0.11":
      user     => root,
      group    => root,
      alias    => "install_passenger",
      before   => [File["passenger_conf"],Exec["passenger_apache_module"]],
      unless   => "ls /usr/local/lib/ruby/gems/1.9.1/gems/passenger-3.0.11/"
  }

exec {
  "/usr/local/bin/passenger-install-apache2-module --auto":
    user     => root,
    group    => root,
    path     => "/bin:/usr/bin:/usr/local/apache2/bin/",
    alias    => "passenger_apache_module",
    before   => File["passenger_conf"],
    unless   => "ls /usr/local/lib/ruby/gems/1.9.1/gems/\
passenger-3.0.11/ext/apache2/mod_passenger.so"
}

  file {
    "/etc/apache2/conf.d/passenger.conf":
      mode     => 644,
      owner    => root,
      group    => root,
      alias    => "passenger_conf",
      notify   => Service["apache2"],
      source   => "puppet:///modules/passenger/passenger.conf"
  }
}
```

As usual, we'll also add an include to our manifests/site.pp to get Puppet to use our new module.

```
puppetrails/with_passenger/manifests/site.pp
Exec {
  path => "/usr/local/sbin:/usr/local/bin:/usr/sbin:/usr/bin:/sbin:/bin"
}
include apache2
include massiveapp
include mysql
include passenger
```

Now we can run Puppet and install the Passenger gem and module.

```
app $ sudo puppet apply --verbose manifests/site.pp
info: Applying configuration version '1319451008'
notice: /Stage[main]/Passenger/Exec[/usr/local/bin/\
  passenger-install-apache2-module --auto]/returns: executed successfully
info: FileBucket adding {md5}b72cb12ea075df2ca1ae66e824fa083b
info: /Stage[main]/Passenger/File[/etc/apache2/conf.d/passenger.conf]: \
  Filebucketed /etc/apache2/conf.d/passenger.conf to puppet \
  with sum b72cb12ea075df2ca1ae66e824fa083b
notice: /Stage[main]/Passenger/File[/etc/apache2/conf.d/passenger.conf]/content: \
  content changed '{md5}b72cb12ea075df2ca1ae66e824fa083b' \
  to '{md5}47757e49ad1ea230630a935d41459b08'
info: /etc/apache2/conf.d/passenger.conf: Scheduling refresh of Service[apache2]
notice: /Stage[main]/Apache2/Service[apache2]/ensure: \
  ensure changed 'stopped' to 'running'
notice: /Stage[main]/Apache2/Service[apache2]: Triggered 'refresh' from 1 events
notice: Finished catalog run in 35.59 seconds
```

We'll add these scripts to our ever-expanding Git repository.

We've installed Passenger and explored some of the Passenger configuration settings. We've also learned about a few more Puppet capabilities, including the exec resource type and the unless parameter. Next we'll make some organizational improvements to our Puppet manifests.

3.7 Managing Multiple Hosts with Puppet

Our manifests/site.pp is getting to be a little messy. We have a mix of two different things in there; we have an exec resource declaration that applies globally, and we have module include directives for our MassiveApp server. And if we wanted to manage another server from the same Puppet repository, we'd need some place to put that.

The answer is to use a Puppet concept called *nodes*. Puppet nodes are containers for resources; a node has a name and a set of directives, although we usually try to restrict them to module inclusion.

To get started with nodes, we'll need a new manifest/nodes.pp file in which we'll define a node for our app host.

puppetrails/manifests/nodes.pp
```
node "app" {
  include apache2
  include mysql
  include massiveapp
  include passenger
}
```

The node name, which must be unique, must be the same as the host name of the server. With our nodes.pp file, we can add as many hosts as we like, and each can include different modules. We can also trim down our site.pp considerably now.

puppetrails/withoutnodes/site.pp
```
Exec {
    path => "/usr/local/sbin:/usr/local/bin:/usr/sbin:/usr/bin:/sbin:/bin"
}
import "nodes.pp"
```

Nodes provide a convenient way to separate hosts. We use them on all but the smallest Puppet installations.

3.8 Updating the Base Box

Clearly Puppet is going to be useful for the rest of this book; we'll always want to install it to manage everything else. That being the case, let's update our Vagrant base box to include a basic Puppet installation. This will save us a few steps every time we build out a new VM.

Since we're enhancing our base box, we need to fire up a new VM that's built from that base box. So, we'll create a new working directory with a simple Vagrantfile.

```
$ mkdir ~/deployingrails/updatedvm/ && cd ~/deployingrails/updatedvm/
$ vagrant init lucid64_with_ruby193
A `Vagrantfile` has been placed in this directory. You are now
ready to `vagrant up` your first virtual environment! Please read
the comments in the Vagrantfile as well as documentation on
`vagrantup.com` for more information on using Vagrant.
```

Now we can start the VM and ssh in.

```
$ vagrant up
«lots of output»
$ vagrant ssh
vm $
```

We need a Puppet user and the Puppet gem, so let's set up both of them.

```
vm $ sudo useradd --comment "Puppet" --no-create-home \
--system --shell /bin/false puppet
vm $ sudo gem install puppet -v 2.7.12 --no-rdoc --no-ri
Fetching: facter-1.6.5.gem (100%)
Fetching: puppet-2.7.12.gem (100%)
Successfully installed facter-1.6.5
Successfully installed puppet-2.7.12
2 gems installed
```

That's the only enhancement we're making, so we'll exit, package up the VM, and replace our old base box with our new Puppet-capable box.

```
vm $ exit
$ vagrant package
«lots of output»
$ vagrant box remove lucid64_with_ruby193
[vagrant] Deleting box 'lucid64_with_ruby193'...
$ vagrant box add lucid64_with_ruby193 package.box
[vagrant] Downloading with Vagrant::Downloaders::File...
[vagrant] Copying box to temporary location...
«lots of output»
```

A quick test is in order, so let's clean up our working directory, re-create it, and fire up a new VM with a minimal Vagrantfile.

```
$ vagrant destroy --force
$ cd ../
$ rm -rf updatedvm && mkdir updatedvm
$ cd updatedvm
$ vagrant init lucid64_with_ruby193
«some output»
$ vagrant up
«lots of output»
$ vagrant ssh
vm $
```

Finally, the test: is Puppet installed?

```
vm $ gem list puppet

*** LOCAL GEMS ***

puppet (2.7.12)
```

That's what we want to see. We've updated our base box to include Puppet, and now we'll save a few steps on future VMs since Puppet will be ready to go.

3.9 Where to Go Next

What we've done so far has only scratched the surface of the Puppet universe. There are a few important areas for future exploration: the Puppet language itself, the PuppetMaster and Puppet Dashboard, and the Puppet module ecosystem.

The Puppet Configuration Language

So far we've seen the basics of the Puppet language. We've looked at classes, resource types, nodes, and parameters. There's a lot more to the Puppet DSL and manifest structure, though; modules can include ERB templates that can use variables to produce different files, classes can define functions that can clear out great swathes of duplicated resource declarations, and there are a variety of control flow features such as if and switch statements. On a more macro level, Puppet *environments* can help partition manifests and settings that are for a staging environment from those intended for a production environment. For larger and more complicated server farms, Puppet features such as virtual resources and stored configurations are quite useful, and there's even a concept of "stages," which can ensure that certain setup resources get applied before any other resources.

So, there's a lot to explore past what we've shown here. Still, even with only the concepts introduced thus far, you can build out a reasonable server cluster and get many of the benefits of formalizing configuration using Puppet. But if you find that your manifests are getting repetitive or unwieldy, it's good to know that Puppet has much more to offer.

PuppetMaster and Puppet Dashboard

One important element of Puppet that we haven't discussed is the concept of a PuppetMaster, which is a service that runs on a central host; the Puppet-Master controls access to all the manifests. The other hosts that are configured via Puppet run a Puppet client that connects to the PuppetMaster, pulls down the appropriate configuration directives, and applies any necessary changes. Authentication between the client and server are handled by SSL certificates that each host submits and that can be signed on the PuppetMaster.

We haven't discussed configuring and running a PuppetMaster here because, for getting started, the idea of formalizing a server's packages and files into Puppet manifests brings the largest benefit. It's also possible to run even a medium-sized Puppet setup without a PuppetMaster; simply transferring the Puppet manifests from server to server with git or with rsync will answer the needs of many shops. But using a PuppetMaster is generally recommended, and there are a variety of tutorials showing how to set up a single host as a PuppetMaster or even a cluster of PuppetMasters for failover.

Along the same lines, the Puppet Dashboard is an open source Rails application that supplies an HTML view into the nodes, classes, and hosts on which Puppet is running. Each time a Puppet agent runs, it can report status to the Dashboard so that you can see the state of each host, whether any errors occurred, or whether there were local configuration changes that the Puppet agent overwrote with the latest manifests. Small to medium Puppet installations can run the PuppetMaster and the Puppet Dashboard on the same host. Running the Puppet Dashboard is not required to operate an effective Puppet system, but it provides much needed visibility into the host status.

Open Source Puppet Modules

More than 250 open source Puppet modules are currently available on PuppetForge.[5] As the PuppetForge website says, "Skilled Puppet users have already written many Puppet modules to automate the deployment and configuration of many popular applications. You can reuse these modules in your own infrastructure, saving time and effort." That's true enough, and studying the source code of these modules is a great way to get a feel for how others have solved configuration problems using Puppet.

That said, it's worth learning enough of the Puppet language to write a few simple modules to get started. Many of the modules on PuppetForge were written by advanced Puppet users and are intended to work on a variety of operating systems; if your system has straightforward needs and only a single operating system to support, writing several modules using basic package, exec, service, and file resources may be enough to get you started with automation. But whether you use the modules from PuppetForge or not, they're a great resource and are always available for you to study.

3.10 Conclusion

In this chapter we've gotten an introduction to Puppet, the system configuration utility. We've seen how it automates and formalizes the installation and configuration of various system components, and we've built a basic set of Puppet manifests to prepare a VM for the deployment of MassiveApp.

In the next chapter, we'll look at deploying MassiveApp onto our newly configured VM using the popular Ruby deployment tool Capistrano.

---

5.   http://forge.puppetlabs.com/

Puppet repositories are organized by creating a collection of modules. Each module can be included in a node with an include directive, such as include apache2. Each module contains at least one manifest in the manifests and, optionally, some files in the files directory. Manifests contain class declarations, which contain resource declarations that are composed of types and parameters.

Running Puppet

You can apply Puppet manifest to a system using the following:

```
$ sudo puppet apply --verbose manifests/site.pp
```

Or, to do a test run with more output, use --noop with --verbose.

```
$ sudo puppet apply --noop --verbose manifests/site.pp
```

Sample Apache Manifest

Here's a sample Apache manifest that ensures Apache is installed, has a custom configuration file in place, and starts on boot:

puppetrails/apache_package_file_service/modules/apache2/manifests/init.pp
```
class apache2 {
  package {
    "apache2":
      ensure => present,
      before => File["/etc/apache2/apache2.conf"]
  }

  file {
    "/etc/apache2/apache2.conf":
      owner   => root,
      group   => root,
      mode    => 644,
      source  => "puppet:///modules/apache2/apache2.conf"
  }

  service {
    "apache2":
      ensure    => true,
      enable    => true,
      subscribe => File["/etc/apache2/apache2.conf"]
  }
}
```

Passenger Settings

Here are some basic Passenger settings; you'll want some variation on these in your Apache configuration:

```
PassengerUseGlobalQueue on
PassengerMaxPoolSize 5
PassengerPoolIdleTime 900
PassengerMaxRequests 10000
```

CHAPTER 4

Basic Capistrano

Developing a world-class web application isn't going to do much good if we
aren't able to find a way for the world to see it. For other web frameworks,
this can often be a tedious and time-consuming process. Application code
needs to be updated, database schemas need to be migrated, and application
servers must be restarted. We could do all of this manually by sshing into the
server, pulling the latest code from the repository, running database migration
tasks, and restarting the application server. Even better, we could write some
shell scripts that would automatically perform these tasks for us. But why
do all that when we could be spending time improving MassiveApp instead?
The good news is that we don't have to do all that.

Battle-tested and used for deploying many of today's Rails apps, Capistrano
(originally authored by Jamis Buck and now ably maintained by Lee Hambley)
is the tool that Rails developers have used for years to get their applications
from development to production on a daily basis. It was built from the start
for deploying Rails applications, and it has all the tools we need to get MassiveApp deployed and to help keep deployments running smoothly afterward.
Capistrano's library of tasks, plugins, and utilities has also evolved over the
years with the rest of the Rails ecosystem, and thus Capistrano continues to
meet the deployment needs of Rails applications both new and old.

In the previous chapter, we set up a VM for running MassiveApp. Now we'll
use Capistrano to deploy MassiveApp from our workstation to the VM we
created. Capistrano's responsibility is to prepare the server for deployment
and then deploy the application as updates are made. It does this by executing
tasks as Unix shell commands over an SSH connection to the server. Tasks
are written in a Ruby DSL, so we can leverage the full power of Ruby and the
libraries and gems it has available when writing our deployment scripts.

Let's see what it takes to get Capistrano up and running, and we'll get MassiveApp deployed to our VM for the first time.

4.1 Setting Up Capistrano

The first thing we'll do is install Capistrano on our machine. We'll install Capistrano on the machine we're deploying *from*, not the server we're deploying *to*. All of the things that Capistrano does are invoked as shell commands via an SSH connection, so other than a user account, Capistrano doesn't need anything special on the server to do its work.

When Capistrano connects to the server, it can use an SSH key pair to authenticate the connection attempt. For that to work, we need to have an SSH private key loaded in our keyring that is authorized with a public key on the server for the user Capistrano tries to connect as. Otherwise, if there is no key pair being used or the key fails to authenticate, Capistrano will surface a password prompt every time it runs a command. Having to enter a password multiple times during a deployment is annoying at best and at worst will prevent us from deploying hands-free when it comes to continuous deployment practices. So, to avoid those password prompts, we're going to have Capistrano connect to our VM via the vagrant user account. That account already has a public key in place, so we'll be able to connect right in.

Since we're going to be installing MassiveApp, let's move into the directory we cloned in Section 1.3, *Learning with MassiveApp*, on page 7.

```
$ cd ~/deployingrails/massiveapp
```

The master branch of the repository has all the Capistrano files in place, but we'll build them from scratch here. We have a branch in this repository that contains MassiveApp without Capistrano configuration.

```
$ git branch -a
  before_capistrano
* master
  remotes/origin/HEAD -> origin/master
  remotes/origin/before_capistrano
  remotes/origin/master
```

So, let's switch over to that before_capistrano branch.

```
$ git checkout before_capistrano
Branch before_capistrano set up to track\
remote branch before_capistrano from origin.
Switched to a new branch 'before_capistrano'
```

Like most Ruby libraries and applications, Capistrano comes as a gem. We could install Capistrano using gem install capistrano, but since we're using Bundler for MassiveApp, let's ensure Capistrano always gets installed by adding it to our Gemfile.

```
group :development do
  gem 'capistrano', '~> 2.11.2'
end
```

We add the capistrano gem to the development group since it's not one of MassiveApp's runtime dependencies; thus, there's no need to have it bundled with the application when we deploy. Now we'll get Capistrano and its dependencies in place with Bundler.

```
$ bundle
«...»
Installing net-ssh (2.2.1)
Installing net-scp (1.0.4)
Installing net-sftp (2.0.5)
Installing net-ssh-gateway (1.1.0)
Installing capistrano (2.11.2)
«...»
Your bundle is complete! Use `bundle show [gemname]`
 to see where a bundled gem is installed.
```

To ensure that Capistrano is installed and also to get a handy list of Capistrano's options, let's run cap -h.

```
$ cap -h
Usage: cap [options] action ...
    -d, --debug            Prompts before each remote command execution.
    -e, --explain TASK     Displays help (if available) for the task.
    -F, --default-config   Always use default config, even with -f.
    -f, --file FILE        A recipe file to load. May be given more than once.
    -H, --long-help        Explain these options and environment variables.
«and many more options»
```

We can see more detailed help information with cap -H; here's an example:

```
$ cap -H
-----------------------------
Capistrano
-----------------------------

Capistrano is a utility for automating the execution of commands across multiple
remote machines. It was originally conceived as an aid to deploy Ruby on Rails
web applications, but has since evolved to become a much more general-purpose
tool.
«and much more »
```

MassiveApp Dependencies

MassiveApp uses a MySQL database to store data and thus depends on the mysql2 gem. This gem is a native extension (that is, it includes a component written in C that must be compiled), so it may cause the Bundler run to fail if the appropriate MySQL libraries aren't installed. Many Rails developers will have those libraries in place, but if it does fail, the fix will depend on how MySQL is installed. For example, if it's installed via Homebrew,[a] things will probably just work, whereas if it's installed from source, you may have to ensure that Bundler can find the MySQL shared object libraries and header files.

a.   http://mxcl.github.com/homebrew/

Now we'll set up MassiveApp with Capistrano. The Capistrano deploy process needs some supporting files, and happily Capistrano can generate some example files when we run the capify command.

```
$ capify .
[add] writing './Capfile'
[add] writing './config/deploy.rb'
[done] capified!
```

The capify command created two files for us. The first file, Capfile, lives in our project's root directory and takes care of loading Capistrano's default tasks, any tasks that might be found in plugins (which Capistrano calls *recipes*), the Rails asset pipeline tasks, and our primary deployment script in config/deploy.rb. Here's the content of Capfile; it's just a few lines:

capistrano/Capfile
```
load 'deploy' if respond_to?(:namespace) # cap2 differentiator

# Uncomment if you are using Rails' asset pipeline
# load 'deploy/assets'

Dir[
'vendor/gems/*/recipes/*.rb',
'vendor/plugins/*/recipes/*.rb'].each { |plugin| load(plugin) }

load 'config/deploy' # remove this line to skip loading any of the default tasks
```

The code in Capfile calls the Ruby Kernel#load() method, but that means something different here. It's not just loading up Ruby source code from files. For its own purposes, Capistrano overrides Ruby's default behavior to load its configuration files as well as ones that you specify. Capistrano's redefined load() can also be used to load arbitrary strings containing Ruby code (for example, load(:string => "set :branch, 'release-42'")) and even blocks to be evaluated.

For our first change, MassiveApp is a Rails 3.2 application, so we do want to use the asset pipeline. Therefore, let's uncomment this line in the Capfile:

```
load 'deploy/assets'
```

That's it for the Capfile. The other file that was generated is config/deploy.rb; this contains MassiveApp's deployment script. Next we'll take a look at the settings contained in deploy.rb and learn how to configure them for deploying MassiveApp to our VM.

4.2 Making It Work

The capify command adds a few comments and default settings to config/deploy.rb. We're going to change almost everything, though, and we can learn more about Capistrano if we just start with a blank slate. So, let's open config/deploy.rb in an editor and delete all the contents.

Now that we have an empty config/deploy.rb, we can build out the Capistrano deployment configuration for MassiveApp. MassiveApp is a Rails 3 application and thus uses Bundler, so we need to include the Bundler Capistrano tasks. This line takes care of that:

capistrano/config/deploy.rb
```
require 'bundler/capistrano'
```

Next we set a Capistrano *variable*. Capistrano variables are more or less like Ruby variables; setting a variable makes it available to other parts of the deployment script. Let's set an application variable that we'll use by plugging it into various other parts of the script; this will ensure we'll have directory names that match the application name. We'll usually set this to something "Unixy" (in other words, lowercase, no spaces, no odd characters) like massiveapp.

capistrano/config/deploy.rb
```
set :application, "massiveapp"
```

Deploying MassiveApp means getting the code from the source code repository onto a server, so we need to tell Capistrano where that code lives. Let's add the scm setting with a value of :git. This setting can be a symbol or a string (for example, "git"), but we find symbols more readable. This is followed by the repository. For MassiveApp, this is the GitHub URL since that's where our repository resides.

capistrano/config/deploy.rb
```
set :scm, :git
set :repository, "git://github.com/deployingrails/massiveapp.git"
```

We're deploying to one server, so we need to tell Capistrano where it is. Capistrano has the concept of *roles*, which define what purpose a particular host serves in an environment. For example, some servers may be application servers, some may be database servers, and some may be catchall utility boxes. The VM we've set up will act as a web, application, and database server, so we'll configure it with both those roles by setting the server variable to those role names.

capistrano/config/deploy.rb
```
server "localhost", :web, :app, :db, :primary => true
```

Capistrano needs to connect via SSH to the server to which it's deploying code, but there's a wrinkle here since we're using Vagrant. When we set up the VM with Vagrant, we saw some output when we ran our first vagrant up. Here's the relevant part of that output:

```
[default] Forwarding ports...
[default] -- 22 => 2222 (adapter 1)
```

So, the default Vagrant configuration we're using has forwarded port 2222 on our host to the standard ssh port 22 on the guest VM. We'll need to tell Capistrano about this, so in the next line we tell Capistrano to connect to the port that Vagrant is forwarding. This is followed by the path to the private key that comes with Vagrant. This will save us from having to type in the virtual machine's password.

capistrano/config/deploy.rb
```
ssh_options[:port] = 2222
ssh_options[:keys] = "~/.vagrant.d/insecure_private_key"
```

We need to deploy as an existing user and group, so the next few lines contain those settings. We'll also add a deploy_to setting that tells Capistrano where MassiveApp will live on the virtual machine; this matches the directory path that we created with Puppet in Section 3.5, *Creating the MassiveApp Rails Directory Tree*, on page 47. Also, since we're deploying to a directory that the vagrant user already owns, we won't need to use sudo, so we'll turn that off.

capistrano/config/deploy.rb
```
set :user, "vagrant"
set :group, "vagrant"
set :deploy_to, "/var/massiveapp"
set :use_sudo, false
```

Since we're going to deploy code, we need a way to move the code from the Git repository to the VM. These next few lines use what Capistrano calls the *copy strategy* to move the code up to the VM. The copy strategy consists of cloning the Git repository to a temporary directory on the local machine and, since we've also set copy_strategy to export, removing the .git directory. Removing the .git directory makes the deploy payload smaller and, more importantly, prevents our entire Git repository from being accessible to someone who hacks into our server. The copy strategy then compresses the source code and copies the compressed file to the VM where it is uncompressed into the deployment target directory. This is a convenient way to put the code onto the VM since the code export is done locally; we don't need to depend on the VM being able to connect to the remote Git repository or even having Git installed.

capistrano/config/deploy.rb
```
set :deploy_via, :copy
set :copy_strategy, :export
```

So far, we've seen Capistrano variable settings; now it's time to add some tasks. When we deploy new code to the VM, we need to tell Passenger to load our new code into new application instances. We'll do this with a few task declarations.

This series of tasks starts with a namespace() declaration. This allows us to group the Passenger-related tasks logically, and it lets us declare other start and stop tasks to manage other services without those declarations clashing with the Passenger task names. The stop and start tasks are empty since Passenger will serve up MassiveApp as soon as the code is in place, but the restart task contains a single command that signals Passenger to restart MassiveApp so our new code will be loaded. And we need a task to copy our database.yml file into place, so we'll put that here as well as a before directive that will force that task to be called as part of a deployment.

capistrano/config/deploy.rb
```
namespace :deploy do
  task :start do ; end
  task :stop do ; end
  desc "Restart the application"
  task :restart, :roles => :app, :except => { :no_release => true } do
    run "#{try_sudo} touch #{File.join(current_path,'tmp','restart.txt')}"
  end
  desc "Copy the database.yml file into the latest release"
  task :copy_in_database_yml do
    run "cp #{shared_path}/config/database.yml #{latest_release}/config/"
  end
end
before "deploy:assets:precompile", "deploy:copy_in_database_yml"
```

We'll look at more tasks later, but that wraps up our initial tour of a minimal config/deploy.rb. Now we'll actually use it!

4.3 Setting Up the Deploy

Now that the deployment configuration is in place, we'll need a VM on which to deploy it. From the previous chapter, let's create a Vagrantfile in ~/deployingrails/ massiveapp/; we'll put a few basic settings in here.

```
capistrano/Vagrantfile
Vagrant::Config.run do |config|
  config.vm.customize ["modifyvm", :id, "--name", "app", "--memory", "512"]
  config.vm.box = "lucid64_with_ruby193"
  config.vm.host_name = "app"
  config.vm.forward_port 22, 2222, :auto => true
  config.vm.forward_port 80, 4567
  config.vm.network :hostonly, "33.33.13.37"
  config.vm.share_folder "puppet", "/etc/puppet", "../massiveapp_ops"
end
```

As we discussed in *Instances Need Unique Names*, on page 22, Vagrant allows only one VM at a time to have a particular name. So, if there's still a VM named app running from previous examples, now is a good time to go back and destroy that VM. With that done, let's fire up the new VM and connect into it.

```
$ vagrant up
«...»
[default] Mounting shared folders...
[default] -- v-root: /vagrant
[default] -- puppet: etc/puppet
«...»
$ vagrant ssh
«...»
app $
```

And now we'll set it up as a MassiveApp server using the Puppet manifests that we built in the previous chapter.

```
app $ cd /etc/puppet
app $ sudo puppet apply --verbose manifests/site.pp
«lots of output»
```

With that VM in place, we're getting closer to a code deploy. We set deploy_to to /var/massiveapp, but that directory isn't quite ready yet. For Capistrano to deploy to a server, it needs to have a subdirectory structure in place. This directory structure will be used for the application code releases and for assets that are shared by the application between releases.

Let's use Capistrano to create these directories for us by running the deploy:setup task.

```
$ cap deploy:setup
  * executing `deploy:setup'
  * executing "mkdir -p /var/massiveapp /var/massiveapp/releases
  /var/massiveapp/shared /var/massiveapp/shared/system
  /var/massiveapp/shared/log /var/massiveapp/shared/pids &&
  chmod g+w /var/massiveapp /var/massiveapp/releases
  /var/massiveapp/shared /var/massiveapp/shared/system
  /var/massiveapp/shared/log /var/massiveapp/shared/pids"
    servers: ["localhost"]
    [localhost] executing command
    command finished in 4ms
```

Running the deploy:setup task created the following directory structure in the /var/massiveapp directory:

```
- /releases
- /shared
  |- /log
  |- /system
  |- /pids
```

Each time we deploy, Capistrano will create a new subdirectory in the releases directory and place the source code for MassiveApp there. The shared directory will contain various, well, shared resources. Thus, shared/log will contain MassiveApp's log files, and shared/system will contain any files that need to be kept from deployment to deployment. We also have shared/config, which we created with Puppet and which contains MassiveApp's database.yml.

We've built out a basic Capistrano configuration file, we've used Capistrano to create some directories on our VM, and we're getting close to deploying some actual code. That's what's coming up next.

4.4 Pushing a Release

Now that we have our config/deploy.rb file ready to go and the initial directory structure in place, let's get MassiveApp out on the virtual machine. The task to run is deploy:cold; it's named cold because we're deploying MassiveApp for the first time. And remember when we included require 'bundler/capistrano' in config/deploy.rb? With that in place, the deploy:cold task will run bundle:install to get our MassiveApp gems into place. It's an after_deploy *life-cycle hook* on deploy:finalize_update, so it'll be run on subsequent deploys as well.

We'll unpack the deploy flow in this section, but Figure 2, *The deploy:code task flow*, on page 70 is an overview of what happens. The top-level task is deploy:cold, and that triggers various other dependent tasks.

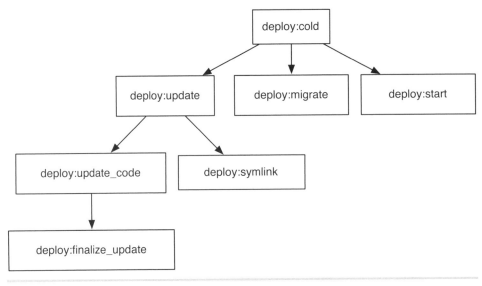

Figure 2—The **deploy:code** task flow

Deploying with Capistrano produces a torrent of output, but it's worth reading through it at least once to get familiar with what Capistrano is doing. We get things rolling by invoking the task.

```
$ cap deploy:cold
«lots of output»
```

First, deploy:cold runs a dependent task called deploy:update, which in turn runs deploy:update_code. This task exports MassiveApp's code from our Git repository by cloning the repository and deleting the .git directory.

```
capistrano/deploy_cold_output.txt
 * executing `deploy:cold'
 * executing `deploy:update'
** transaction: start
 * executing `deploy:update_code'
   executing locally:
   "git ls-remote
   git://github.com/deployingrails/massiveapp.git HEAD"
   command finished in 388ms
 * getting (via export) revision
   1d45e7a7609386da0b56cbd9299eb6e1ea73edee
   to /var/folders/dE/dEW2lQWVGMeQ5tBgIlc5l++++TU/-Tmp-/20120322202531
   executing locally:
   git clone -q git://github.com/deployingrails/massiveapp.git
   /var/folders/dE/dEW2lQWVGMeQ5tBgIlc5l++++TU/-Tmp-/20120322202531
   && cd /var/folders/dE/dEW2lQWVGMeQ5tBgIlc5l++++TU/-Tmp-/20120322202531
   && git checkout -q -b deploy 1d45e7a7609386da0b56cbd9299eb6e1ea73edee
```

```
&& rm -Rf /var/folders/dE/dEW2lQWVGMeQ5tBgIlc5l++++TU/-Tmp-/20120322202531/.git
command finished in 187ms
```

Next, the source code gets packaged, compressed, and moved (using sftp) up
to the VM. The filename is based on a timestamp with granularity down to
the second. Each releases subdirectory name is based on this timestamp, so
this allows us to deploy frequently without directory conflicts.

capistrano/deploy_cold_output.txt
```
    compressing /var/folders/dE/dEW2lQWVGMeQ5tBgIlc5l++++TU/-Tmp-/20120322202531
    to /var/folders/dE/dEW2lQWVGMeQ5tBgIlc5l++++TU/-Tmp-/20120322202531.tar.gz
    executing locally: tar czf 20120322202531.tar.gz 20120322202531
    command finished in 10ms
    servers: ["localhost"]
** sftp upload
   /var/folders/dE/dEW2lQWVGMeQ5tBgIlc5l++++TU/-Tmp-/20120322202531.tar.gz
   -> /tmp/20120322202531.tar.gz
   [localhost] sftp upload
   /var/folders/dE/dEW2lQWVGMeQ5tBgIlc5l++++TU/-Tmp-/20120322202531.tar.gz
   -> /tmp/20120322202531.tar.gz
   [localhost] sftp upload
   /var/folders/dE/dEW2lQWVGMeQ5tBgIlc5l++++TU/-Tmp-/20120322202531.tar.gz
   -> /tmp/20120322202531.tar.gz done
 * sftp upload complete
```

Then, Capistrano uncompresses the code into the releases directory, which we
created when we ran deploy:setup. After the code is uncompressed, Capistrano
deletes the tar file. At this point, MassiveApp's code is in the correct location
to be served up.

capistrano/deploy_cold_output.txt
```
 * executing "cd /var/massiveapp/releases &&
   tar xzf /tmp/20120322202531.tar.gz && rm /tmp/20120322202531.tar.gz"
   servers: ["localhost"]
   [localhost] executing command
   [localhost] sh -c 'cd /var/massiveapp/releases
   && tar xzf /tmp/20120322202531.tar.gz
   && rm /tmp/20120322202531.tar.gz'
   command finished in 14ms
```

Capistrano then sets up a symbolic link to a shared/assets subdirectory.

capistrano/deploy_cold_output.txt
```
 * executing `deploy:finalize_update'
   triggering before callbacks for `deploy:finalize_update'
 * executing `deploy:assets:symlink'
 * executing "rm -rf /var/massiveapp/releases/20120322202531/public/assets &&\\\n
   mkdir -p /var/massiveapp/releases/20120322202531/public &&\\\n
   mkdir -p /var/massiveapp/shared/assets &&\\\n
   ln -s /var/massiveapp/shared/assets
```

```
/var/massiveapp/releases/20120322202531/public/assets"
servers: ["localhost"]
[localhost] executing command
[localhost] sh -c
'rm -rf /var/massiveapp/releases/20120322202531/public/assets &&\
[localhost] mkdir -p /var/massiveapp/releases/20120322202531/public &&\
[localhost] mkdir -p /var/massiveapp/shared/assets &&\
[localhost] ln -s /var/massiveapp/shared/assets
/var/massiveapp/releases/20120322202531/public/assets'
command finished in 9ms
```

Once that's done, the deploy:finalize_update task sets permissions and creates several symbolic links.

capistrano/deploy_cold_output.txt
```
* executing "chmod -R g+w /var/massiveapp/releases/20120322202531"
  servers: ["localhost"]
  [localhost] executing command
  [localhost] sh -c 'chmod -R g+w /var/massiveapp/releases/20120322202531'
  command finished in 5ms
* executing "rm -rf /var/massiveapp/releases/20120322202531/log
  /var/massiveapp/releases/20120322202531/public/system
  /var/massiveapp/releases/20120322202531/tmp/pids
  &&\\\n    mkdir -p /var/massiveapp/releases/20120322202531/public
  &&\\\n    mkdir -p /var/massiveapp/releases/20120322202531/tmp"
  servers: ["localhost"]
  [localhost] executing command
  [localhost] sh -c
  'rm -rf /var/massiveapp/releases/20120322202531/log
  /var/massiveapp/releases/20120322202531/public/system
  /var/massiveapp/releases/20120322202531/tmp/pids &&\
  [localhost] mkdir -p /var/massiveapp/releases/20120322202531/public &&\
  [localhost] mkdir -p /var/massiveapp/releases/20120322202531/tmp'
  command finished in 7ms
* executing "ln -s /var/massiveapp/shared/system
  /var/massiveapp/releases/20120322202531/public/system"
  servers: ["localhost"]
  [localhost] executing command
  [localhost] sh -c 'ln -s /var/massiveapp/shared/system
  /var/massiveapp/releases/20120322202531/public/system'
  command finished in 5ms
* executing "ln -s /var/massiveapp/shared/log
  /var/massiveapp/releases/20120322202531/log"
  servers: ["localhost"]
  [localhost] executing command
  [localhost] sh -c 'ln -s /var/massiveapp/shared/log
  /var/massiveapp/releases/20120322202531/log'
  command finished in 5ms
* executing "ln -s /var/massiveapp/shared/pids
  /var/massiveapp/releases/20120322202531/tmp/pids"
  servers: ["localhost"]
```

```
[localhost] executing command
[localhost] sh -c 'ln -s /var/massiveapp/shared/pids
/var/massiveapp/releases/20120322202531/tmp/pids'
command finished in 5ms
```

During this step, the public/system directory gets symlinked to shared/system. This means that anything in shared/system will be available through MassiveApp's document root to anyone who guesses the filename. So, that's a good place to put shared public documents, such as press releases or documentation manuals that need to be available across deployments. But it's not a good place to put sensitive data, such as an environment-specific database.yml file (not that either of your authors has made that mistake...or, perhaps, will ever make that mistake again).

Here's the output of the Bundler command bundle that we discussed earlier; this installs MassiveApp's gems on the VM:

capistrano/deploy_cold_output.txt
```
  triggering after callbacks for `deploy:finalize_update'
* executing `bundle:install'
* executing "ls -x /var/massiveapp/releases"
  servers: ["localhost"]
  [localhost] executing command
  [localhost] sh -c 'ls -x /var/massiveapp/releases'
  command finished in 5ms
* executing "cd /var/massiveapp/releases/20120322202531
  && bundle install
  --gemfile /var/massiveapp/releases/20120322202531/Gemfile
  --path /var/massiveapp/shared/bundle
  --deployment --quiet --without development test"
  servers: ["localhost"]
  [localhost] executing command
  [localhost] sh -c 'cd /var/massiveapp/releases/20120322202531
  && bundle install
  --gemfile /var/massiveapp/releases/20120322202531/Gemfile
  --path /var/massiveapp/shared/bundle
  --deployment --quiet --without development test'
  command finished in 259ms
```

Next the Rails asset pipeline precompiles the static assets; these files get placed into the /var/massiveapp/shared/assets/ directory that Capistrano created earlier. This can take a while for projects that have many CSS or JavaScript files. Just before this happens, we copy the database.yml file into place since the Rails environment requires it.

capistrano/deploy_cold_output.txt
```
  triggering after callbacks for `deploy:update_code'
* executing `deploy:assets:precompile'
  triggering before callbacks for `deploy:assets:precompile'
```

```
* executing `deploy:copy_in_database_yml'
* executing "cp /var/massiveapp/shared/config/database.yml
  /var/massiveapp/releases/20120514044142/config/"
  servers: ["localhost"]
  [localhost] executing command
  command finished in 5ms
* executing "cd /var/massiveapp/releases/20120322202531
  && bundle exec rake RAILS_ENV=production RAILS_GROUPS=assets assets:precompile"
  servers: ["localhost"]
  [localhost] executing command
  [localhost] sh -c
  'cd /var/massiveapp/releases/20120322202531
  && bundle exec rake RAILS_ENV=production RAILS_GROUPS=assets assets:precompile'
  command finished in 11332ms
```

Then comes the magic moment when the current symbolic link is created. Since the Apache DocumentRoot points to current/public/, this makes the application available.

capistrano/deploy_cold_output.txt

```
  * executing `deploy:create_symlink'
  * executing `deploy:symlink'
[Deprecation Warning] This API has changed, please
  hook `deploy:create_symlink` instead of `deploy:symlink`.
  * executing "rm -f /var/massiveapp/current
    && ln -s /var/massiveapp/releases/20120322202531 /var/massiveapp/current"
    servers: ["localhost"]
    [localhost] executing command
    [localhost] sh -c 'rm -f /var/massiveapp/current
    && ln -s /var/massiveapp/releases/20120322202531 /var/massiveapp/current'
    command finished in 9ms
```

Since Puppet just created the massiveapp_production database, it's empty. So, Capistrano runs all the migrations to get our tables into place.

capistrano/deploy_cold_output.txt

```
  * executing `deploy:migrate'
  * executing "cd /var/massiveapp/releases/20120322202531 &&
    bundle exec rake RAILS_ENV=production  db:migrate"
    servers: ["localhost"]
    [localhost] executing command
    [localhost] sh -c 'cd /var/massiveapp/releases/20120322202531
    && bundle exec rake RAILS_ENV=production  db:migrate'
** [out :: localhost] ==  CreateUsers: migrating ==========
** [out :: localhost] -- create_table(:users)
** [out :: localhost] -> 0.0022s
** [out :: localhost] ==  CreateUsers: migrated (0.0023s) =
** [out :: localhost]
** [out :: localhost] ==  CreateBookmarks: migrating ======
** [out :: localhost] -- create_table(:bookmarks)
** [out :: localhost] -> 0.0035s
```

```
** [out :: localhost] -- add_index(:bookmarks, :user_id)
** [out :: localhost] -> 0.0040s
** [out :: localhost] ==  CreateBookmarks: migrated (0.0075s) =
** [out :: localhost]
** [out :: localhost] ==  CreateShares: migrating ==========
** [out :: localhost] -- create_table(:shares)
** [out :: localhost] -> 0.0023s
** [out :: localhost] -- add_index(:shares, :bookmark_id)
** [out :: localhost] -> 0.0038s
** [out :: localhost] -- add_index(:shares, :shared_by_id)
** [out :: localhost] -> 0.0034s
** [out :: localhost] -- add_index(:shares, :shared_with_id)
** [out :: localhost] -> 0.0034s
** [out :: localhost] ==  CreateShares: migrated (0.0130s) =
** [out :: localhost]
** [out :: localhost] ==  RenameUsersToAccounts: migrating =
** [out :: localhost] -- rename_table(:users, :accounts)
** [out :: localhost] -> 0.0011s
** [out :: localhost] ==  RenameUsersToAccounts: migrated (0.0011s) =
** [out :: localhost]
   command finished in 1581ms
```

At last Capistrano calls deploy:start, which we've previously defined to do nothing.

capistrano/deploy_cold_output.txt
```
* executing `deploy:start'
```

Done! MassiveApp is deployed to the virtual machine. If we open a browser to localhost:4567, we'll see MassiveApp in action.

Now that the first deploy is done, we can deploy in the future with another task, deploy.

```
$ cap deploy
  * executing `deploy'
  * executing `deploy:update'
 ** transaction: start
  * executing `deploy:update_code'
    executing locally: "git ls-remote
      git://github.com/deployingrails/massiveapp.git HEAD"
    command finished in 109ms
«and much more»
```

The difference between deploy and deploy:cold is that deploy:cold triggers the deploy:migrate task and also calls deploy:start rather than deploy:restart. We can run deploy:migrations to do a normal deploy but run any pending migrations as well, although at the cost of the increased deploy time because of the time it takes to run that task.

Now we've deployed MassiveApp and thoroughly explored the Capistrano deployment process. Next we'll look more closely at some Capistrano concepts that we've only glanced at thus far: tasks, hooks, and roles.

4.5   Exploring Roles, Tasks, and Hooks

Getting Capistrano to deploy MassiveApp was a success. Now we'll dive a little deeper into Capistrano's use of tasks, hooks, and roles.

Capistrano Tasks

In the example of a Capistrano task in config/deploy.rb where we defined a series of tasks to manage MassiveApp's restarts. Here's that section of the file:

```
capistrano/config/deploy.rb
namespace :deploy do
  task :start do ; end
  task :stop do ; end
  desc "Restart the application"
  task :restart, :roles => :app, :except => { :no_release => true } do
    run "#{try_sudo} touch #{File.join(current_path,'tmp','restart.txt')}"
  end
  desc "Copy the database.yml file into the latest release"
  task :copy_in_database_yml do
    run "cp #{shared_path}/config/database.yml #{latest_release}/config/"
  end
end
before "deploy:assets:precompile", "deploy:copy_in_database_yml"
```

Working from the top down, we first see a namespace() declaration. A namespace can be any symbol and lets you group tasks by functionality area. For example, the thinking_sphinx RubyGem contains a number of tasks all declared within the thinking_sphinx namespace. On that same line, we see that the namespace() method accepts a block. This block can contain more namespace declarations as well as task declarations. We can declare a namespace several times in our script if we want to add tasks to that namespace at different points. In that respect, redeclaring a namespace is much like reopening a Ruby class.

Inside the deploy namespace, you see the actual tasks: stop, start, and restart. stop and start are both *no-ops*. That is, they pass in an empty block and thus do nothing. The restart task, on the other hand, has some code and a few interesting features.

- It's prefixed by a desc() method call with a String parameter. With this method call in place, a user running cap -T will see the task listed along with its description. Without a description in place, a user would need to remember to run cap -vT, which displays tasks that don't have descriptions. Who's going to remember that extra flag? Thus, we'll define a description for all but the most trivial tasks.

- There's a :roles => :app parameter. This indicates that this task will be run only on servers that are listed in the :app role. That's because there's no need to try to restart Passenger unless a server is running MassiveApp. For example, we might have a utility server that needs the MassiveApp code deployed for cron jobs but isn't serving requests over HTTP. There's no need to touch tmp/restart.txt on that server.

- There's also an :except => { :no_release => true } clause. This prevents the task from being executed on servers that are not part of the release process. For example, we may have a server running a message queue that is not affected by releases, but we still may want to execute certain tasks on that server. In that case, we would mark that server as being release-free (for example, role :message_queue, "my.mq.server", :no_release => true), and deploy: restart wouldn't affect it.

- Finally, there's the body of the task. This contains a call to the run() method, which executes the given String as a shell script on the appropriate servers. The command contains a reference to the current_path() method. That's the way to interpolate values into the commands that we want to execute on the remote servers.

The Capistrano wiki[1] contains a good deal of information on the various commands a task can call, and that set of commands will vary based on the Capistrano plugins and extensions that are installed. We'll see many more examples of tasks in this book, though, and we'll call out the interesting bits.

Capistrano Hooks

Most Rails developers are used to seeing ActiveRecord's callback methods. For example, the callback method before_save() provides a way for an ActiveRecord model to execute some code just prior to being saved. These callback methods are sometimes referred to as *hooks* since they allow model code to "hook" into ActiveRecord's object life-cycle management.

Capistrano has a similar feature called a deployment *hook*. This is a piece of code that runs before or after a particular task. You've seen a hint at one of these already; the first few lines of config/deploy.rb in Section 4.4, *Pushing a*

---

1. https://github.com/capistrano/capistrano/wiki

Release, on page 69 contained a require statement that brought in the Bundler Capistrano tasks. To be accurate, it brought in the Bundler Capistrano *task*; as of this writing, there's only one. That single task is a deploy:update_code *after hook* that causes the bundle:install task to be run after the deploy:update_code task is completed. It makes sense to run bundle:install at that point since by then the Gemfile is in place. Given that there's an after hook, you won't be surprised to hear that *before hooks* also exist for the purpose of, well, running code before a task.

Hooks are as useful with Capistrano as they are with ActiveRecord. For example, if we're feeling cautious, we might want our deployment script to prompt for confirmation before deploying the code. To do this, we could register a before_deploy hook for a task that does just that. Here's the code; let's place this in a new file called lib/deploy/confirm_deploy.rb:

capistrano/lib/deploy/confirm_deploy.rb
```
namespace :deploy do
  desc "Make sure the user really wants to deploy"
  task :confirm do
    if Capistrano::CLI.ui.ask("Are you sure you want to deploy?") == "yes"
      puts "OK, here goes!"
    else
      puts "Exiting"
      exit
    end
  end
end
```

In this example, the task uses Capistrano's Capistrano::CLI utility to prompt the user for input and exit if the user doesn't type yes. To get Capistrano to see this task, though, we need to modify the Capfile to load it. So, let's open the Capfile and add one more line so that Capistrano will load everything in the lib/deploy directory. Now the Capfile looks like this:

capistrano/cap2/Capfile
```
load 'deploy' if respond_to?(:namespace) # cap2 differentiator
Dir['vendor/plugins/*/recipes/*.rb'].each { |plugin| load(plugin) }
load 'config/deploy' # remove this line to skip loading any of the default tasks
Dir.glob("lib/deploy/*.rb").each {|f| load f }
```

Now we'll declare a hook to call this task from our config/deploy.rb. We'll add this as the last line of that file:

```
before :deploy, "deploy:confirm"
```

Now we can see this task in action. Let's run the cap deploy task and wait for the prompt.

```
$ cap deploy
  * executing `deploy'
    triggering before callbacks for `deploy'
  * executing `deploy:confirm'
Are you sure you want to deploy?
no
Exiting
```

This task definition and the hook consisted of only a few lines of code, but they needed to go somewhere. We could have put the code right into config/deploy.rb, and for such a short bit of code that wouldn't be a terrible solution. But these sorts of things build up over time, and to keep our config/deploy.rb from growing, we prefer to put the code in the lib/deploy directory. Then we can give the file an intention-revealing name like confirm_deploy.rb, and someone browsing that directory will be able to get a quick idea of what's in there. We put the task definition in that file and put the actual hook (that is, before :deploy, "deploy:confirm") into the config/deploy.rb file. That way, all the logic is contained in config/deploy.rb, and the lib/deploy directory acts as a set of libraries that don't do anything unless explicitly invoked.

The downside of putting things in a separate directory like this is that now all our tasks aren't defined in one place. But there are enough useful plugins and utilities in the Capistrano ecosystem that we've found we're loading Capistrano code from other directories anyway. We think the organizational benefits outweigh the initial loss of visibility, and putting all the hooks in config/deploy.rb makes a big difference.

Capistrano Roles

Previously (in Section 4.2, *Making It Work*, on page 65) we saw a server() declaration that configured localhost to act as both the application and the database for MassiveApp. We can use Capistrano's role feature whenever we want a task to run on one set of servers but not on another. One way to write this is as follows:

```
server "servername", :some_role_name, :another_role_name
```

This is a nice shortcut when we have only one host to work with. The following is an alternate method when we have a variety of servers in different roles:

```
role :some_role_name, "servername"
role :another_role_name, "servername"
```

Once we declare a role, we can use it in task declarations. For example, suppose we wanted the deploy:confirm task to run only on servers configured in the app role. We could use this declaration to accomplish that:

```
task :confirm, :roles => :app do
```

We can also use environment variables to take advantage of role declarations. For example, to make a workers:refresh task run only on servers that are configured with the worker role, we could do this:

```
$ ROLES=worker cap workers:refresh
```

The role name can be any valid Ruby symbol. The built-in Capistrano tasks center around three predefined roles.

- app is for tasks that run on application servers. deploy:cold, deploy:update_code, and deploy:restart are all tasks that run on servers in this role.

- db is for tasks that run on database servers. An example of this is deploy:migrate.

- web is for tasks that run on web servers, that is, servers dedicated to serving static content. deploy:web:enable and deploy:web:disable are the only standard tasks that use this role.

4.6 Conclusion

We've written a Capistrano script and deployed MassiveApp to our virtual machine. Having seen an entire successful deployment run means that the flood of Capistrano output is no longer a mystery. Better still, we now have a basic understanding of the elements that make up a Capistrano deployment script (tasks, variables, and so on), and we'll be able to modify that script to meet future needs.

There are a variety of alternatives to Capistrano that are appropriate for very large deployment scenarios; Twitter's murder[2] is one such alternative. We've found that Capistrano provides a great place to start and can get an application a long way before one of the other solutions needs to be evaluated. When an application has gotten to the size where it outgrows Capistrano, there's usually a dedicated operations team tasked with thinking about making the code-to-server delivery as smooth as possible.

With this foundation in place, we'll spend the next chapter looking at some more advanced Capistrano techniques and tools.

---

2. https://github.com/lg/murder

## CHAPTER 5

Advanced Capistrano

Now that we've configured Capistrano to do the heavy lifting when it comes to deploying MassiveApp, we can sit back and enjoy the show, right? Well, as you can probably guess, not quite. Deployment, like any other area of software development, benefits from constantly iterating and improving the code and configuration. When refactoring our Capistrano configuration, Capistrano provides a number of facilities that will aid us in both making deployments faster and maintaining MassiveApp once it's deployed. In this chapter, we'll take a look at some of these advanced features, techniques, and best practices with Capistrano to round out MassiveApp's deployment process.

Not all these Capistrano techniques will be useful in every deployment scenario. For example, we'll discuss multistage deployments, which are needed only when deploying an application to more than one environment. But we'll discuss the situations in which each feature would come in handy, and these are all good tools to have at the ready.

5.1 Deploying Faster by Creating Symlinks in Bulk

Sometimes we'll see variables defined in block form; here's an example:

```
set(:deploy_to) { "/var/massiveapp/deploy/#{name}" }
```

Blocks are used in Capistrano for variables whose values must be lazy-loaded. They become especially useful when you must interpolate the value of another Capistrano variable and as a rule of thumb should always be used whenever a reference to another Capistrano variable is made.

Let's look at a more complex use of block variables and speed up our deploys at the same time. As part of the default deployment process, Capistrano symlinks certain directories in the #{deploy_to}/shared directory after updating the application code. By default, each of these symlinks is created using a separate call to run, which in turn creates a separate SSH connection to make each symlink. Establishing and tearing down these SSH connections can take some time. Using Capistrano's block variables, though, we can replace the symlink task with one that gives us more speed, as well as additional flexibility.

Here's a set of variables assignments that show all the directories that need to be cleaned up, created, or removed during a deploy. There are a lot, so if we can avoid making a connection for each, our deploys will be much faster.

capistrano2/sample_variables.rb
```
set :cleanup_targets, %w(log public/system tmp)
set :release_directories, %w(log tmp)
set :release_symlinks do
  {
    "config/settings/#{stage}.yml" => 'config/settings.yml',
    "config/database/#{stage}.yml" => 'config/memcached.yml',
  }
end
set :shared_symlinks, {
  'log'     => 'log',
  'pids'    => 'tmp/pids',
  'sockets' => 'tmp/sockets',
  'system'  => 'public/system'
}
```

To get started, let's redefine the deploy:symlink task. We'll include a description, and we'll run this task with the same restrictions as the built-in tasks, only on app servers.

capistrano2/lib/deploy/deploy_symlink_override.rb
```
namespace :deploy do
  desc "Create symlinks to stage-specific configuration files and shared resources"
  task :symlink, :roles => :app, :except => { :no_release => true } do
  end
end
```

Now we can fill in the body of the task. We'll iterate over the cleanup_targets array and create a shell command to remove each of the target files/directories.

```
symlink_command = cleanup_targets.map { |target| \
  "rm -fr #{current_path}/#{target}" }
```

Next we'll do the same with the release_directories variable; it contains directories to be re-created on each deploy.

```
symlink_command += release_directories.map { |directory| "mkdir -p #{directory} }
```

Then we build more commands from the release_symlinks variable that contains symlinks that should be created from items in the release directory. These will typically be stage-specific configuration files that we don't mind checking in to our repository. The -s flag tells the ln utility to create a symlink, and the -f flag tells ln that if the symlink exists, it should remove and re-create it.

```
symlink_command += release_symlinks.map { |from, to| \
  "rm -fr #{current_path}/#{to} && \
  ln -sf #{current_path}/#{from} #{current_path}/#{to}" }
```

We build still more commands from the data in shared_symlinks. In this variable, *from* is relative to shared_path, and *to* is relative to the current_path.

```
symlink_command += shared_symlinks.map { |from, to| \
  "rm -fr #{current_path}/#{to} && \
  ln -sf #{shared_path}/#{from} #{current_path}/#{to}" }
```

Finally, we concatenate all of these into a single shell command that runs all of the directory and symlink commands at once.

```
run "cd #{current_path} && #{symlink_command.join(' && ')}"
```

Here's the entire task that we've built up line by line:

```
capistrano2/deploy_task.rb
namespace :deploy do
  desc "Create symlinks to stage-specific configuration files and shared resources"
  task :symlink, :roles => :app, :except => { :no_release => true } do
    symlink_command = cleanup_targets.map \
      { |target| "rm -fr #{current_path}/#{target}" }
    symlink_command += release_directories.map \
      { |directory| "mkdir -p #{directory} }
    symlink_command += release_symlinks.map \
      { |from, to| "rm -fr #{current_path}/#{to} && \
        ln -sf #{current_path}/#{from} #{current_path}/#{to}" }
    symlink_command += shared_symlinks.map \
      { |from, to| "rm -fr #{current_path}/#{to} && \
        ln -sf #{shared_path}/#{from} #{current_path}/#{to}" }
    run "cd #{current_path} && #{symlink_command.join(' && ')}"
  end
end
```

This technique nicely separates the configuration data values from the code that processes them, making the deployment configuration more readable. It's a win on both performance and clarity.

5.2 Uploading and Downloading Files

Capistrano has a handy set of functions available for transferring files to and from remote machines. The simplest of these is get, which we can use to fetch a file from a remote server.

capistrano2/get.rb
```
desc "Download the production log file"
task :get_log do
  get "#{current_path}/log/production.log", \
    "#{Time.now.strftime("%Y%m%d%H%M")}.production.log"
end
```

We can also fetch an entire directory tree with the recursive option.

capistrano2/get_recursive.rb
```
desc "Download the entire log directory"
task :get_log_directory do
  get "#{current_path}/log/", "tmp/", :recursive => true
end
```

get will connect to only one server, but for connecting to multiple servers, we can use download. However, if we download files with the same name from multiple servers, they'll just overwrite each other. Fortunately, Capistrano supports a simple macro; it replaces $CAPISTRANO:HOST$ with the name of the host to which Capistrano is connecting. So, we can write our download task with this macro in the destination filename, and we'll get a series of files all prefixed with the appropriate host name.

capistrano2/download.rb
```
desc "Download the production log file"
task :download_log do
  download "#{current_path}/log/production.log",\
    "$CAPISTRANO:HOST$.production.log"
end
```

Capistrano also gives us an upload command for transferring files to remote servers. The $CAPISTRANO:HOST$ string works with upload, so we can give each server a specific maintenance page by placing a few files in a local directory.

```
$ ls tmp/maintenance_pages/
maintenance.html.server1.com maintenance.html.server2.com
maintenance.html.server3.com
```

Then we'll reference that file in a task that uses upload, and each server will receive the appropriate file.

capistrano2/upload.rb
```
desc "Upload the host-specific maintenance pages to each server"
task :upload_maintenance_page do
  upload "tmp/maintenance.html.$CAPISTRANO:HOST$", "#{deploy_to}/maintenance.html"
end
```

Sometimes we need to upload not a file but instead just the contents of a string. In those cases, we can use the put() method. To demonstrate this, let's write a small task to copy the current Git revision to the remote servers. We can find the Git revision with rev-parse.

```
$ git rev-parse HEAD
956fe36157c57060414e4f9804bb79fc6f1cae90 # Or some such SHA
```

And we'll upload it to our VM using put().

capistrano2/put.rb
```
desc "Put the current revision onto the server"
task :put_revision do
  put `git rev-parse HEAD`.strip, "#{current_path}/public/REVISION"
end
```

With these handy Capistrano features, there's no reason to resort to shelling out to scp to move files or data around.

5.3   Restricting Tasks with Roles

We've seen the default app, web, and db Capistrano roles and some examples of how they're used by various built-in Capistrano tasks. However, sometimes we have jobs that don't fit into those three categories, and for those situations we can define and use a new server role. Let's set up some roles for using Redis.[1]

A basic Redis configuration has an instance running on one server. We'll define a new redis role by naming it and supplying the hosts to which it applies.

```
role :redis, "redismaster.mydomain"
```

Now we'll use this new role in a task declaration.

```
task :rewrite_aof, :roles => :redis do |t|
  # send in the bgrewriteaof command
end
```

This means that the rewrite_aof task will be run only on our redismaster.mydomain host. We could also specify several host names on one line if we had multiple instances.

```
role :redis, "redis1.mydomain", "redis2.mydomain"
```

Here's another scenario. Suppose we have several hosts running Redis for gathering statistics and an additional host running an instance that we use for Resque. To accommodate this setup, we can attach attributes to the role declarations to differentiate those hosts.

---

1.   An excellent open source key-value store; read all about it at http://redis.io.

```
role :redis, "resque.mydomain", {:resque => true}
role :redis, "stats1.mydomain", "stats2.mydomain", {:stats => true}
```

To get a weekly summary for the stats hosts, let's declare a task that further restricts the hosts on which it's run.

```
task :weekly_summary, :roles => :redis, :only => {:stats => true} do |t|
  # calculate weekly statistics
end
```

For the ultimate in flexibility, we can pass a block to a role declaration, and that block will be evaluated when the script is running. This is handy when the list of servers to which a role applies is not known until runtime. For example, we'll want to run bgrewriteaof on all our Redis servers, and the list of those servers might be stored in a separate YAML file.

```
servers:
  redis:
    - 192.168.10.10
    - 192.168.10.11
    - 192.168.10.14
```

We'll read those servers in with a block associated with our role declaration. In this case, we need to wrap the role name in parentheses so the Ruby parser can tell where the arguments to role() end and where the block starts.

```
role(:redis) {YAML.load(File.read("config/servers.yml"))["servers"]["redis"] }
```

Now when we run a task that is declared for that role, we'll be sure to get the latest server list.

Roles also give us the ability to run a task on a restricted set of servers using the ROLES environment variable. For example, we can run the deploy:setup task only on servers in the utility role like this:

```
$ cap deploy:setup ROLES=utility
  * executing `deploy:setup'
  [ ... some boilerplate output ... ]
    servers: ["utilitybox.mydomain.com"]
    [utilitybox.mydomain.com] executing command
    command finished
```

Roles provide a convenient and standard way to restrict a task to a subset of servers. When we find a Capistrano deploy file that contains if statements, we usually take a closer look to see whether they can be replaced with roles.

5.4 Deploying to Multiple Environments with Multistage

For a small project, we usually have to deploy to only one environment, namely, production. For larger projects, though, we'll have a quality assurance environment, and sometimes we'll have a performance testing environment and maybe a sales demonstration environment, and, generally, we'll be deploying to multiple environments.

We like to solve this problem with a technique called Capistrano *multistage*. Multistage lets us specify a different Capistrano configuration for each environment we're deploying to while continuing to share the common settings in config/deploy.rb.

Older versions of Capistrano required that capistrano-ext be installed via a separate gem, but multistage was built into Capistrano as of version 2.10.0. Since we're using a newer version than that, we'll jump right into configuring multistage by modifying config/deploy.rb. Let's set two variables and require multistage's code. The first variable, stages, is an Array of all the environments that we'll be deploying to. The second variable, default_stage, is the stage that Capistrano will deploy to if we run cap deploy without specifying a stage. Lastly, we require the multistage extension. Here's how that looks at the top of config/deploy.rb with two stages, beta and production:

```
set :stages, %w(beta production)
set :default_stage, "beta"
require 'capistrano/ext/multistage'
```

We've told Capistrano that we have several stages, so now we need to define them. Let's create a new directory to hold our stage configuration; multistage will look for these in config/deploy/ by default, so we'll create that directory.[2]

```
$ mkdir config/deploy/
```

Now we can add a new file to that directory with the custom settings for our beta environment. In this case, the only thing different about beta is that it's on a different server, so let's put that setting into config/deploy/beta.rb.

```
server "beta.mydomain.com", :web, :app, :db, :primary => true
```

And we'll set the same variable in our production stage configuration, config/deploy/production.rb.

```
server "mydomain.com", :web, :app, :db, :primary => true
```

---

2. We could use a different directory with set :stage_dir, "some_directory".

We're setting the server name in both our environment files, so we can remove that setting from config/deploy.rb.

Now a deploy to the beta environment doesn't require an environment name.

```
$ cap deploy
«output»
```

By explicitly specifying the beta environment, we get the same result.

```
$ cap beta deploy
«output»
```

And to deploy to production, we use the following:

```
$ cap production deploy
«output»
```

We can expand our list of stages as needed, and we can move any of the Capistrano variable settings into our individual stage deployment files. Those files get loaded after config/deploy.rb, so any settings in those files will override the settings in config/deploy.rb.

When we run cap, the stage names (beta, production, and so on) look a bit like they're parameters to the cap command, but the stages are really just tasks. When we run Capistrano with multistage enabled, multistage programmatically defines a task for each stage that's listed; we can see this happening in the Capistrano source code in lib/capistrano/ext/multistage.rb.

```
stages.each do |name|
  desc "Set the target stage to `#{name}'."
  task(name) do
    # and some more code is here
  end
end
```

Since Capistrano invokes tasks from left to right, the stage task (for example, beta) is executed before the task that we want to run (for example, deploy) in that stage.

Multistage provides a simple and effective way to deploy to multiple environments; it's something we find useful in all but the smallest projects.

5.5 Capturing and Streaming Remote Command Output

Everything is going great with MassiveApp, and new user registrations are flooding in. However, MassiveApp still has its share of hiccups in production, and you've grown tired of opening up a new SSH session, tailing logs, and performing other simple server maintenance tasks.

Sometimes we need to get a bit closer to the metal when diagnosing problems in production. Although logging into our server via SSH is usually an option, you will find that it's often more convenient to be able to run small tasks directly from your working directory. Capistrano provides the capture and stream methods for just this purpose. capture lets us run a remote command on a server and get back the output as a string, while stream allows us to keep the session open and get an ongoing dump of the command's standard output. Both methods take the same options as run.

Using Capture

Let's take a look at capture. Let's say we'd like to see the amount of free memory on our production server. Typically, we would log in and run something like the following:

```
vm $ free -m
             total      used      free    shared   buffers    cached
Mem:           998       931        67         0        70       494
«More output»
```

We can use this to create a diagnostic task in Capistrano that displays the information in a nicer form.

capistrano2/lib/deploy/diagnostics.rb
```
namespace :diagnostics do
  desc "Display free memory"
  task :memory_usage do
    mem = capture("free -m | grep Mem").squeeze.split(' ')[1..-1]
    total, used, free, shared, buffers, cached = mem

    puts "Memory on #{role} (in MBs)"
    puts "Total: #{total}"
    puts "Used: #{used}"
    puts "Free: #{free}"
    puts "Shared: #{shared}"
    puts "Buffers: #{buffers}"
    puts "Cached: #{cached}"
  end
end
```

Using capture in this way means we don't have to employ hackery like running commands and piping the output to a file. It's a cleaner and more efficient way of getting command results.

Capturing a Stream

stream lets us get a constantly updated output of the command we want to run. A simple use case for this is tailing our production logs. We can take advantage of variable interpolation to make a task that will tail the correct log regardless of the environment in which multistage has placed us.

```
capistrano2/stream.rb
namespace :logs do
  desc "Tail the Rails log for the current stage"
  task :tail, :roles => :app do
    stream "tail -f #{current_path}/log/#{stage}.log"
  end
end
```

capture and stream are two simple and extremely useful commands with quite a few use cases. A good rule of thumb is that any command you find yourself running more than once on the server is a candidate for one of these methods, especially if you need to run the command on more than one box at once.

5.6 Running Commands with the Capistrano Shell

We've seen ways to transfer files and content to and from our application servers, and we've seen how Capistrano is communicating with our application servers over an ssh connection. But Capistrano can do more than just transfer files and run single commands; it can also run shell commands interactively using the Capistrano shell. Let's see how that works.

First we need a place to start a few VMs.

```
$ mkdir -p ~/deployingrails/capshell/
$ cd ~/deployingrails/capshell/
```

Now we'll create a Vagrantfile with three VMs; the shell is much more interesting on multiple VMs since we can run commands on all of them. We'll use VMs with only 256MB of memory since we won't be running MassiveApp on them. We'll also set them up so that we're forwarding a specific port from our host computer to each VM. (See Figure 3, *Creating a Vagrantfile with three VMS*, on page 91.) Let's fire them up.

```
$ vagrant up
[app1] Importing base box 'lucid64'...
«and lots more as three VMs boot up»
```

We'll clone MassiveApp into this directory so that we'll have a Capistrano configuration in place.

```
$ git clone -q git@github.com:deployingrails/massiveapp.git .
```

---

capistrano2/cap_shell/Vagrantfile

```
Vagrant::Config.run do |config|
  (1..3).each do |i|
    config.vm.define "app#{i}".to_sym do |c|
      c.vm.customize ["modifyvm", :id, "--name", "app#{i}", "--memory", "256"]
      c.vm.box = "lucid64"
      c.vm.host_name = "app#{i}"
      c.vm.forward_port 22, 2322+i
    end
  end
end
```

Figure 3—Creating a Vagrantfile with three VMS

Now let's modify the Capistrano configuration so that it knows about our three VMs. To do this, we just need to replace our single server setting with three hosts, which is easy enough since we can embed Ruby code in our config/deploy.rb file.

```
(1..3).each do |i|
  server "app#{i}", :web, :app, :db, :primary => true, :port => 2322+i
end
```

And since we have three VMs running locally, we'll need to add those host names to our /etc/hosts file.

```
127.0.0.1 app1 app2 app3
```

We're set up for testing the Capistrano shell. First we start it with cap shell.

```
$ cap shell
cap shell
* executing `shell'
====================================================================
Welcome to the interactive Capistrano shell! This is an experimental
feature, and is liable to change in future releases. Type 'help' for
a summary of how to use the shell.
--------------------------------------------------------------------
cap>
```

As the prompt promises, we can get some help easily enough.

```
cap> help
--- HELP! -----------------------------------------------------
"Get me out of this thing. I just want to quit."
-> Easy enough. Just type "exit", or "quit". Or press ctrl-D.

"I want to execute a command on all servers."
-> Just type the command, and press enter. It will be passed,
   verbatim, to all defined servers.
«and lots more»
```

That last help item looks promising. Let's run our first cap shell command and see how much disk space is available on the root partition of each server.

```
cap> df -kh /
 ** [out :: app1:2323] Filesystem          Size  Used Avail Use% Mounted on
 ** [out :: app1:2323] /dev/sda1            38G  913M   36G   3% /
 ** [out :: app2:2324] Filesystem          Size  Used Avail Use% Mounted on
 ** [out :: app2:2324] /dev/sda1            38G  913M   36G   3% /
 ** [out :: app3:2325] Filesystem          Size  Used Avail Use% Mounted on
 ** [out :: app3:2325] /dev/sda1            38G  913M   36G   3% /
```

When we entered the command into the shell, Capistrano opened a connection to each VM, ran the command, and displayed the results prefixed by the server name on which it ran. Our config/deploy.rb lists vagrant as the account to use for Capistrano's connection, and we can see that our commands are being run as that account by executing whoami.

```
cap> whoami
 ** [out :: app2:2324] vagrant
 ** [out :: app3:2325] vagrant
 ** [out :: app1:2323] vagrant
```

We can run a command on a subset of our servers by prefixing the command with an on clause. The servers are uniquely identified by the host names and the ports.

```
cap> on app1:2323,app2:2324 ls -l
 ** [out :: app2:2324] total 0
 ** [out :: app1:2323] total 0
```

Let's see how to run a Capistrano task on each server from within the shell. We'll add a simple task to our config/deploy.rb file.

```
task :sayhi do
  run "echo 'hello'"
end
```

Then restart the Capistrano shell, and we can invoke that task on each server by prefixing the task name with an exclamation point.

```
cap> !sayhi
[establishing connection(s) to app1:2323, app2:2324, app3:2325]
 ** [out :: app3:2325] hello
 ** [out :: app2:2324] hello
 ** [out :: app1:2323] hello
```

Finally, we can exit from the shell with the quit command.

```
cap> quit
exiting
$
```

Just to wrap up this multiserver demonstration, outside the Capistrano shell we can also invoke a single command on a set of servers using Capistrano's invoke task.

```
$ cap invoke COMMAND="df -kh /"
  * executing `invoke'
  * executing "df -kh /"
    servers: ["app1", "app2", "app3"]
    [app2:2324] executing command
** [out :: app2:2324] Filesystem            Size  Used Avail Use% Mounted on
** [out :: app2:2324] /dev/sda1              38G  913M   36G   3% /
    [app3:2325] executing command
** [out :: app3:2325] Filesystem            Size  Used Avail Use% Mounted on
** [out :: app3:2325] /dev/sda1              38G  913M   36G   3% /
    [app1:2323] executing command
** [out :: app1:2323] Filesystem            Size  Used Avail Use% Mounted on
** [out :: app1:2323] /dev/sda1              38G  913M   36G   3% /
    command finished in 30ms
```

Or we can use invoke to get a quick approximation of the earlier log tailing example.

```
$ cap invoke COMMAND="tail -f #{current_path}/log/production.log"
  * executing `invoke'
  * executing "tail -f \#{current_path}/log/production.log"
    servers: ["app1", "app2", "app3"]
    [app1:2323] executing command
    [app1:2323] sh -c 'tail -f #{current_path}/log/production.log'
    [app3:2325] executing command
    [app3:2325] sh -c 'tail -f #{current_path}/log/production.log'
    [app2:2324] executing command
    [app2:2324] sh -c 'tail -f #{current_path}/log/production.log'
```

With the Capistrano shell and other related utilities, there's almost never a need to ssh from server to server.

5.7   Conclusion

We've reviewed a variety of Capistrano features and techniques in this chapter, and we now have a solid grasp on not just how to set up a basic deployment but also how to use some of the more interesting Capistrano capabilities.

## CHAPTER 6

Monitoring with Nagios

MassiveApp is deployed and serving the needs of its user base. At least, we're pretty sure that it's serving the needs of the user base, because we're so excited about it that we're manually watching log files, refreshing pages to see new user counts, and generally hovering over the system to make sure that all is well. But we can do this for only so long; eventually we'll get wrapped up in coding the next big feature and forget to check the server load. And while we're not watching things, that's when a surge of activity is likely to bring MassiveApp to its knees.

What we need is someone to check on the server and let us know whether anything strange is happening; we need monitoring. But since we don't have the budget for a person to do that, we'll need an automated solution instead. Effective monitoring will provide us with feedback when MassiveApp's hardware, system services, or application code behaves in an unexpected manner. In this context, "unexpected" may mean that a service has crashed or is using too much memory, or it may mean something "good," such as a huge influx of new users. Either way, if something out of the ordinary is happening, a good monitoring solution will let us know about it.

We're going to use Nagios[1] for our monitoring system; here's why:

- It has flexible notifications and scheduling, lots of plugins to check the status of all sorts of services, a web interface to let us examine the state of the system, and a variety of reporting graphs and tables. All these features will come in handy as our monitoring needs evolve.

- It has a solid security model. We can configure it to tunnel remote status checks over ssh, and the web interface has a variety of security-related directives that let us lock things down.

---

1. http://nagios.org

- It scales. If it works well for a large site like Wikipedia,[2] it will work for us. Nagios has various features (such as passive checks) that are built specifically to make large installations effective and efficient.

- Commercial support is available. We won't need it to start with, but as MassiveApp expands, it may be nice to have someone on call who does Nagios configuration and tuning for a living.

- Finally, it's open source and free. A popular application like MassiveApp is going to need a lot of servers; the last thing we want is a per-CPU licensing scheme that gobbles up our profits.

That's our justification; now let's get Nagios running.

6.1 A MassiveApp to Monitor

We're going to use Puppet to manage our Nagios resources, so we need to make sure our Puppet Git repository is ready to receive our commits. We can switch to the without_nagios branch of our massiveapp_ops repository; this branch contains all this book's code except for the Nagios configuration. Here are the commands to do that:

```
$ cd ~/deployingrails/massiveapp_ops
$ git checkout --track origin/without_nagios
Branch without_nagios set up to track remote branch without_nagios from origin.
Switched to a new branch 'without_nagios'
```

Now we can add our Nagios configuration to this repository.

We want to monitor MassiveApp, and MassiveApp (being massive and all) will run on a number of servers. To simulate this with VMs, we'll set up one VM that's running MassiveApp and one VM that's running Nagios and monitoring the other VM. We'll need a Vagrantfile that starts two VMs that use host-only networking to communicate. Let's begin by creating a new directory to hold the VMs.

```
$ mkdir ~/deployingrails/nagios
$ cd ~/deployingrails/nagios
```

Here's our Vagrantfile with our two VM definitions. We forward port 4568 to the nagios VM so that we'll be able to browse to either box. We'll also use the custom base box that we built in *Building a Custom Base Box*, on page 16 for both VMs.

---

2. http://nagios.wikimedia.org/

monitoring/dual_vm/Vagrantfile
```
Vagrant::Config.run do |config|
  config.vm.define :app do |app_config|
    app_config.vm.customize ["modifyvm", :id,
      "--name", "app", "--memory", "512"]
    app_config.vm.box = "lucid64_with_ruby193"
    app_config.vm.host_name = "app"
    app_config.vm.forward_port 22, 2222, :auto => true
    app_config.vm.forward_port 80, 4567
    app_config.vm.network :hostonly, "33.33.13.37"
    app_config.vm.share_folder "puppet", "/etc/puppet", "../massiveapp_ops"
  end
  config.vm.define :nagios do |nagios_config|
    nagios_config.vm.customize ["modifyvm", :id,
      "--name", "nagios", "--memory", "512"]
    nagios_config.vm.box = "lucid64_with_ruby193"
    nagios_config.vm.host_name = "nagios"
    nagios_config.vm.forward_port 22, 2222, :auto => true
    nagios_config.vm.forward_port 80, 4568
    nagios_config.vm.network :hostonly, "33.33.13.38"
    nagios_config.vm.share_folder "puppet", "/etc/puppet", "../massiveapp_ops"
  end
end
```

With that file in our ~/deployingrails/nagios directory, we can start the VMs.

```
$ vagrant up
«lots of output as both VMs are started»
```

We can verify that the VMs are up by connecting into the nagios VM and then connecting over the app VM.

```
$ vagrant ssh nagios
nagios $ ssh 33.33.13.37
The authenticity of host '33.33.13.37 (33.33.13.37)' can't be established.
RSA key fingerprint is ed:d8:51:8c:ed:37:b3:37:2a:0f:28:1f:2f:1a:52:8a.
Are you sure you want to continue connecting (yes/no)? yes
Warning: Permanently added '33.33.13.37' (RSA) to the list of known hosts.
vagrant@33.33.13.37's password:
Last login: Wed Nov  9 03:48:36 2011 from 10.0.2.2
app $
```

Next we need to set up MassiveApp so that Nagios will have something to monitor. From Chapter 3, *Rails on Puppet*, on page 27, we have a Git repository containing manifests to get MassiveApp's services running. Our VMs are both sharing in that repository, so we just need to run Puppet on the app VM.

```
$ vagrant ssh app
app $ cd /etc/puppet
app $ sudo puppet apply manifests/site.pp
«lots of output as services are installed»
```

The nagios VM already has Puppet installed and we haven't built our Puppet module yet, so there's nothing to do on that end.

We haven't deployed MassiveApp yet, but we have plenty of things to monitor already: disk space, memory usage, and so forth. Next we'll get Nagios installed and monitoring those basic resources.

6.2 Writing a Nagios Puppet Module

Nagios' architecture is based around a server and multiple agents. The server is a single host that's the center of the monitoring system; it receives and reacts to data collected by agents running on each monitored machine. In our MassiveApp setup, the Nagios server is on nagios, and we'll have an agent running on app. Nagios also monitors the system it's running on (that is, nagios) out of the box, so we get that for free.

We want to set up Nagios on our nagios VM, but we also want to automate the installation and configuration so that we'll know exactly how we set it up. So, let's build a new Puppet module that does all the tedious work for us. Let's connect into the nagios VM, move to the /etc/puppet directory to get started, and create a new module.

```
$ vagrant ssh nagios
nagios $ cd /etc/puppet/
nagios $ mkdir -p {modules/nagios/manifests,modules/nagios/files}
```

We'll create a nagios class in modules/nagios/manifests/init.pp to hold our resource definitions.

monitoring/class_only/modules/nagios/manifests/init.pp
```
class nagios {
}
```

We're setting up the Nagios server, so we won't put any resources in init.pp. Instead, we'll create a new server class and use that to provision our VM. This starts as an empty class declaration in modules/nagios/manifests/server.pp.

monitoring/class_only/modules/nagios/manifests/server.pp
```
class nagios::server {
}
```

Ubuntu's package repository has a Nagios package, so let's add a resource declaration to our server class. This will bring in other Nagios packages as dependencies.

monitoring/with_package/modules/nagios/manifests/server.pp
```
class nagios::server {
  package {
    "nagios3":
      ensure => present
  }
}
```

Since we're adding a new module, we also need to add this to our mani-fests/nodes.pp file. We'll also install Apache (in addition to Nagios) on the nagios node since Nagios surfaces an HTML interface that we'll want to use.

monitoring/initial_node/manifests/nodes.pp
```
node "app" inherits basenode {
  include apache2
  include massiveapp
  include memcached
  include mysql
  include passenger
}

node "nagios" {
  include apache2
  include nagios::server
}
```

Let's go ahead and run Puppet; this will get the Apache and Nagios packages in place.

```
nagios $ sudo puppet apply --verbose manifests/site.pp
info: Applying configuration version '1302145355'
notice: /Stage[main]/Nagios::Server/\
  Package[nagios3]/ensure: created
```

The packages are installed, but we want to ensure that the Nagios server will start when our VM reboots. So, let's open modules/nagios/manifests/server.pp and add a service resource that's enabled.

monitoring/with_service/modules/nagios/manifests/server.pp
```
class nagios::server {
  package {
    "nagios3":
      ensure => present
  }
  service {
    "nagios3":
      ensure      => running,
      hasrestart  => true,
      enable      => true,
      hasstatus   => true,
```

```
      restart      => "/etc/init.d/nagios3 reload",
      require      => Package["nagios3"]
  }
}
```

Let's go ahead and run Puppet to get our service definition installed.

A *check* is the term that Nagios uses for the process of examining something's status. The Nagios web interface is our window into the checks and their results, so we need to ensure that Apache can serve up that web interface. Nagios comes with an Apache virtual host configuration file that does the job, but it allows Nagios to be accessed using the URL /nagios on any domain that's hosted by that server. We prefer to run Nagios on its own domain (nagios.somehost.com) so that it won't interfere with anything else that we put on that host. To do that, we'll need a virtual host definition. This will be a static file in our Puppet module; let's copy in the default Apache configuration file.

```
nagios $ cp /etc/nagios3/apache2.conf modules/nagios/files/
```

Now we'll make some changes to modules/nagios/files/apache2.conf. We'll add a <VirtualHost> element and delete all the commented-out lines; once that's done, we have a relatively small file.

```
monitoring/modules/nagios/files/apache2.conf
NameVirtualHost *:80
<VirtualHost *:80>
  ServerName nagios.localhost
  ScriptAlias /cgi-bin/nagios3 /usr/lib/cgi-bin/nagios3
  ScriptAlias /nagios3/cgi-bin /usr/lib/cgi-bin/nagios3
  DocumentRoot /usr/share/nagios3/htdocs/
  Alias /nagios3/stylesheets /etc/nagios3/stylesheets
  Alias /nagios3 /usr/share/nagios3/htdocs
  <DirectoryMatch (/usr/share/nagios3/htdocs\
  |/usr/lib/cgi-bin/nagios3|/etc/nagios3/stylesheets)>
    Options FollowSymLinks
    DirectoryIndex index.html
    AllowOverride AuthConfig
    Order Allow,Deny
    Allow From All
    AuthName "Nagios Access"
    AuthType Basic
    AuthUserFile /etc/nagios3/htpasswd.users
    require valid-user
  </DirectoryMatch>
</VirtualHost>
```

The Apache configuration includes an AuthType Basic directive. This sets up HTTP basic authentication, which is a good idea since it protects the Nagios installation from prying eyes. For that to work, though, we need to create a text file with a username and password. We'll use the Apache utility htpasswd for this, and we'll store that file in our Nagios module's files directory. Let's create a password file with one user, nagiosadmin, with a password of nagios.

```
nagios $ htpasswd -cmb modules/nagios/files/htpasswd.users nagiosadmin nagios
```

We need a Puppet file resource to get the Apache configuration file in place and another file resource to handle the htpasswd.users file. Let's add those entries to modules/nagios/manifests/server.pp. We have a notify attribute for the Apache service on the apache2.conf entry, so when that file changes, Apache will be restarted.

monitoring/with_files/modules/nagios/manifests/server.pp

```
class nagios::server {
  package {
    "nagios3":
      ensure => present
  }
  service {
    "nagios3":
      ensure      => running,
      hasrestart  => true,
      enable      => true,
      hasstatus   => true,
      restart     => "/etc/init.d/nagios3 reload",
      require     => Package["nagios3"]
  }
  file {
    "/etc/nagios3/apache2.conf":
      source  => "puppet:///modules/nagios/apache2.conf",
      owner   => root,
      group   => root,
      mode    => 644,
      notify  => Service["apache2"];
    "/etc/nagios3/htpasswd.users":
      source  => "puppet:///modules/nagios/htpasswd.users",
      owner   => www-data,
      group   => nagios,
      mode    => 640,
      require => [Package["apache2"],Package["nagios3"]];
  }
}
```

After running Puppet again to get those in place, Nagios is running on the VM, and we need to configure our workstation so we can browse into it. We'll do this by adding an entry to our /etc/hosts file, so let's open that file on the host machine and add this line:

```
127.0.0.1 nagios.localhost
```

Now we can open our browser to http://nagios.localhost:4568/, and we'll see a basic authentication dialog for a username and password. We'll enter the same values as we put in the htpasswd file (nagiosadmin for the username and nagios for the password), and then we can see the Nagios web interface.

The front page of the Nagios interface has two frames. The one on the right is more or less an advertisement for a Nagios support provider, so the one on the left is the one we're more interested in. The left frame has links to pages that display various aspects of the systems being monitored. Nagios refers to servers it's monitoring as *hosts*, so when we click the Host Details link, we see a list of servers. Somewhat unexpectedly, there are two servers listed on that page: localhost and gateway. That's because Nagios is monitoring the VM that it's running on, and it's also pinging the IP address that's configured as the default route on the VM. Both servers are listed with a green background, which means that all is well. We can click either of the host names and see details about when Nagios last checked that host and how long the check took. We can also see a variety of links deeper into the data that Nagios gathers about the host.

Let's explore a little more. Nagios refers to the items that it is monitoring as *services*, so if we click the Service Detail link in the left panel, we can see a list of services such as disk space, the ssh daemon, the count of logged-in users, and a few others. Clicking an individual service, such as Disk Space, takes us to another details page showing the time the service was last checked and the results of that check. As with the host detail page, we can go digging a lot deeper, but since we just started Nagios, not much data is available yet.

But there is one useful option we can try at this point. On the right side of the page for an individual service, there's a "Re-schedule the next check of this service" link. This link lets us do an immediate check of a service without waiting for Nagios' next scheduled check to run. If we click that link, we see another page that tells us we're about to force a service check. Let's click the Commit button to force a check, and...hm, no check. Instead, we get an error message: "Sorry, but Nagios is currently not checking for external commands, so your command will not be committed." Let's fix that.

The issue is that Nagios locks down some options by default. In this case, there's a check_external_commands variable in the Nagios configuration file that we need to enable. So, let's get back into the Puppet mind-set and make that happen. First we'll copy the default Nagios configuration file into our Nagios module.

```
nagios $ cp /etc/nagios3/nagios.cfg modules/nagios/files/
```

Now we can make our change. Let's open modules/nagios/files/nagios.cfg, find the check_external_commands variable, change the value from 0 to 1, and save the file. We're partway there, but we need to manage this file with Puppet as well. So, let's open modules/nagios/manifests/server.pp and add a new file resource. We're using a notify attribute so that Nagios will be restarted when the configuration file changes.

```
monitoring/with_cfg_file/modules/nagios/manifests/server.pp
class nagios::server {
  package {
    "nagios3":
      ensure => present
  }
  service {
    "nagios3":
      ensure      => running,
      hasrestart  => true,
      enable      => true,
      hasstatus   => true,
      restart     => "/etc/init.d/nagios3 reload",
      require     => Package["nagios3"]
  }
  file {
    "/etc/nagios3/apache2.conf":
      source  => "puppet:///modules/nagios/apache2.conf",
      owner   => root,
      group   => root,
      mode    => 644,
      notify  => Service["apache2"];
    "/etc/nagios3/htpasswd.users":
      source  => "puppet:///modules/nagios/htpasswd.users",
      owner   => www-data,
      group   => nagios,
      mode    => 640,
      require => [Package["apache2"],Package["nagios3"]];
    "/etc/nagios3/nagios.cfg":
      source  => "puppet:///modules/nagios/nagios.cfg",
      owner   => nagios,
      group   => nagios,
      mode    => 644,
      require => [Package["apache2"],Package["nagios3"]],
      notify  => [Service["apache2"],Service["nagios3"]]
  }
}
```

Now we can run Puppet and try our Commit button again. We see some progress; at least we're getting a different error message: Error: Could not stat() command file '/var/lib/nagios3/rw/nagios.cmd'! In other words, Nagios uses a file as a signal that commands need to be run, and this file doesn't have the proper permissions. Back into modules/nagios/manifests/server.pp we go, and this time we're adding a file resource that's setting the permissions on the nagios.cmd file and also a user resource that adds the www-data user to the nagios group.

```
class nagios::server {
  package {
    "nagios3":
      ensure => present
  }
  service {
    "nagios3":
      ensure      => running,
      hasrestart  => true,
      enable      => true,
      hasstatus   => true,
      restart     => "/etc/init.d/nagios3 reload",
      require     => Package["nagios3"]
  }
  file {
    "/etc/nagios3/apache2.conf":
      source  => "puppet:///modules/nagios/apache2.conf",
      owner   => root,
      group   => root,
      mode    => 644,
      notify  => Service["apache2"];
    "/etc/nagios3/htpasswd.users":
      source  => "puppet:///modules/nagios/htpasswd.users",
      owner   => www-data,
      group   => nagios,
      mode    => 640,
      require => [Package["apache2"],Package["nagios3"]];
    "/etc/nagios3/nagios.cfg":
      source  => "puppet:///modules/nagios/nagios.cfg",
      owner   => nagios,
      group   => nagios,
      mode    => 644,
      require => [Package["apache2"],Package["nagios3"]],
      notify  => [Service["apache2"],Service["nagios3"]];
    "/var/lib/nagios3/rw":
      ensure  => directory,
      owner   => nagios,
      group   => www-data,
      mode    => 710,
      require => Package["nagios3"];
  }
  user {
    "www-data":
      groups  => "nagios",
      notify  => Package["apache2"],
```

```
        require => Package["nagios3"],
    }
}
```

We run Puppet, click Commit one more time, and now we have success. We see a message along the lines of "Your command request was successfully submitted to Nagios for processing." We can verify that the check ran by clicking Service Detail and then Disk Space, and the Last Check Time field will show a very recent timestamp. So, now we can force a check at any time. This is especially handy when we're adding new service checks and want to ensure that things are working.

We have Nagios running on a server, it's monitoring itself, and we can browse the web interface and see what's going on. Next we need to get Nagios to monitor what's happening on our app VM. But first we'll catch our breath by looking at some general monitoring concepts.

6.3 Monitoring Concepts in Nagios

Let's think about monitoring scenarios in general; doing this will give us an introduction to a few more Nagios terms. It will also set up our expectations for what concepts our monitoring framework will support. We want to keep track of various servers; as we've seen, these are Nagios *hosts*. We'll need to partition these hosts; for example, once our infrastructure exceeds a certain size, we'll have some servers that are less critical than others. Nagios provides a way to group hosts via the aptly named *hostgroups*. With hostgroups, we can configure Nagios to send an SMS for a production database server problem but send an email for an issue with the standby performance testing server.

As we continue to think through the monitoring domain, we know our hosts are running various programs (which, as we've seen, Nagios calls *services*) that we're keeping an eye on. Nagios checks services using *commands*. If something goes wrong, someone needs to be notified; that lucky person is a *contact*. Perhaps we have someone else on the team who also needs to know when things break; in that case, both people would be part of a *contact group*.

Monitoring disk space is different than monitoring CPU load, and both of those are different than monitoring a network service like MySQL. Nagios addresses the need to monitor different types of services by providing *plugins* and an open plugin architecture. The default Nagios installation comes with more than sixty plugins including check_tcp, check_mailq, check_file_age, and many more. And that's just the tip of the iceberg. When putting a new service in place, a quick Internet search for *nagios some_service_name* usually finds a variety of approaches to monitoring that service. As an example, there are currently thirty-two different MySQL monitoring plugins that check everything from replication lag to connection counts to temporary table creation. So, before rolling your own Nagios plugin, take a quick look to see what's out there.

Any monitoring system you choose (or write) will involve these general domain concepts (hosts, services, commands, contacts) in some form or another. Even a simple cron job that pings a server once a minute and emails on failure falls under these general categories; there's a host that's receiving a service check, and a failure results in a contact receiving a notification. If you inherit a simple monitoring setup that consists of a few shell scripts, take heart; you have a place to start, and you at least know what your predecessor considered important enough to monitor.

This isn't an exhaustive list of monitoring concepts or Nagios concepts. If we flip through a Nagios reference manual, we'll see chapters on time periods, macros, host dependencies, and much more. The takeaway is that we need to monitor our existing services and make a practice of thinking about monitoring for any new services. We need to keep the vision in mind; we're setting things up so that we'll know when our systems are reaching their limits and we'll constantly improve the monitoring system. At the very least, we'll have a nice system to hand off when our inevitable promotion occurs.

Now that we've covered some monitoring concepts and Nagios terms, we'll enhance the monitoring for our nagios VM.

6.4 Monitoring Local Resources

A basic form of monitoring is a simple check to ensure that a server is up. The Nagios setup that we've configured for nagios has this in place for any other servers that we add. We don't ping the nagios VM; the Nagios server being down means that notifications wouldn't go out anyway. But it's a good place to start with other servers. Some firewalls will drop pings or, to be more specific, all Internet Control Message Protocol (ICMP) packets. If that was the case, we'd pick some other network service to check. ssh is one good candidate; if the ssh service is not responding, the server is probably having other issues as well.

Once we know the system is up, the next step is to see whether we're approaching any operating system–level resource limits. By this we mean things such as disk space, process count, and CPU load average. The default setup includes these checks, and we really don't want to run a system without

Watching the Watcher

Nagios will faithfully monitor MassiveApp, but if the Nagios server goes down, how will we find out? Rather than depending on our customers, we'll use a server in another data center or a service like Pingdom[a] to check up on Nagios. There will be some additional setup cost and time, but it's worth it to be the first to know.

---

a.   http://www.pingdom.com/

them. Sometimes a load average alert will be our first indicator that a flood of traffic has come our way.

Our Nagios setup has default values at which it alerts, and for most use cases those values are pretty reasonable. For example, the disk space check sends a "warning" alert when only 20 percent of disk space remains and sends a "critical" alert when 10 percent remains. But maybe we'd like to be a bit more prudent. Let's try it by editing the Nagios configuration and changing the alert value.

Nagios creates a /etc/nagios3/conf.d directory that contains a few default configuration files. One of these files, localhost_nagios2.cfg (despite its name, it works fine with Nagios 3), contains the setting for the disk space alert threshold. Let's get this file into our Nagios Puppet module so we can track our changes. First we'll create a new directory in modules/nagios/files/. We're creating a conf.d directory that contains a hosts directory; this will let us put all our host configuration in one location.

```
nagios $ mkdir -p modules/nagios/files/conf.d/hosts
```

Now we can copy localhost_nagios2.cfg into our new directory, although we'll drop the Nagios version.

```
nagios $ cp /etc/nagios3/conf.d/localhost_nagios2.cfg \
  modules/nagios/files/conf.d/hosts/localhost.cfg
```

Let's open modules/nagios/files/conf.d/hosts/localhost.cfg and locate the following section:

```
define service {
  use                   local-service
  service_description   Disk Space
  check_command         check_all_disks!20%!10%
}
```

This is a Nagios *object definition*, and it consists of an object name, service, that contains *variables* and their *values*. The use variable is Nagios' way of implementing inheritance; it causes this service check to inherit variables from the local-service *template* that's defined earlier in /etc/nagios3/conf.d/hosts/local-host.cfg. That template in turn inherits from another generic-service template (defined in /etc/nagios3/conf.d/generic-service_nagios2.cfg), which sets default variable values such as a 24/7 notification period. Any of those variables can be overridden at any level, and using templates in this manner can greatly reduce duplication in Nagios object definitions.

The check_command variable has a value that specifies the alerting thresholds. Let's change the 20% to something very high, like 99%, and save the file.

Now the change is in our Puppet file tree, so we need to manage it with our Puppet module. Let's open modules/nagios/manifests/server.pp and add a new section to our list of file resources. We'll have other files to manage in the conf.d directory tree, so we'll set the recurse attribute to true. We'll also remove the old localhost_nagios2.cfg file using another file resource with the ensure attribute set to absent.

monitoring/with_nagios_cfg/modules/nagios/manifests/server.pp
```
class nagios::server {
  package {
    "nagios3":
      ensure => present
  }
  service {
    "nagios3":
      ensure     => running,
      hasrestart => true,
      enable     => true,
      hasstatus  => true,
      restart    => "/etc/init.d/nagios3 reload",
      require    => Package["nagios3"]
  }
  file {
    "/etc/nagios3/apache2.conf":
      source  => "puppet:///modules/nagios/apache2.conf",
      owner   => root,
      group   => root,
      mode    => 644,
      notify  => Service["apache2"];
    "/etc/nagios3/htpasswd.users":
      source  => "puppet:///modules/nagios/htpasswd.users",
      owner   => www-data,
      group   => nagios,
      mode    => 640,
      require => [Package["apache2"],Package["nagios3"]];
    "/etc/nagios3/nagios.cfg":
      source  => "puppet:///modules/nagios/nagios.cfg",
      owner   => nagios,
```

```
      group   => nagios,
      mode    => 644,
      require => [Package["apache2"],Package["nagios3"]],
      notify  => [Service["apache2"],Service["nagios3"]];
    "/var/lib/nagios3/rw":
      ensure  => directory,
      owner   => nagios,
      group   => www-data,
      mode    => 710,
      require => Package["nagios3"];
    "/etc/nagios3/conf.d":
      source  => "puppet:///modules/nagios/conf.d/",
      ensure  => directory,
      owner   => nagios,
      group   => nagios,
      mode    => 0644,
      recurse => true,
      notify  => Service["nagios3"],
      require => Package["nagios3"];
    "/etc/nagios3/conf.d/localhost_nagios2.cfg":
      ensure  => absent;
  }
  user {
    "www-data":
      groups  => "nagios",
      notify  => Package["apache2"],
      require => Package["nagios3"],
  }
}
```

We've made our changes, so let's run Puppet to get those in place and restart Nagios.

Now, let's force Nagios to check this service right away rather than waiting for the next scheduled check. We can do this through the web interface since earlier we set up Nagios to allow external commands. First we'll click the Service Detail link in the left pane; then click Disk Space in the right pane to take us to the disk space check details. Then we'll click "Re-schedule the next check of this service" and submit the form on the next page via the Commit button. Now when we go back to the Service Detail page again, we see the Disk Space status is highlighted in yellow and the Status column value is Warning.

Changing the disk space warning threshold to 99 percent was a good way to ensure Nagios was functioning, but alerting at this level is probably just a bit much for normal operation. Let's back out that change by editing modules/nagios/files/conf.d/hosts/localhost.cfg, changing the service definition, and forcing another check through the web interface. Then we'll see the Disk Space status line go back to a more placid green.

We've seen that Nagios is checking the basic system status, and we've successfully modified a monitoring threshold to suit our preferences. This is the virtuous cycle of monitoring. We're aware of what we're monitoring, we're getting alerted when something exceeds a threshold, and then we're resolving the alert.

Now we'll go a little deeper and set up monitoring for services on both our VMs.

6.5 Monitoring Services

The MassiveApp server itself may be up and running, but that doesn't mean everything is working. MassiveApp uses a variety of network services (Apache, MySQL, memcached), and if any of those are offline, MassiveApp will be either slow or go down completely. By setting up separate monitors for each service, we'll get a specific alert if one component shuts down, and we'll know what needs to be restarted or tuned.

Some services can be monitored by a simple port check. We can get a good comfort level that the service is available by ensuring that it is responding to attempts to connect to it on its configured TCP port. One example of a service that fits this profile is ssh. There's a service check for ssh in the default configuration file for localhost (located in /etc/nagios3/conf.d/localhost.cfg); here's what it looks like:

```
define service {
  use                 local-service
  service_description ssh
  check_command       check_ssh
}
```

The check_command variable is set to check_ssh; that's one of Nagios' built-in plugins. By default, this plugin connects to the ssh daemon and puts the response in the Status Information field of the Nagios web interface.

Monitoring ssh

Let's take a closer look at using the check_ssh plugin. It provides a reasonable default strategy, but it can also ensure that the ssh daemon provides a particular response. Nagios provides a convenient way to experiment with a plugin's options; plugins are just files stored in /usr/lib/nagios/plugins, so we can test check_ssh from the shell without tweaking a configuration file. Let's do that now; we'll run the check_ssh plugin without any options.

```
nagios $ /usr/lib/nagios/plugins/check_ssh
check_ssh: Could not parse arguments
Usage:check_ssh [-46] [-t <timeout>] [-r <remote version>]
 [-p <port>] <host>
```

We got an error message since we didn't pass in any arguments, but we also see the parameters that this plugin accepts. It requires a host parameter; let's try that.

```
nagios $ /usr/lib/nagios/plugins/check_ssh localhost
SSH OK - OpenSSH_5.3p1 Debian-3ubuntu4 (protocol 2.0)
```

That's better; the plugin connected to the ssh daemon and received a version string in response. This is the standard ssh daemon output, so we could get this same response if we used telnet to connect to an ssh daemon. That's also the output we see in the Nagios web interface for the status of this check. Let's see how it looks when we send in some bad data; the -r option checks for a particular ssh version, so we can use that to get a warning.

```
nagios $ /usr/lib/nagios/plugins/check_ssh -r 0.1 localhost
SSH WARNING - OpenSSH_5.3p1 Debian-3ubuntu4 (protocol 2.0)
 version mismatch, expected '0.1'
```

And for an outright failure, let's try to connect to port 23. This is the standard telnet port, which is insecure in exciting ways. But even if it were running, it wouldn't respond in a way that would satisfy the check_ssh plugin.

```
nagios $ /usr/lib/nagios/plugins/check_ssh -p 23 localhost
Connection refused
```

This script failure won't affect the Nagios dashboard since we're running these checks out of band; we can experiment without fear of causing notifications to be sent or ugly colors to appear in the web interface.

Let's also ensure that check_ssh can check the status of the ssh daemon running on our app VM. To make this easier, we'll add a host name entry to our nagios VM's /etc/hosts; that way, we won't have to type our app's IP address repeatedly.

```
33.33.13.37 app
```

With that in place, we can run the check_ssh plugin against app.

```
nagios $ /usr/lib/nagios/plugins/check_ssh app
SSH OK - OpenSSH_5.3p1 Debian-3ubuntu4 (protocol 2.0)
```

That's as expected; the app VM was built from the same base box as the nagios VM, so it should be the same version. To get Nagios to do that same check automatically, we'll add a new hosts file for our app box. Of course, we'll manage that with Puppet, so let's create modules/nagios/files/conf.d/hosts/app.cfg with the new *host* object definition. We'll inherit from another built-in Nagios template, generic-host, and we'll give our new host the name app.

monitoring/nagios_cfg_only_host_def/modules/nagios/files/conf.d/hosts/app.cfg
```
define host{
  use        generic-host
  host_name app
  alias      app
  address    33.33.13.37
}
```

We need to check ssh, so we'll add a new service definition to that file. The only thing that changes from our localhost service definition is the host name that we're checking.

monitoring/nagios_cfg_host_and_service/modules/nagios/files/conf.d/hosts/app.cfg
```
define host{
  use        generic-host
  host_name app
  alias      app
  address    33.33.13.37
}
define service {
  use generic-service
  host_name app
  service_description SSH
  check_command check_ssh
}
```

Now we'll run Puppet, which will deploy these new files and restart Nagios. Once that's done, we can look at the web interface, and there we see our new app host with our ssh check.

We know how to run a Nagios script from the command line, we know what it looks like when it succeeds, and we've seen the failure modes for one particular plugin. We've also added our first remote monitor. Next we'll set up monitoring for more MassiveApp services.

Monitoring Remote Services with NRPE

Our app VM is running some services that aren't listening on an external interface; they're listening only on 127.0.0.1 since MassiveApp is the only thing that needs to access them. That means our nagios VM can't access them directly to see whether they're running; something like check_ssh just won't work. What we need is a way to tunnel from nagios over to app and check those services locally. Fortunately Nagios provides a means to do this via an *addon* named the Nagios Remote Plugins Executor (NRPE). Architecturally, NRPE consists of a *monitoring host* (that is, our nagios VM), which communicates with an NRPE daemon process on a *remote host* (that is, our app VM) that we want to monitor. The NRPE daemon handles running the Nagios checks and returns the results to the monitoring host.

We can start getting those pieces in place by adding another package, nagios-nrpe-plugin, to our nagios::server class. Our server.pp file is getting pretty long, so rather than displaying the entire file, here's the package resource declaration:

```
package {
  ["nagios3", "nagios-nrpe-plugin"]:
    ensure => present
}
```

Once we run Puppet, we have the monitoring host plugin in place. Now over on app we can set up the other end by defining a nagios::client class in modules/nagios/manifests/client.pp and requiring that the NRPE daemon and the Nagios plugins be installed. We need the NRPE daemon so that the monitoring host will have something to contact, and we'll need the Nagios plugins since those provide the logic for checking all the resources.

monitoring/client_only_package/modules/nagios/manifests/client.pp
```
class nagios::client {
  package {
    ["nagios-nrpe-server","nagios-plugins"]:
      ensure => present
  }
}
```

We also need to include this class in our app node definition, so we'll open manifests/nodes.pp on app and add an include directive to our app node.

monitoring/manifests/nodes.pp
```
node "app" inherits basenode {
  include apache2
  include massiveapp
  include memcached
  include mysql
  include nagios::client
  include passenger
}
node "nagios" {
  include apache2
  include nagios::server
}
```

We can run Puppet on app, and the NRPE daemon will be installed and started. That's not quite enough, though; NRPE doesn't know which machine we're running our Nagios server on. We need to modify the NRPE configuration file so that it knows which machine should be allowed to connect and request resource status information. Let's copy /etc/nagios/nrpe.cfg into modules/nagios/files/nrpe.cfg and change the allowed_hosts variable to 33.33.13.38.

```
allowed_hosts=33.33.13.38
```

We want the NRPE daemon to restart when we make configuration file changes like this one, so let's set up the NRPE configuration file in Puppet the same way we did with Apache in *Restarting Apache on Configuration Changes*, on page 41. Here's our modules/nagios/manifests/client.pp file with the same package-file-service pattern for the NRPE configuration file and the NRPE daemon:

monitoring/client_with_pfs/modules/nagios/manifests/client.pp
```
class nagios::client {
  package {
    ["nagios-nrpe-server","nagios-plugins"]:
      ensure => present
  }
  file {
    "/etc/nagios/nrpe.cfg":
      owner   => root,
      group   => root,
      mode    => 644,
      source  => "puppet:///modules/nagios/nrpe.cfg"
  }
  service {
    "nagios-nrpe-server":
      ensure    => true,
      enable    => true,
      subscribe => File["/etc/nagios/nrpe.cfg"]
  }
}
```

A Puppet run will move over our modified nrpe.cfg and restart the NRPE daemon.

```
app $ sudo puppet apply --verbose manifests/site.pp
info: Applying configuration version '1321765051'
info: FileBucket adding \
  {md5}a82e7fc5d321a0dd0830c2981e5e5911
info: /Stage[main]/Nagios::Client/File\
  [/etc/nagios/nrpe.cfg]: Filebucketed /etc/nagios/nrpe.cfg \
  to puppet with sum a82e7fc5d321a0dd0830c2981e5e5911
notice: /Stage[main]/Nagios::Client/File\
  [/etc/nagios/nrpe.cfg]/content: content changed \
  '{md5}a82e7fc5d321a0dd0830c2981e5e5911' to '{md5}c49d23685c60ca537e750349ae26e599'
info: /etc/nagios/nrpe.cfg: Scheduling refresh of \
```

```
Service[nagios-nrpe-server]
notice: /Stage[main]/Nagios::Client/Service\
  [nagios-nrpe-server]: Triggered 'refresh' from 1 events
notice: Finished catalog run in 0.40 seconds
```

We can verify that the NRPE daemon on app is accessible from nagios by running the NRPE plugin from a shell on nagios. We'll invoke this plugin just like we did with check_ssh; we need to pass in at least a host parameter.

```
nagios $ /usr/lib/nagios/plugins/check_nrpe -H app
NRPE v2.12
```

That looks promising. What else can we check on app? We can see all the plugins that NRPE can run out of the box by looking at our nrpe.cfg file on app.

```
app $ grep "^command\[" modules/nagios/files/nrpe.cfg
command[check_users]=/usr/lib/nagios/plugins/check_users -w 5 -c 10
command[check_load]=/usr/lib/nagios/plugins/check_load -w 15,10,5 -c 30,25,20
command[check_hda1]=/usr/lib/nagios/plugins/check_disk -w 20% -c 10% -p /dev/hda1
command[check_zombie_procs]=/usr/lib/nagios/plugins/check_procs -w 5 -c 10 -s Z
command[check_total_procs]=/usr/lib/nagios/plugins/check_procs -w 150 -c 200
```

Back on nagios, let's give that first plugin, check_users, a whirl from the shell. check_users will monitor the number of logged-in users on a host and alert if there are too many, so it shouldn't be alerting yet.

```
nagios $ /usr/lib/nagios/plugins/check_nrpe -H app -c check_users
USERS OK - 1 users currently logged in |users=1;5;10;0
```

The check is able to run on app when we run it manually; now we'll configure Nagios to run it automatically. Let's edit modules/nagios/files/hosts/app.cfg and add a new service check. Normally the command name is the same as the plugin name. In this case, though, the check_nrpe plugin defines two commands. We can see these two command definitions in /etc/nagios-plugins/config/check_nrpe.cfg; there's one command defined for when we pass arguments to the plugin and one when we don't. In this case, we're calling check_users and not passing any arguments, so we'll use check_nrpe_1arg. It's "1 arg" because the host name to check is always passed to the check command.

monitoring/check_nrpe_commands.cfg
```
# this command runs a program $ARG1$ with arguments $ARG2$
define command {
  command_name   check_nrpe
  command_line   /usr/lib/nagios/plugins/check_nrpe \
    -H $HOSTADDRESS$ -c $ARG1$ -a $ARG2$
}

# this command runs a program $ARG1$ with no arguments
define command {
```

```
command_name  check_nrpe_1arg
command_line  /usr/lib/nagios/plugins/check_nrpe \
   -H $HOSTADDRESS$ -c $ARG1$
}
```

With that background, we can add our service check in modules/nagios/mfiles/conf.d/ hosts/app.cfg.

```
define service {
  use generic-service
  host_name app
  service_description Current Users
  check_command check_nrpe_1arg!check_users
}
```

We'll rerun Puppet to get our configuration files in place; now we can look back at the HTML interface, and there's our Current Users service check showing green for app.

We can run local and remote checks, so our Nagios coverage is improving quickly. Next we'll define a new service check for memcached that uses the NRPE daemon that we just configured.

Monitoring Memcached Remotely

We need a monitoring check for memcached that uses NRPE, so over on app let's open up modules/nagios/files/nrpe.cfg and add the following command definition:

```
command[check_memcached]=/usr/lib/nagios/plugins/check_tcp \
  -p 11211 -e "VERSION" -E -s "version\n" -w2 -c5
```

This service check uses the check_tcp plugin to monitor the memcached status. check_tcp is a flexible plugin that we can use to keep an eye on many different TCP-based services. In this case, we're sending in quite a few options.

- The -p 11211 parameter is a mandatory port argument; check_tcp needs to know what port we're checking.

- -e "VERSION" tells the plugin what to expect in return.

- -E tells check_tcp to send a carriage return after sending quit to close the connection.

- -s "version\n" indicates what text to send once the plugin connects to the port.

- -w2 -c5 triggers a warning status if memcached doesn't respond in two seconds and a critical state if it doesn't respond in five seconds.

Let's run Puppet on app to get that new command definition into NRPE's command set. Once that's done, over on nagios we can add this check into our app configuration in modules/nagios/files/conf.d/hosts/app.cfg.

```
define service {
  use generic-service
  host_name app
  service_description memcached
  check_command check_nrpe_1arg!check_memcached
}
```

Now we can run Puppet on nagios, and we can see our new app memcached check in place in the HTML interface.

We've gotten two things out of crafting this check. First, we can see that Nagios can check not only that a service is up but also that it's properly answering queries. Second, we can see that we won't always need to download (or write) a plugin for a new service; in many cases, we can build one using Nagios' existing built-in plugins.

Next we'll look at a more Rails-specific check that will tell us whether Passenger memory usage is getting out of hand.

Monitoring Passenger

We're running MassiveApp with Passenger, and though of course we've written MassiveApp's code perfectly, there may be memory leaks in the libraries that we're using. To catch any problems, we'll write a Nagios plugin that checks the memory size of each Passenger process.

This is the first time we're adding a new plugin rather than using an existing plugin. But the testing process is the same. We'll write our plugin, run it a few times to ensure it's working, and then integrate it into our Puppet configuration. Passenger is running only on app, so let's start there and put our plugin in /usr/lib/nagios/plugins/check_passenger. The first version will just require the appropriate libraries and display a dump of the Passenger process list. Passenger comes with a utility class that supplies us with the process information, so we'll use that here.

monitoring/check_passenger_print
```
#!/usr/local/bin/ruby

require 'rubygems'
gem 'passenger'
require 'phusion_passenger'
require 'phusion_passenger/platform_info'
require 'phusion_passenger/admin_tools/memory_stats'
```

```
require 'optparse'

include PhusionPassenger

puts AdminTools::MemoryStats.new.passenger_processes.inspect
```

When we run this on our VM, we get a jumbled list of Object#inspect() output. It's not pretty, but now we know we're able to find the Passenger processes.

```
app $ ruby /usr/lib/nagios/plugins/check_passenger
[#<PhusionPassenger::AdminTools::MemoryStats::Process:0x000000025ba200 @pid=22218,
«many more lines»
```

We want to flag only those processes with high memory usage, so we'll need to tell the script what constitutes "high" memory usage. We can do this with arguments that we'll parse using the Ruby standard library's optparse.

monitoring/check_passenger
```
options = {:warning_threshold => 80, :critical_threshold => 100}
OptionParser.new do |opts|
  opts.banner = "Usage: check_passenger [options]"
  opts.on("-w N", "--warning", "Warning threshold in MB") do |w|
    options[:warning_threshold] = w.to_i
  end
  opts.on("-c N", "--critical", "Critical threshold in MB") do |c|
    options[:critical_threshold] = c.to_i
  end
end.parse!
```

We'll also need some code to search the Passenger process list for large processes. Each object in that list is an instance of the Ruby standard library Process class and has an rss() accessor that tells us how much memory it's using. This code also includes the Nagios-specific bits, that is, the output and the exit code. The output is important because Nagios will display it in the web interface. The exit code is important since Nagios uses that to determine the monitored item's state: ok, warning, or critical.

monitoring/check_passenger
```
msg, exit_code = if procs.find { |p| p.rss > options[:critical_threshold]*1000 }
  count = procs.count {|p|p.rss > options[:critical_threshold]*1000 }
  ["CRITICAL - #{count} #{pluralize('instance', count)} \
    #{singularize('exceed', count)} #{options[:critical_threshold]} MB", 2]
elsif procs.find {|p| p.rss > options[:warning_threshold]*1000 }
  count = procs.count {|p|p.rss > options[:warning_threshold]*1000 }
  ["WARNING - #{count} #{pluralize('instance', count)} \
    #{singularize('exceed', count)} #{options[:warning_threshold]} MB", 1]
else
  ["OK - No processes exceed #{options[:warning_threshold]} MB", 0]
end
```

Our complete check will conform to Nagios' requirements by printing a message and exiting with the appropriate status code.

monitoring/check_passenger

```ruby
#!/usr/local/bin/ruby

require 'rubygems'
gem 'passenger'
require 'phusion_passenger'
require 'phusion_passenger/platform_info'
require 'phusion_passenger/admin_tools/memory_stats'
require 'optparse'

include PhusionPassenger

def pluralize(str, count)
  if count > 1
    "#{str}s"
  else
    str
  end
end

def singularize(str, count)
  if count > 1
    str
  else
    "#{str}s"
  end
end

options = {:warning_threshold => 80, :critical_threshold => 100}
OptionParser.new do |opts|
  opts.banner = "Usage: check_passenger [options]"
  opts.on("-w N", "--warning", "Warning threshold in MB") do |w|
    options[:warning_threshold] = w.to_i
  end
  opts.on("-c N", "--critical", "Critical threshold in MB") do |c|
    options[:critical_threshold] = c.to_i
  end
end.parse!

procs = AdminTools::MemoryStats.new.passenger_processes

msg, exit_code = if procs.find { |p| p.rss > options[:critical_threshold]*1000 }
  count = procs.count {|p|p.rss > options[:critical_threshold]*1000 }
  ["CRITICAL - #{count} #{pluralize('instance', count)} \
    #{singularize('exceed', count)} #{options[:critical_threshold]} MB", 2]
elsif procs.find {|p| p.rss > options[:warning_threshold]*1000 }
  count = procs.count {|p|p.rss > options[:warning_threshold]*1000 }
```

```
  ["WARNING - #{count} #{pluralize('instance', count)} \
    #{singularize('exceed', count)} #{options[:warning_threshold]} MB", 1]
else
  ["OK - No processes exceed #{options[:warning_threshold]} MB", 0]
end

puts "PASSENGER #{msg}"
exit exit_code
```

And here's a test run with a low warning threshold to ensure we'll see some output:

```
app $ ruby /usr/lib/nagios/plugins/check_passenger -w 10
PASSENGER WARNING - 1 instance    exceeds 10 MB
```

Our check works, so the next step is to add it to our Puppet Nagios module. We want to invoke the plugin via NRPE, so as with our memcached check, we'll need to make changes on both app and nagios. We'll put check_passenger in a new modules/nagios/files/plugins/ directory in our module. Then we'll add another file resource to modules/nagios/manifests/client.pp that will move our script into place, and we'll ensure that the package is installed before we try to copy our script into place. Here's our completed client.pp:

monitoring/modules/nagios/manifests/client.pp
```
class nagios::client {
  package {
    ["nagios-nrpe-server","nagios-plugins"]:
      ensure => present,
      before => [File["/etc/nagios/nrpe.cfg"],\
      File["/usr/lib/nagios/plugins/check_passenger"]]
  }
  file {
    "/etc/nagios/nrpe.cfg":
      owner   => root,
      group   => root,
      mode    => 644,
      source  => "puppet:///modules/nagios/nrpe.cfg";
    "/usr/lib/nagios/plugins/check_passenger":
      source  => "puppet:///modules/nagios/plugins/check_passenger",
      owner   => nagios,
      group   => nagios,
      mode    => 755;
  }
  service {
    "nagios-nrpe-server":
      ensure    => true,
      enable    => true,
      subscribe => File["/etc/nagios/nrpe.cfg"]
  }
}
```

Now we'll define a new Nagios command that points to our script. We'll put the command definition in our Nagios Puppet module in modules/nagios/files/ conf.d/commands.cfg, and for the command definition we just need to name it and give Nagios the command's path.

monitoring/commands.cfg
```
define command {
  command_name check_passenger
  command_line /usr/lib/nagios/plugins/check_passenger
}
```

We also need to tell NRPE to make the new check available, so we'll add a new command to modules/nagios/files/nrpe.cfg.

command[check_passenger]=**/usr/lib/nagios/plugins/check_passenger -w 10**

The last piece of the puzzle is to configure nagios to run this new command as part of the app checks. This is another service definition like the memcached definition in *Monitoring Remote Services with NRPE*, on page 112, and we'll put this in app.cfg.

monitoring/nagios-service-definitions
```
define service {
  use generic-service
  host_name app
  service_description Passenger
  check_command check_nrpe_1arg!check_passenger
}
```

Remember how we used the Puppet recurse attribute for managing the conf.d file resource? Since that's in place, we can rerun Puppet, the new Nagios configuration file will be moved into the /etc/nagios3/conf.d/hosts directory, and Nagios will be restarted.

And that's it. With those elements in place, a new Passenger service shows up in the web interface, and Nagios will check Passenger every few minutes and alert us if any Passenger processes are exceeding our memory thresholds. Currently, it's warning since we set the threshold to a low value, but we can easily bump that up in modules/nagios/files/nrpe.cfg to a more reasonable level.

We've seen how to monitor servers and services with Nagios. Next, we'll look at monitoring MassiveApp.

6.6 Monitoring Applications

The monitoring techniques we've seen have all been useful with any application; check_disk is helpful for a Ruby on Rails application, a Java application, or a static website, and check_passenger is useful for any Rails application. But Nagios can also monitor an application's specific data thresholds. Let's see how that's done.

We've seen how Nagios uses plugins to bring in new functionality, and we've written our own plugin to monitor Passenger memory usage. Now we'll write another plugin to check MassiveApp's activity. Actually, most of the logic will be in MassiveApp; we'll write just enough of a plugin to connect to MassiveApp and report a result.

For the specifics of this check, consider MassiveApp's daily growth rate in terms of accounts. In any twenty-four hours, we get around a dozen new accounts. If we get many more than that, we want to get an alert so we can think about firing up more servers.

We could do this check in a few different ways. We could query the MySQL database directly, but although that would avoid the performance impact of loading up the Rails framework, it would mean we couldn't use our ActiveRecord models with their handy scopes and such. We could use HTTP to hit a controller action, but then we'd want to ensure that the action could be accessed only by Nagios. So, we'll keep it simple by using a Rake task. First we'll declare the task; we can put this in lib/tasks/monitor.rake. We're namespacing the task inside nagios; this keeps all our Nagios-related tasks in one place.

```
monitoring/task_only/lib/tasks/monitor.rake
namespace :nagios do
  desc "Nagios monitor for recent accounts"
  task :accounts => :environment do
  end
end
```

Next let's count the number of "recently" created accounts; in this case, "recently" means "in the past twenty-four hours." We can do this with a straightforward ActiveRecord query.

```
monitoring/task_and_query/lib/tasks/monitor.rake
namespace :nagios do
  desc "Nagios monitor for recent accounts"
  task :accounts => :environment do
    recent = Account.where("created_at > ?", 1.day.ago).count
  end
end
```

In this plugin, we'll ask for a warning if we get more than fifty new accounts in a day, and we'll consider it critical if we get more than ninety in a day.

monitoring/lib/tasks/monitor.rake
```ruby
namespace :nagios do
  desc "Nagios monitor for recent accounts"
  task :accounts => :environment do
    recent = Account.where("created_at > ?", 1.day.ago).count
    msg, exit_code = if recent > 90
      ["CRITICAL", 2]
    elsif recent > 50
      ["WARNING", 1]
    else
      ["OK", 0]
    end
    puts "ACCOUNTS #{msg} - #{recent} accounts created in the past day"
    exit exit_code
  end
end
```

We have the Rake task in MassiveApp's codebase now; next up, we need Nagios to be able to run it. We can do this with a simple Bash script. We'll name this script check_recent_accounts and put our nagios Puppet module in modules/nagios/files/plugins/ alongside our check_passenger plugin. That script needs to run our Rake task using the --silent flag to prevent the usual "(in /path/to/the/app)" Rake output message since that would confuse Nagios. It also needs to relay the exit code from the Rake task on to Nagios. We can do that using the Bash special parameter $?, which holds the exit code of the last command executed.

monitoring/modules/nagios/files/check_recent_accounts
```bash
#!/bin/bash
cd /var/massiveapp/current/
RAILS_ENV=production /usr/bin/rake --silent nagios:accounts
exit $?
```

Switching back into Puppet mind-set, we'll add another file resource to our nagios::client class that will move our script into place.

monitoring/check_recent_accounts.pp
```
"/usr/lib/nagios/plugins/check_recent_accounts":
   source  => "puppet:///modules/nagios/plugins/check_recent_accounts",
   owner   => nagios,
   group   => nagios,
   mode    => 755;
```

And as with check_passenger, we'll want to ensure the package is installed before attempting to copy our script into place. (See Figure 4, *Ensure the package is installed*, on page 124)

We'll also need to add the new command to nrpe.cfg.

```
command[check_recent_accounts]=/usr/lib/nagios/plugins/check_recent_accounts
```

```
package {
  ["nagios-nrpe-server","nagios-plugins"]:
    ensure => present,
    before => [File["/etc/nagios/nrpe.cfg"],\
    File["/usr/lib/nagios/plugins/check_recent_accounts"],\
    File["/usr/lib/nagios/plugins/check_passenger"]]
}
```

Figure 4—Ensure the package is installed

Let's run Puppet to get the script and the new nrpe.cfg in place. We can get into the console and add a few test accounts just to get data to work with.

```
app $ ./script/rails console production
Loading production environment (Rails 3.2.2)
ruby-1.9.3-p194 :001 >\
 70.times {|i| Account.create!(:email => "test#{i}@example.com") }; nil
```

Now we can execute a trial run of this plugin in the same way that we've exercised other plugins; we'll just run it from the shell.

```
app $ /usr/lib/nagios/plugins/check_recent_accounts
ACCOUNTS WARNING - 70 accounts created in the past day
```

We need to tell Nagios about our new check, so we'll add it to commands.cfg.

```
monitoring/commands.cfg
define command {
  command_name check_recent_accounts
  command_line /usr/lib/nagios/plugins/check_recent_accounts
}
```

And we'll add this to our app checks:

```
monitoring/nagios-service-definitions
define service {
  use generic-service
  service_description Recent Accounts
  host_name app
  check_command check_nrpe_1arg!check_recent_accounts
}
```

Another Puppet run, and everything is in place; now Nagios will let us know if (or when) we get a mad rush of new users.

This is the sort of check that needs to be run only once for MassiveApp. That is, when MassiveApp grows to encompass a few servers, we won't run this on each server as we'd do with check_ssh and check_passenger. Instead, we'd designate one host to run this check and to alert us if the thresholds were exceeded.

6.7   Where to Go Next

This whirlwind tour of Nagios has hit on the high points, but there are some interesting areas for future investigation. The ones we think are important are learning more about notifications and escalations, further exploring the standard Nagios interface, and selecting the appropriate Nagios tools and services to meet the needs of your system.

Notifications and Escalations

Nagios allows for a variety of notification mechanisms and strategies; SMS and email are built in, but plugins are available for notifying via IRC, Twitter, Campfire, and more. We can also set up per-person notification schedules so that a particular person doesn't receive notifications on their regular day off or receives only critical notifications for critical hosts on that day. Using contacts, hosts, and hostgroups to tune notifications can prevent everyone from seeing and eventually ignoring too many notifications.

If a notification is sent and not handled within a certain time period, Nagios can then escalate that notification to another group. An initial notification might go to a help-desk support group, and if the problem persists, another notification can be sent to a sysadmin group. Nagios has serviceescalation and hostescalation objects to help manage the escalation schedules and strategies.

One system failing can cause others to fail and result in an avalanche of notifications. We can manage this by setting up dependencies so that if one system drops offline, Nagios will suppress the messaging for dependent services. Nagios allows for both host and service dependencies to further throttle messaging as needed. And in a pinch, we can even disable messaging systemwide if something has gone terribly wrong.

Exploring the Standard Nagios Interface

We touched on a few areas of the built-in Nagios interface, but there's a lot more to see there. It includes pages that provide a topological map of the monitored hosts, it has an interface that enables access via a Wireless Markup Language client, and it even includes a (somewhat gratuitous) Virtual Reality Markup Language view. More practically, there are pages showing event histograms, a history of all notifications, histories of all log entries, and the ability to view event trends over time. It also allows for planned downtime windows to be created that will suppress notifications during that time. So, although the Nagios interface sometimes appears a bit dated, there's a lot of functionality there.

For those who want enhancements to the standard interface, there are several tools (NagVis, NDOUtils, exfoliation, NagiosGraph, and more) that can supply different views into the data that Nagios collects. Several of these enhancements show additional data; for example, NagiosGraph can display a timeline of the performance reported by each Nagios check.

Nagios Ecosystem

Nagios has a rich ecosystem of options to meet various needs. For example, connecting a central host to monitored hosts may not be the right solution for everyone. Nagios also provides an alternative way, *passive checks*, that uses the Nagios Service Check Acceptor to report checks to the central monitoring server. With passive checks, the Nagios server doesn't reach out to agents. Instead, other processes push check results into a directory where the server picks them up. This can work well for large installations and those where the server doesn't have access to the hosts that need to be monitored.

We've looked at a few plugins and written a simple one. But some of the plugins open doors to entire new areas of functionality; for example, the check_snmp plugin enables Simple Network Management Protocol integration. The Nagios Exchange[3] includes hundreds of ready-made plugins; it's worth reviewing the recent releases section occasionally to see what people are writing for Nagios.

6.8 Conclusion

In this chapter, we've discussed what monitoring is and why it's important. We've talked about a particular open source monitoring tool, Nagios, and why we like to use it to monitor our applications. Then we looked at using Nagios to monitor servers, services, and MassiveApp.

Nagios is a large system with a lot of functionality, and there are several good books on it; *Nagios: System and Network Monitoring [Bar08]* is excellent, as is *Learning Nagios 3.0 [Koc08]*. We've already seen the Nagios Puppet module and have a functioning monitoring system, so between a book or two, the Internet, and the system we have in place, we can get a fairly capable monitoring setup.

Here are a few closing thoughts on monitoring in general. Maintaining and enhancing a monitoring infrastructure may not initially appear to be exciting tasks. As the monitoring people, most of the time we're tweaking thresholds, adding monitors that may alert us once every six months, or navigating the

---

3. http://exchange.nagios.org/

somewhat less than impressive web interfaces that most monitoring tools seem to have. There's not a lot of sizzle in this kind of work.

But that said, keeping a monitoring system up-to-date is an important part of deploying our applications. If we're familiar with our monitoring tools, we'll be able to respond to outages by thinking about what checks we can add that will prevent that type of downtime. When our application gets new functionality or rolls out a new component, we'll be in a good frame of mind to add monitors preemptively to ensure the usage patterns are what we expect. Being on the team that keeps the monitoring infrastructure running gives us many windows into the entire system, and that's a great perspective to have.

6.9   For Future Reference

Nagios Architecture Overview

Nagios operates in a host/agent model, with a central host monitoring other hosts that are running Nagios' command execution agent, NRPE. Nagios provides a web interface to view system status but also sends alerts in a variety of ways. Nagios monitors hosts, which are organized into hostgroups, using commands that check services. New commands can be implemented as plugins, which are simply programs that can be written in any language as long as they conform to the Nagios output format.

Defining Nagios Objects

Nagios is configured via a directory tree of configuration files in which templates declare a variety of objects such as hosts, commands, and services. A sample host definition includes the host name and IP address and specifies a parent template that provides default values.

```
define host{
  use        generic-host
  host_name  app
  alias      app
  address    33.33.13.37
}
```

We use a service object to define a service check.

```
define service {
  use generic-service
  host_name app
  service_description SSH
  check_command check_ssh
}
```

Checking a remote service that can be accessed only locally requires NRPE. Here's a check parameter that uses NRPE:

```
check_command check_nrpe_1arg!check_users
```

Adding a new check to NRPE also requires that the command be defined in NRPE's configuration file, nrpe.cfg. Here's an example:

```
command[check_passenger]=/usr/lib/nagios/plugins/check_passenger -w 10
```

Checking Rails with Nagios

For checks specific to Rails applications, plugins can be written as Rake tasks that print a message such as ThingToCheck WARNING - 42 somethings occurred. This output message will be displayed in the Nagios interface. The task should also exit with a status code of 0 for an OK status, 1 for a WARNING status, and 2 for a CRITICAL status. Such a task can then be invoked with a Bash script as follows:

```
#!/bin/bash
cd /path/to/apps/current/
RAILS_ENV=production /usr/bin/rake --silent task:name
exit $?
```

This script can be invoke via NRPE by defining a new command in nrpe.cfg.

## CHAPTER 7

Collecting Metrics with Ganglia

MassiveApp is written and ready to go. And with the monitoring system that we put in place in Chapter 6, *Monitoring with Nagios*, on page 95, we can be confident knowing that we'll be alerted if our hardware is overloaded or if we get a flood of new users.

That's a good situation, but it's not the whole story. The monitoring system will send an alert because some threshold (load average, process count, and so on) has been exceeded. However, we want to be able to predict when we'll run low on a system resource based on our past usage trends; an upcoming shortage of disk space is something we can easily see by looking at a graph of disk free space shrinking over the course of a few weeks. And if the number of processes on a server crosses a monitoring threshold and causes an alert, is it because the process count has been slowly increasing for the past few weeks, or is this a sudden spike? To answer these questions, we need to gather and display metrics about the MassiveApp infrastructure.

We're going to use Ganglia[1] for collecting information about our servers for a number of reasons.

- Ganglia has been around for a while and is designed to scale; it's been monitoring large (2,000 nodes) distributed server clusters for more than ten years. The University of California – Berkeley monitors several large clusters and has a publicly available Ganglia web view.[2]

- It comes with a solid collection of metric-gathering scripts, and many additional plugins are available. It also can accept custom data via simple shell scripts, Python modules, and even a Ruby client.

---

1. http://ganglia.sourceforge.net
2. http://monitor.millennium.berkeley.edu/

- The basic Ganglia installation provides immediate value; ten minutes after we get Ganglia running on a new server, we're seeing interesting system-level metrics.

- It's open source and free, so as MassiveApp grows, we can fix any bugs we find, and we won't need to worry about licensing fees.

7.1 Setting Up a Metrics VM

In the same way as we did with the Nagios examples, we'll want to store everything in Puppet. We can use a branch on this book's massiveapp_ops repository that has everything except the Ganglia module. Here's how to get that:

```
$ cd ~/deployingrails/massiveapp_ops
$ git checkout --track origin/without_ganglia
Branch without_ganglia set up to track remote branch without_ganglia from origin.
Switched to a new branch 'without_ganglia'
```

We'll want to have our metrics collection host separated from our MassiveApp application hosts, so let's set up two virtual machines. One VM will run MassiveApp, and the other will run Ganglia. This is much like the setup that we did in Chapter 6, *Monitoring with Nagios*, on page 95 where we put the Nagios server on a nagios VM and MassiveApp on an app VM. Let's create a directory to hold our VMs.

```
$ mkdir ~/deployingrails/ganglia && cd ~/deployingrails/ganglia
```

Now we need a Vagrantfile with two VM definitions—one to run MassiveApp and one to run our Ganglia server. We'll use host-based networking, we'll forward host port 4567 to app guest port 80 and host port 4569 (to avoid conflicting with the monitoring VM) to ganglia guest port 80, and we'll mount our Puppet repository into /etc/puppet.

metrics/Vagrantfile
```
Vagrant::Config.run do |config|
  config.vm.define :app do |app_config|
    app_config.vm.customize ["modifyvm", :id,
      "--name", "app", "--memory", "512"]
    app_config.vm.box = "lucid64_with_ruby193"
    app_config.vm.host_name = "app"
    app_config.vm.forward_port 22, 2222, :auto => true
    app_config.vm.forward_port 80, 4567
    app_config.vm.network :hostonly, "33.33.13.37"
    app_config.vm.share_folder "puppet", "/etc/puppet", "../massiveapp_ops"
  end
  config.vm.define :ganglia do |ganglia_config|
```

```
    ganglia_config.vm.customize ["modifyvm", :id,
      "--name", "ganglia", "--memory", "512"]
    ganglia_config.vm.box = "lucid64_with_ruby193"
    ganglia_config.vm.host_name = "ganglia"
    ganglia_config.vm.forward_port 22, 2222, :auto => true
    ganglia_config.vm.forward_port 80, 4569
    ganglia_config.vm.network :hostonly, "33.33.13.38"
    ganglia_config.vm.share_folder "puppet", "/etc/puppet", "../massiveapp_ops"
  end
end
```

As we mentioned in Section 4.3, *Setting Up the Deploy*, on page 68, Vagrant allows only one VM to have a particular name at a time, so if there's an existing app VM, now would be a good time to go back and destroy it. With that done, we'll start both VMs and connect into ganglia.

```
$ vagrant up
«lots of output as both VMs are started»
$ vagrant ssh ganglia
ganglia $
```

And we'll verify that we can communicate between VMs by starting an ssh session from ganglia into app.

```
ganglia $ ssh 33.33.13.37
«ssh warnings»
vagrant@33.33.13.37's password:
Last login: Sat Oct 22 21:41:02 2011 from 10.0.2.2
app $
```

Now that our VMs are running, we'll set up Ganglia and start gathering metrics.

7.2 Writing a Ganglia Puppet Module

So, we need metrics, and we're going to use Ganglia to collect them. Using the techniques that we've picked up over the course of the past few chapters, let's build a Puppet module that will install and configure Ganglia. That will also provide us with what we'll need to build out any other servers.

Our VM is running Ubuntu 10.04, and that OS version has three packages that are necessary for our Ganglia installation.

- ganglia-monitor: This package contains the gmond daemon that gathers metrics from the host on which it's running. We'll need to install this package on any server for which we want to collect metrics, so it'll go on both ganglia and app.

- gmetad: This package receives and stores data sent to it from the gmond daemons. We need only one of these per cluster of servers, so this will go on ganglia.

- ganglia-webfrontend: This package creates and displays charts and graphs from the information that gmetad has stored. Like the gmetad, we need only one of these for each server cluster, so this will go on ganglia as well.

To start gathering and viewing metrics, we'll need to set up all three of those packages on our ganglia VM. Let's open a shell session into ganglia, move into the Puppet base directory, and create a new Puppet module directory.

```
ganglia $ cd /etc/puppet/
ganglia $ mkdir -p {modules/ganglia/manifests,modules/ganglia/files}
```

To download and install the three Ganglia packages, let's create our new module's configuration file: modules/ganglia/manifests/init.pp. As with Nagios, we'll just put a placeholder class here.

```
class ganglia {
}
```

Let's make a server class in modules/ganglia/manifests/server.pp to hold our package declarations.

metrics/only_packages/modules/ganglia/manifests/server.pp
```
class ganglia::server {
  package {
    ["ganglia-monitor", "ganglia-webfrontend","gmetad"]:
      ensure  => installed
  }
}
```

We also need to define a new Puppet node (refer to Section 3.7, *Managing Multiple Hosts with Puppet*, on page 54 for more on Puppet nodes) and include our new module, so let's open manifests/nodes.pp and add this to the end of the file:

```
node "ganglia" inherits basenode {
  include ganglia::server
}
```

With that in place, we can run Puppet, and it will install our Ganglia packages.

```
ganglia $ sudo puppet apply --verbose manifests/site.pp
«various other messages»
info: Applying configuration version '1299475416'
notice: /Stage[main]/Ganglia/Package[gmetad]/ensure: \
  ensure changed 'purged' to 'present'
notice: /Stage[main]/Ganglia/Package[ganglia-webfrontend]/ensure: \
```

```
    ensure changed 'purged' to 'present'
notice: /Stage[main]/Ganglia/Package[ganglia-monitor]/ensure: \
    ensure changed 'purged' to 'present'
```

Installing these packages does more than put the Ganglia program files in place. The installation scripts also start the gmetad and gmond services. For the ganglia-webfrontend service to be available, though, we need to create a symbolic link so the Apache configuration file will be loaded when Apache starts. We'll do that via Puppet using a file resource in modules/ganglia/manifests/server.pp.

metrics/server_with_symlink/modules/ganglia/manifests/server.pp
```
class ganglia::server {
  package {
    ["ganglia-monitor", "ganglia-webfrontend","gmetad"]:
      ensure  => installed
  }
  file {
    "/etc/apache2/conf.d/ganglia.conf":
      ensure  => link,
      target  => "/etc/ganglia-webfrontend/apache.conf",
      notify  => Service["apache2"];
  }
}
```

That will cause the default Ganglia Apache configuration file to be loaded when Apache starts. The default configuration file, however, doesn't contain a virtual host declaration. Without that, any time we want to access the Ganglia web pages, we'll need to browse to localhost:4569/ganglia. But if we add a virtual host declaration, we can then browse in through the host name ganglia.localhost.

So let's set that up with a custom Apache configuration file in modules/ganglia/files/apache.conf. Here's the Apache configuration file that we'll put in modules/ganglia/files/apache.conf:

metrics/modules/ganglia/files/apache.conf
```
<VirtualHost *:80>
  ServerName ganglia.localhost
  DocumentRoot /usr/share/ganglia-webfrontend
  Alias /ganglia /usr/share/ganglia-webfrontend
</VirtualHost>
```

We'll need to put that in the /etc/ganglia-webfrontend directory, so let's enhance our manifest to handle that. In this updated resource declaration, our symlink resource depends on our custom Apache configuration file being in place, and a change either to the symlink or to apache.conf will cause the Apache service to be restarted.

metrics/server_with_apache/modules/ganglia/manifests/server.pp

```
class ganglia::server {
  package {
    ["ganglia-monitor", "ganglia-webfrontend","gmetad"]:
      ensure  => installed
  }
  file {
    "/etc/ganglia-webfrontend/apache.conf":
      source  => "puppet:///modules/ganglia/apache.conf",
      owner   => root,
      group   => root,
      mode    => 644,
      notify  => Service["apache2"];
    "/etc/apache2/conf.d/ganglia.conf":
      ensure  => link,
      target  => "/etc/ganglia-webfrontend/apache.conf",
      require => File["/etc/ganglia-webfrontend/apache.conf"],
      notify  => Service["apache2"];
  }
}
```

We'll also want Apache on this node, so we'll modify our ganglia node definition in manifests/nodes.pp to reflect that.

```
node "ganglia" inherits basenode {
  include apache2
  include ganglia::server
}
```

Let's run Puppet to get everything in place.

```
ganglia $ sudo puppet apply --verbose manifests/site.pp
info: Applying configuration version '1299477369'
notice: /Stage[main]/Ganglia/File[/etc/apache2/conf.d/ganglia.conf]/ensure: \
  created
info: /Stage[main]/Ganglia/File[/etc/apache2/conf.d/ganglia.conf]: \
  Scheduling refresh of Service[apache2]
notice: /Stage[main]/Apache/Service[apache2]: \
  Triggered 'refresh' from 1 events
```

Although Ganglia is now running and accessible via the virtual host we defined, we need to do a little more work configuring Ganglia before we can gather any metrics. Ganglia requires that we define a *cluster* that contains the servers on which we're collecting data. Defining a cluster is pretty painless; we just need to make some changes to the Ganglia configuration files. So, we'll do some manual configuration and backfill that into Puppet.

Let's open /etc/ganglia/gmond.conf, move to the cluster definition on line 20, and change the cluster name to MassiveApp:

```
cluster {
  name    = "MassiveApp"
  owner   = "unspecified"
  latlong = "unspecified"
  url     = "unspecified"
}
```

We also need to tell the gmond to publish its data using its IP address; if we don't do that, it'll show up in the Ganglia UI as localhost. So, a few lines after the cluster definition, there's a udp_send_channel definition that we'll modify to contain a host and port.

```
udp_send_channel {
  host = 33.33.13.38
  port = 8649
}
```

We want gmond to listen for metrics published from other gmond instances like the one that we'll set up on app. We can accomplish that by configuring udp_receive_channel to listen on the standard gmond port.

```
udp_recv_channel {
  port = 8649
}
```

The gmetad will need to talk to this gmond to get the data that's being collected, so let's change the gmond tcp_accept_channel to listen on port 8650.

```
tcp_accept_channel {
  port = 8650
}
```

And since we've set that port for gmetad to communicate with, we need to open /etc/ganglia/gmetad.conf and add a data source so that gmetad will know where to look. This setting is located around line 40.

```
data_source "MassiveApp" localhost:8650
```

We also need to run our gmetad as the ganglia user since that's the account that the package sets up as the owner of the data directories, so we'll modify the setuid_username setting on line 93.

```
setuid_username "ganglia"
```

We've modified the configuration; next we'll capture those changes in our Puppet manifests. Let's copy the gmond.conf file into modules/ganglia/files/gmond_server.cond, and we'll preserve our gmetad.conf file by copying it into modules/ganglia/files/gmetad.conf. Then let's open modules/ganglia/manifests/server.pp and add two more file resources; then gmond.conf and gmetad.conf will be managed by Puppet.

metrics/server_with_gmond_gmetad/modules/ganglia/manifests/server.pp
```
class ganglia::server {
  package {
    ["ganglia-monitor", "ganglia-webfrontend","gmetad"]:
      ensure  => installed
  }
  file {
    "/etc/ganglia-webfrontend/apache.conf":
      source  => "puppet:///modules/ganglia/apache.conf",
      owner   => root,
      group   => root,
      mode    => 644,
      notify  => Service["apache2"];
    "/etc/apache2/conf.d/ganglia.conf":
      ensure  => link,
      target  => "/etc/ganglia-webfrontend/apache.conf",
      require => File["/etc/ganglia-webfrontend/apache.conf"],
      notify  => Service["apache2"];
    "/etc/ganglia/gmond.conf":
      source  => "puppet:///modules/ganglia/gmond_server.conf",
      owner   => root,
      group   => root,
      mode    => 644,
      notify  => Service["ganglia-monitor"],
      require => Package["ganglia-monitor"];
    "/etc/ganglia/gmetad.conf":
      source  => "puppet:///modules/ganglia/gmetad.conf",
      owner   => root,
      group   => root,
      mode    => 644,
      notify  => Service["gmetad"],
      require => Package["gmetad"];
  }
}
```

We added notify attributes so that changes to the configuration files would restart the services. For that to work, though, we need to define those service resources in our server.pp.

metrics/server_with_services/modules/ganglia/manifests/server.pp
```
class ganglia::server {
  package {
    ["ganglia-monitor", "ganglia-webfrontend","gmetad"]:
      ensure  => installed
  }
  file {
    "/etc/ganglia-webfrontend/apache.conf":
      source  => "puppet:///modules/ganglia/apache.conf",
      owner   => root,
      group   => root,
```

```
    mode     => 644,
    notify   => Service["apache2"];
  "/etc/apache2/conf.d/ganglia.conf":
    ensure   => link,
    target   => "/etc/ganglia-webfrontend/apache.conf",
    require  => File["/etc/ganglia-webfrontend/apache.conf"],
    notify   => Service["apache2"];
  "/etc/ganglia/gmond.conf":
    source   => "puppet:///modules/ganglia/gmond_server.conf",
    owner    => root,
    group    => root,
    mode     => 644,
    notify   => Service["ganglia-monitor"],
    require  => Package["ganglia-monitor"];
  "/etc/ganglia/gmetad.conf":
    source   => "puppet:///modules/ganglia/gmetad.conf",
    owner    => root,
    group    => root,
    mode     => 644,
    notify   => Service["gmetad"],
    require  => Package["gmetad"];
  }
  service {
    ["ganglia-monitor", "gmetad"]:
      hasrestart => true
  }
}
```

With the new file and the service definitions in place, running Puppet will install our customized configuration files and restart our services. Let's go ahead and run Puppet to apply those changes.

To see Ganglia in action, we need to add a new ganglia.localhost entry on the host machine (that is, the laptop) like we did in Section 6.2, *Writing a Nagios Puppet Module*, on page 98. Let's open /etc/hosts, add that entry, and save the file.

```
127.0.0.1 ganglia.localhost
```

Now we can browse to http://ganglia.localhost:4569/ to see the information that Ganglia presents.

Ganglia Web Interface

The front page of the Ganglia web interface contains a set of graphs of aggregated metrics from across the entire cluster. For example, one of these graphs displays the aggregated network bandwidth used by all the hosts. In this case, we have only one host in the cluster (so far), so there's not a lot of aggregation going on. But it does give us a quick view into the VM's activity, and the page refreshes itself every five minutes to show the latest numbers.

The front page also contains a specific metric's graph for a single system just below the cluster graphs. Again, in this case, we have only one system, so Ganglia displays the load_one metric (that is, the load average for the past one minute) for our VM. If we click that load_one graph, the view changes to a collection of graphs showing the thirty-three metrics that Ganglia has gathered. Some of these are more interesting than others; for example, the network_report graph displays the bytes per second flowing in and out of the network interface, while boottime shows just the time that the host was last started.

Above the aggregated graphs are a few controls that allow us to select a time scale consisting of hour, day, week, month, or year. This corresponds to the scale along the x-axis of the graphs. The scale setting travels with us between pages, so if we select day and click a host-specific graph, we see graphs of all the metrics for the past day.

Now that we've explored the web interface a bit, we can see that we have a basic Ganglia system installed and configured. This already provides us with some useful low-level metrics, and next we can improve visibility by expanding the cluster to include our app VM.

Monitoring a Remote Host with Ganglia

Our ganglia VM is running all three Ganglia packages. But a cluster that consists of only one server isn't much of a cluster. Let's configure app so that we're seeing metrics for that host as well.

First we need to ssh into app, run Puppet, and then deploy MassiveApp to this machine. That will put the database, tables, and application in place. Once that's done, we'll have something to monitor.

app isn't our metrics server, so all we need to run there is the gmond daemon that's provided by ganglia-monitor. Here's the class declaration to put in modules/ganglia/manifests/client.pp with the package resource:

```
metrics/client_with_packages/modules/ganglia/manifests/client.pp
class ganglia::client {
  package {
    "ganglia-monitor":
      ensure  => installed
  }
}
```

We want to ensure the service is started, so let's also add a service resource.

```
metrics/client_with_service/modules/ganglia/manifests/client.pp
class ganglia::client {
  package {
    "ganglia-monitor":
      ensure  => installed
  }
  service {
    "ganglia-monitor":
      hasrestart => true
  }
}
```

We need to set up gmond on app so that it will report metrics. Let's start by copying the basic configuration file into our module. We can use this configuration file for any other Ganglia client hosts that we set up, so we'll name it gmond_client.conf.

```
app $ cp /etc/ganglia/gmond.conf modules/ganglia/files/gmond_client.conf
```

We want app to join our cluster, so let's edit modules/ganglia/files/gmond_client.conf and modify the cluster definition so that it matches the cluster we defined in gmond.conf on ganglia.

```
cluster {
  name = "MassiveApp"
  owner = "unspecified"
  latlong = "unspecified"
  url = "unspecified"
}
```

We also want app to report to the gmond running on ganglia, so we'll set it up to send data there. Let's delete the contents of the udp_send_channel configuration and replace it with a configuration setting that points to the ganglia VM.

```
udp_send_channel {
  host = 33.33.13.38
  port = 8649
}
```

We don't want app to receive metrics data from any other hosts, so in that same file we'll delete the contents of both the udp_recv_channel and tcp_accept_channel blocks. We would delete them entirely, but some older versions of Ganglia crash if those blocks aren't present. Finally, we need Puppet to move this file into place, so we'll add a new file resource to modules/ganglia/manifests/client.pp.

```
metrics/client_with_config/modules/ganglia/manifests/client.pp
class ganglia::client {
  package {
```

```
    "ganglia-monitor":
      ensure  => installed
  }
  service {
    "ganglia-monitor":
      hasrestart => true
  }
  file {
    "/etc/ganglia/gmond.conf":
      source  => "puppet:///modules/ganglia/gmond_client.conf",
      owner   => root,
      group   => root,
      mode    => 644,
      notify  => Service["ganglia-monitor"],
      require => Package["ganglia-monitor"];
  }
}
```

The app node doesn't include our Ganglia client class yet, so we'll add this to the app node in manifests/nodes.pp:

```
include ganglia::client
```

We can then run Puppet on app, and the gmond on app will begin to publish data to ganglia.

There was a lot less setup required for a Ganglia client host than for a server host. We just installed gmond, we pointed it to our Ganglia server, and we have metrics. This is one of the beauties of Ganglia; a few moments after installing the client daemon, we have useful data.

Next we'll look at using Ganglia plugins to gather more specific metrics.

7.3   Using Ganglia Plugins

Ganglia gathers metrics using *plugins*. It comes with plugins that collect the low-level metrics we've seen so far such as CPU usage, load average, process counts, and so on. The Ganglia user and developer community has accumulated a variety of plugins for higher-level services and applications. MassiveApp uses MySQL, so let's check the Ganglia plugin repository for MySQL plugins and incorporate what we find into our monitoring system.

The Ganglia plugin repository[3] has a good collection of MySQL plugins from which we can choose. There are several different types of plugins, the most straightforward of which are simple scripts that we can run from the command

---

3.   https://github.com/ganglia

line. These are called *gmetric scripts* because they use the gmetric utility that is part of the ganglia-monitor package. So, we'll get a gmetric script in place, we'll run it with a cron job, and it will use gmetric to send new metrics to gmond. Let's start by downloading a MySQL gmetric script. There's a good one written by Vladimir Vuksan.[4] Let's grab that file using curl and put it in the modules/ganglia/files/gmetric directory on app.

```
app $ mkdir modules/ganglia/files/gmetric
app $ curl --silent --output modules/ganglia/files/gmetric/ganglia_mysql_stats.pl \
  https://raw.github.com/ganglia/gmetric\
  /master/database/mysql_stats/ganglia_mysql_stats.pl
```

Before we use this plugin, we need to ensure that it can connect to the MassiveApp MySQL database. Let's open the script and move down to line 19, which contains the command this plugin will use to gather MySQL data. Let's change this line to match our MySQL access controls. After the change, it'll look like this:

```
$stats_command = "/usr/bin/mysqladmin -u root --password=root extended-status";
```

After saving the file and exiting the editor, we can verify that the plugin is working by making the script executable and then running it manually.

```
app $ chmod 755 modules/ganglia/files/gmetric/ganglia_mysql_stats.pl
app $ ./modules/ganglia/files/gmetric/ganglia_mysql_stats.pl
Com_delete = 0 / sec
Com_create_table = 0 / sec
Threads_created = 0 / sec
Key_read_requests = 0 / sec
Bytes_received = 0.0562293274531422 / sec
«lots of other metrics»
```

Now we know that the script can talk to MySQL and bring back some metrics. Let's get this into Puppet by adding new file resources to our Ganglia module's client.pp. We'll add both a directory and the script file itself; we can just append these new file resources to the existing file resource that we've already declared.

metrics/client_with_plugin/modules/ganglia/manifests/client.pp
```
class ganglia::client {
  package {
    "ganglia-monitor":
      ensure  => installed
  }
  service {
    "ganglia-monitor":
      hasrestart => true
  }
```

4.   https://github.com/ganglia/gmetric/blob/master/database/mysql_stats/ganglia_mysql_stats.pl

```
  file {
    "/etc/ganglia/gmond.conf":
      source  => "puppet:///modules/ganglia/gmond_client.conf",
      owner   => root,
      group   => root,
      mode    => 644,
      notify  => Service["ganglia-monitor"],
      require => Package["ganglia-monitor"];
    "/etc/ganglia/gmetric":
      ensure  => directory,
      owner   => root,
      group   => root;
    "/etc/ganglia/gmetric/ganglia_mysql_stats.pl":
      source  => "puppet:///modules/ganglia/gmetric/ganglia_mysql_stats.pl",
      owner   => root,
      group   => root,
      mode    => 755,
      require => File["/etc/ganglia/gmetric"]
  }
}
```

That will put the script in place, but we also need to run it regularly to collect metrics. We can do that with a cron job that runs once a minute. Here's our new client.pp:

metrics/client_with_cron/modules/ganglia/manifests/client.pp
```
class ganglia::client {
  package {
    "ganglia-monitor":
      ensure  => installed
  }
  service {
    "ganglia-monitor":
      hasrestart => true
  }
  file {
    "/etc/ganglia/gmond.conf":
      source  => "puppet:///modules/ganglia/gmond_client.conf",
      owner   => root,
      group   => root,
      mode    => 644,
      notify  => Service["ganglia-monitor"],
      require => Package["ganglia-monitor"];
    "/etc/ganglia/gmetric":
      ensure  => directory,
      owner   => root,
      group   => root;
    "/etc/ganglia/gmetric/ganglia_mysql_stats.pl":
      source  => "puppet:///modules/ganglia/gmetric/ganglia_mysql_stats.pl",
      owner   => root,
```

```
      group   => root,
      mode    => 755,
      require => File["/etc/ganglia/gmetric"]
  }
  cron {
    "ganglia_mysql_stats":
      user    => vagrant,
      minute  => "*",
      command => "/etc/ganglia/gmetric/ganglia_mysql_stats.pl",
      require => File["/etc/ganglia/gmetric/ganglia_mysql_stats.pl"]
  }
}
```

Now we'll run Puppet to create our new files and our cron task. Within a minute we'll see new options (such as Com_select, Bytes_sent, and so on) appear in the metric select box at the top of the Ganglia user interface. Or we can see all the new graphs at once by clicking the load_one graph and scrolling down through the graphs that are specific to our VM.

This is the way we'll want to monitor most services. We look around for an existing Ganglia plugin, install it, and start seeing new metrics. And don't forget to contribute any enhancements back to the plugin author to help future Ganglia users.

Next we'll look at writing our own plugin.

7.4 Gathering Metrics with a Custom Gmetric Plugin

As we've seen, adding new Ganglia plugins is mostly a matter of finding the script, getting it into place, and setting up a cron job to run it regularly. But we won't find any plugins out there for gathering metrics on MassiveApp; if we want those metrics, we'll need to write something ourselves. Fortunately, gmetric makes this a simple task.

In Section 6.6, *Monitoring Applications*, on page 121, we discussed the account creation rate and built a monitor that will alert us when an unexpectedly large number of accounts is being created. The account creation rate seems like a useful metric, so let's use gmetric to gather that information, and we can watch the (hopefully) upward trend.

The basic idea for building a gmetric plugin is to gather metrics, name them, and then publish them to the local gmond process. We can get the number of accounts created recently by querying MySQL. Let's get into the MySQL console and run a query to count those recent accounts.

```
$ mysql -uroot -proot massiveapp_production
Welcome to the MySQL monitor.  Commands end with ; or \g.
Your MySQL connection id is 44
Server version: 5.1.41-3ubuntu12.10 (Ubuntu)

Type 'help;' or '\h' for help. Type '\c' to clear the current input statement.

mysql> select count(id) from accounts where created_at > (now() - interval 1 hour);
+-----------+
| count(id) |
+-----------+
|         0 |
+-----------+
1 row in set (0.00 sec)
```

This returns a count of zero, since our avalanche of users has not yet arrived. But it's enough to show us that we're getting a value back from our query. We can use this as the basis for our plugin.

It's time to start working on the plugin's code. We'll want to put it in the Puppet repository in the modules/ganglia/files/gmetric directory next to our MySQL plugin. Let's open a new file called gmetric_accounts.rb and add the following:

metrics/modules/ganglia/files/gmetric/gmetric_accounts.rb
```ruby
#!/usr/bin/env ruby
def recently_created_record_count
  cmd = 'mysql -uroot -proot --silent '
  cmd += '--skip-column-names massiveapp_production --execute '
  cmd += '"select count(id) from accounts where '
  cmd += 'created_at > (now() - interval 1 hour)"'
  `#{cmd}`.strip
end
```

The first line sets up the path to the Ruby executable. Next, the recently_created_record_count() method takes care of connecting to MySQL and running our query, and it uses the --silent and --skip-column-names options to avoid cluttering the output with column headers and other extraneous information. Once the result is returned, we strip any whitespace in case it has a carriage return appended.

So, now we have our record count; let's publish it to Ganglia. We'll do this by passing a few arguments to the gmetric command-line utility. Let's add another function to gmetric_accounts.rb.

metrics/modules/ganglia/files/gmetric/gmetric_accounts.rb
```ruby
def publish(count)
  puts "Publishing accounts = #{count}" if ARGV.include?("-v")
  system("gmetric --name 'accounts' --value #{count} --type uint16")
end
```

We're running gmetric with a name argument that will be displayed in the Ganglia web interface's metric picker, and we're passing in the actual value that we're publishing. We're also including a metric type; in this case it's uint16. This is an unsigned integer, that is, a positive integer that is capped at 65535. To coin a phrase, that should be enough for anyone.

Our functions are in place, so we just need to call them. Let's add one more line to the file.

metrics/modules/ganglia/files/gmetric/gmetric_accounts.rb

```
publish(recently_created_record_count)
```

That's it for our plugin. We can test it by running it from the command line, and we'll use the -v option to see some output.

```
app $ modules/ganglia/files/gmetric/gmetric_accounts.rb -v
Publishing accounts = 0
```

That's the error-free output we want to see. Now we'll add Puppet resources to put this file in place. Let's open modules/ganglia/manifests/client.pp and add another file resource along with a cron job to gather this metric regularly.

metrics/client_with_gmetric_file_and_cron/modules/ganglia/manifests/client.pp

```
class ganglia::client {
  package {
    "ganglia-monitor":
      ensure  => installed
  }
  service {
    "ganglia-monitor":
      hasrestart => true
  }
  file {
    "/etc/ganglia/gmond.conf":
      source  => "puppet:///modules/ganglia/gmond_client.conf",
      owner   => root,
      group   => root,
      mode    => 644,
      notify  => Service["ganglia-monitor"],
      require => Package["ganglia-monitor"];
    "/etc/ganglia/gmetric":
      ensure  => directory,
      owner   => root,
      group   => root;
    "/etc/ganglia/gmetric/ganglia_mysql_stats.pl":
      source  => "puppet:///modules/ganglia/gmetric/ganglia_mysql_stats.pl",
      owner   => root,
      group   => root,
      mode    => 755,
      require => File["/etc/ganglia/gmetric"];
```

```
  "/etc/ganglia/gmetric/gmetric_accounts.rb":
    source  => "puppet:///modules/ganglia/gmetric/gmetric_accounts.rb",
    owner   => root,
    group   => root,
    mode    => 755,
    require => File["/etc/ganglia/gmetric"]
}
cron {
  "ganglia_mysql_stats":
    user    => vagrant,
    minute  => "*",
    command => "/etc/ganglia/gmetric/ganglia_mysql_stats.pl",
    require => File["/etc/ganglia/gmetric/ganglia_mysql_stats.pl"];
  "gmetric_accounts":
    user    => vagrant,
    minute  => "*",
    command => "/etc/ganglia/gmetric/gmetric_accounts.rb",
    require => File["/etc/ganglia/gmetric/gmetric_accounts.rb"]
  }
}
```

Now we run Puppet to get everything into place, and the account metric will start appearing in the web interface. Granted, it'll be a little dull until the site goes live, but watching that graph trend upward on launch day is just something else to look forward to.

7.5 Producing Metrics with Ruby

We've seen how to funnel metrics into Ganglia by running gmetric and passing in a few arguments. This approach is simple, but the simplicity comes at the price of performance. If we want to collect lots of data, firing off a new process each time we send a value to Ganglia is going to waste CPU and memory on MassiveApp's servers.

A more scalable approach is to use a convenient little Ruby library by Ilya Grigorik named, appropriately enough, gmetric. From the gmetric GitHub page,[5] gmetric is "A pure Ruby client for generating Ganglia 3.1.x+ gmetric meta and metric packets and talking to your gmond/gmetad nodes over UDP protocol." The beauty of gmetric is that since it encapsulates the gmond packet format, we can send plenty of metrics to Ganglia without incurring undue performance penalties.

---

5. https://github.com/igrigorik/gmetric

Let's modify our gmetrics_accounts.rb script to use the gmetric gem to publish metrics. We first need to install gmetric on app; as befits a good system administration tool, it has no dependencies.

```
app $ sudo gem install gmetric
Successfully installed gmetric-0.1.3
1 gem installed
Installing ri documentation for gmetric-0.1.3...
Installing RDoc documentation for gmetric-0.1.3...
```

Since gmetric_accounts.rb is going to use the gmetric gem, we need to add a few lines to the top of the file to bring in RubyGems and gmetric.

```
#!/usr/bin/env ruby

require 'rubygems'
require 'gmetric'
```

Now we'll change the publish() method to send the account value to the gmond on ganglia. We'll do this by calling the send() class method on Ganglia::GMetric and passing in the name, value, and type of the metric we've published.

```
def publish(count)
  puts "Publishing accounts = #{count}" if ARGV.include?("-v")
  Ganglia::GMetric.send("33.33.13.38", 8649, {
    :name => "accounts",
    :type => "uint16",
    :value => count
  })
end
```

As before, we'll test this from the command line; if we create a few test accounts first, we'll get a more interesting metric.

```
app $ modules/ganglia/files/gmetric_gem_accounts.rb -v
Publishing accounts = 21
```

And when we point a browser to the ganglia VM, we can see our graph. Here's the script in its entirety:

```
metrics/modules/ganglia/files/gmetric/gmetric_gem_accounts.rb
#!/usr/bin/env ruby
require 'rubygems'
require 'gmetric'
def recently_created_record_count
  cmd = 'mysql -uroot -proot --silent --skip-column-names '
  cmd += ' massiveapp_production --execute '
  cmd += '"select count(id) from accounts where '
  cmd += 'created_at > (now() - interval 1 hour)"'
  `#{cmd}`.strip.to_i
end
```

```
def publish(count)
  puts "Publishing accounts = #{count}" if ARGV.include?("-v")
  Ganglia::GMetric.send("33.33.13.38", 8649, {
    :name => "accounts",
    :type => "uint16",
    :value => count
  })
end
publish(recently_created_record_count)
```

Running metric_gem_accounts.rb with a cron job and managing the file with Puppet are almost the same as in Section 7.4, *Gathering Metrics with a Custom Gmetric Plugin*, on page 143, so there's no need to rehash that here. The only difference is that we need the gmetric gem to be in place, so we'd add a package resource with the gem provider to ensure it's installed.

```
package {
  "gmetric":
    provider  => "gem",
    ensure    => installed
}
```

Using a Ruby-based in-process network client is a much more efficient way of sending metrics to Ganglia. We favor this technique whenever we're collecting lots of data.

7.6 Where to Go Next

As with the other tools we've covered in this book, we really have room only to scratch the surface of what Ganglia has to offer. For future exploration opportunities, consider looking into Ganglia/Nagios integration and newer versions of Ganglia.

Ganglia and Nagios

You've probably noticed that we're polling servers for data with Nagios and NRPE, and we're using gmond to push data from our servers up to our gmetad. For system-level metrics (CPU activity, process counts, and so on), we're collecting the same data twice—once for monitoring and once for long-term metrics. This works, but it seems like we could do better.

There are several projects working to provide some level of integration between Nagios and Ganglia. Mike Conigliaro's check_ganglia_metric[6] uses a Nagios plugin to connect to Ganglia and trigger alerts based on warning thresholds. For

---

6.   https://github.com/mconigliaro/check_ganglia_metric

another approach, Patrick Dubois' gmond-zmq[7] receives UDP packets from gmond daemons and publishes them on a message queue so that a listener could feed them to Nagios as a passive check. Either of these techniques could help provide tighter coupling between your metrics and your monitoring systems.

We've found that we can run both Ganglia and Nagios on a single server for a while because neither is particularly resource-intensive for small clusters. The monitoring on that server will make it clear when it's time to split them out onto separate boxes, and by then you'll have enough operational experience with both to move either to an appropriately sized replacement server.

Upgrading Ganglia

We've covered the latest stable version of Ganglia that comes with Ubuntu 10.04 and that does what's needed in terms of getting a solid metrics system up and running. But the pace of Ganglia development has picked up recently, and as of this writing, Ganglia 3.3.1 is the newest release. The big win that this release brings is a reworking of the HTML interface with lots of charting improvements, but there's also better Graphite integration, some updated Nagios scripts, and a variety of bug fixes as well. If you're interested in getting even more out of Ganglia, try this newer release on a VM and see whether a production upgrade would pay off for you.

7.7 Conclusion

Ganglia is in place and running on MassiveApp now. As users flock to enjoy MassiveApp, we'll get a continuous stream of metrics that we can use to project new hardware needs, measure resources consumed per account, and calculate the effects of code changes and service tuning. And we have a framework in place for recording new metrics as we add new services and features to MassiveApp.

Metrics are a bit like monitoring in that they run in the background and stay under the radar. But metrics are more fun since they can show us when things are going right as well as when things are going wrong. The more metrics we collect, the better feel we'll have for MassiveApp and how it's faring.

In the next chapter, we'll look at how we can keep MassiveApp running for a long time while avoiding slow performance degradation and cruft.

---

7.   https://github.com/jedi4ever/gmond-zmq

7.8   For Future Reference

Here's a summary of the technical details we've discussed in this chapter.

Ganglia Architecture

Ganglia operates in a server-agent architecture, with a gmond running on each machine for which we're gathering metrics. Each gmond communicates over UDP with a gmetad running on the Ganglia server. The Ganglia server will usually run a web server to provide an HTML interface. Ganglia metrics are collected via plugins, a variety of which are freely available.

gmond Configuration

The Ganglia's server gmond should define a cluster in /etc/ganglia/gmond.conf.

```
cluster {
  name = "MassiveApp"
  owner = "unspecified"
  latlong = "unspecified"
  url = "unspecified"
}
```

It should also listen for metrics from other gmond instances and should publish to the gmetad.

```
udp_send_channel {
  host = 33.33.13.38
  port = 8649
}
udp_recv_channel {
  port = 8649
}
tcp_accept_channel {
  port = 8650
}
```

On each client machine, gmond only needs to join the cluster and send metrics to the central gmond.

```
cluster {
  name = "MassiveApp"
  owner = "unspecified"
  latlong = "unspecified"
  url = "unspecified"
}
udp_send_channel {
  host = 33.33.13.38
  port = 8649
}
```

gmetad Configuration

gmetad needs to define the gmond from which it's pulling data; this is defined in /etc/ganglia/gmetad.conf.

```
data_source "MassiveApp" localhost:8650
```

The gmetad.conf also contains settings for the user account that runs gmetad and a few tuning parameters.

Publishing Metrics with gmetric

Ganglia provides a command-line interface, gmetric, for publishing metrics to a gmond over UDP. For example, assuming we have the count in a local variable called the_count, we can publish the current number of accounts from a Ruby script with the following:

```
system "gmetric --name 'accounts' --value #{the_count} --type uint16"
```

There's also a gmetric RubyGem that will prevent the overhead of execing a process each time we need to publish a metric.

## CHAPTER 8

Maintaining the Application

We've provisioned our servers, deployed MassiveApp, and set up our monitoring and metrics, and things are clicking along nicely. At this point, MassiveApp doesn't have a tremendous amount of data or activity, but we certainly hope that changes over time. So, let's give some thought to what we'll need for ongoing maintenance and what actions we'll take to ensure that MassiveApp stays running. We'll look at managing log files, creating backups, preventing the operational data from getting out of hand, and managing downtime...be it expected or unexpected. By the end of this chapter, we'll have strategies for keeping MassiveApp on an even keel.

We'll start by discussing the task of keeping log files under control, and we'll explore a few simple scripts that will ensure this is something we won't have to bother with.

8.1 Managing Logs

One useful metaphor in maintaining a system is that of "fills and empties." We want to identify all the places where MassiveApp creates data or where a user can create data inside MassiveApp; these are the *fills*. Then, we'll ensure that we have a corresponding set of components that keep those fills from growing to infinity; those are our *empties*. The type of empty varies from fill to fill; we'll want to do something different with our mail server log data than we do with our ever-growing comment list.

So, we need to establish strategies for handling any source of steadily growing data. In some cases, just letting it grow is the right thing to do. For example, a countries table may grow slowly over time, but that growth is slow enough that we can give it a few hundred years before it'll be an issue. The fact that we've deliberately designated it as a data fill that we never empty, though, is a good step.

One significant fill is application and web server logs. If not managed properly, these can chew up tremendous amounts of disk space and be somewhat painful to manage. But we'll set things up so that we never have to worry about them. Let's look at how the default Apache configuration handles logs.

Apache Logs

The stock Apache installation uses a CustomLog directive to control how HTTP requests are logged. Here's the default entry from our VM's /etc/apache2/apache2.conf that shows the location on the filesystem where the log entries appear:

```
CustomLog /var/log/apache2/other_vhosts_access.log vhost_combined
```

That's where the log entries are written, but do they stay there forever? They don't, thanks to *log rotation*. Here's how the log rotation process works. A cron task checks a directory of configuration files to see which files need to be rotated and then operates on those files. For example, a log file originally named secure.log is renamed to secure.log.1, and a new secure.log file is opened. The next rotation results in secure.log.1 being renamed to secure.log.2, secure.log being renamed to secure.log.1, a new secure.log file being opened, and so forth.

Here's the default Apache log rotation configuration file:

```
maintenance/default_apache2_logrotate.d
/var/log/apache2/*.log {
  weekly
  missingok
  rotate 52
  compress
  delaycompress
  notifempty
  create 640 root adm
  sharedscripts
  postrotate
    if [ -f "`. /etc/apache2/envvars ; \
      echo ${APACHE_PID_FILE:-/var/run/apache2.pid}`" ]; then
      /etc/init.d/apache2 reload > /dev/null
    fi
  endscript
}
```

Here's a breakdown of the options in that file:

- The file matching expression /var/log/apache2/*.log tells logrotate which files need to be rotated. In this case, the wildcard indicates that all the files ending in .log in the /var/log/httpd/ directory should be rotated.

- The weekly directive tells logrotate to rotate these files weekly.

- The rotate 52 directive causes logs to be rotated fifty-two times before being deleted.

- compress causes logs to be compressed using gzip.

- delaycompress causes the compression to be delayed until the second time a file is rotated.

- notifempty says not to bother rotating if the log file is empty.

- create 640 root adm sets the permissions on newly created log files.

- sharedscripts causes the postrotate script to be run only once even though there are many files to be rotated.

- postrotate contains a block of shell code that's executed after the logs have been rotated. This code causes Apache to be restarted.

The reload directive in the postrotate block is where we have a problem. A reload will restart Apache, and it will also restart all of our existing Passenger processes. This means that once a week our MassiveApp users will get an unpleasant pause in their experience. That's not a big deal at first, but as MassiveApp grows more popular and as we increase the log rotation to daily or hourly, the problem will get worse.

Fortunately, we can avoid the whole issue using an Apache feature called *piped log rotation*. We'll tell Apache to rotate the main log without needing a restart. We can do this by adding a few directives to our Apache configuration file.

We're customizing apache2.conf, so we'll need to copy it into modules/apache/files and make a change to the CustomLog directive. Let's modify this line so that each log entry is written through the Apache rotatelogs utility, and we'll add the interval in seconds (once a day, so once every 86,400 seconds) at which we want the log to be rotated.

```
CustomLog "|/usr/sbin/rotatelogs \
  /var/log/apache2/other_vhosts_access.log 86400" vhost_combined
```

Since we're modifying apache2.conf, we need to manage it with Puppet. And since we're rolling our own log rotation, let's get rid of the logrotate.d script that was part of the package. We can do both tasks with a few Puppet file resource declarations.

maintenance/modules/apache2/manifests/init.pp

```
class apache2 {
# other resources
  file {
    "/etc/apache2/apache2.conf":
      mode    => "0644",
      owner   => "root",
      group   => "root",
      source  => "puppet:///modules/apache/apache2.conf",
      notify  => Service["apache2"],
      require => Package["apache2"];
    "/etc/logrotate.d/apache2":
      ensure  => absent;
  }
# other resources
}
```

Now we'll run Puppet to apply these changes. We connect into the VM using ssh, navigate to the Puppet directory with cd /etc/puppet, pull the latest changes with git pull, and run Puppet with sudo puppet --verbose --no-daemonize manifests/site.pp. This will get the new apache2.conf file in place, clear out the old logrotate script, and restart Apache. Now we can look in /var/log/apache2 and see there's a new log file with a timestamp named something like other_vhosts_access.log.1304985600. This is our current log file; it'll be rotated nightly, and old files will be compressed. The problem is solved, and we don't have to restart Apache at regular intervals.

We can also use piped log rotation to rotate logs when they reach a certain size, and we can change the format of the log file's name. There's a lot more documentation on the Apache website.[1]

Rails Application Logs

A Rails application under heavy load creates a considerable amount of log data, so we need a strategy for dealing with that data as well. For these files, we like using logrotate, and since a Rails logrotate script doesn't come with any of the standard Linux packages, we'll need to roll our own and get it into place using Puppet.

Earlier we saw the default log rotation script that came with Apache. Our MassiveApp rotation script will have some of the same directives as that script, but we'll make a few changes.

---

1.   http://httpd.apache.org/docs/2.2/programs/rotatelogs.html

- We'll keep only the ten most recent rather than the fifty-two most recent files.

- We'll add code to restart MassiveApp to complete the log rotation.

Here's the log rotation script with those changes:

maintenance/modules/apache2/templates/logrotate_rails.conf.erb
```
<%= current_path %>/log/production.log {
  missingok
  rotate 10
  compress
  delaycompress
  postrotate
    touch <%= current_path %>/tmp/restart.txt
  endscript
}
```

We'll manage this with Puppet, and just in case we change MassiveApp's location, we'll use a Puppet template so we can plug in the path. Let's put the template in modules/massiveapp/templates/massiveapp.logrotate.conf.erb with this content:

maintenance/modules/apache2/templates/logrotate_rails.conf.erb
```
<%= current_path %>/log/production.log {
  missingok
  rotate 10
  compress
  delaycompress
  postrotate
    touch <%= current_path %>/tmp/restart.txt
  endscript
}
```

Now we'll add massiveapp module's init.pp file, which will simply put the log rotation script into place. We're setting the path to MassiveApp in a Puppet variable since that's what the template expects.

maintenance/only_template/modules/massiveapp/manifests/init.pp
```
class massiveapp {

  $current_path = "/var/massiveapp/current"

  file {
    "/etc/logrotate.d/massiveapp.conf":
      owner   => root,
      group   => root,
      mode    => 755,
      content => template("massiveapp/massiveapp.logrotate.conf.erb")
  }
}
```

The shortest built-in time interval that logrotate supplies is daily, so a logrotate script can automatically run only once a day. But let's plan ahead for a time when we're receiving a mighty volume of traffic and work around this limitation with a cron job to run our logrotate script twice a day. We can do this with the -f option, which we can leverage to force the logrotate utility to run our script on demand. Our new Puppet resource, which we'll put in the massiveapp module's init.pp to provision this cron job, specifies our twice-daily cron interval using the Ruby array notation, in other words, [0,12].

maintenance/modules/massiveapp/manifests/init.pp
```
class massiveapp {

  $current_path = "/var/massiveapp/current"

  file {
    "/etc/logrotate.d/massiveapp.conf":
      owner   => root,
      group   => root,
      mode    => 755,
      content => template("massiveapp/massiveapp.logrotate.conf.erb")
  }

  cron {
    "massiveapp_logrotate":
      command => "/usr/bin/logrotate -f /etc/logrotate.d/massiveapp.conf",
      user    => "vagrant",
      hour    => [0,12],
      minute  => "0"
  }

}
```

In the future, we'll be able to look at our metric graphs, determine the times when MassiveApp is least busy, and schedule the log rotations for those times.

Now we can run Puppet to get everything in place, and this cron will ensure that our application logs maintain a reasonable size. As a bonus, we now have a framework for easily reducing our log rotation time interval if need be.

8.2 Archiving Application Data

MassiveApp starts off with just a few records in the database, but over time a few of the tables have the potential to contain lots of rows. One table that is sure to grow quickly is the versions table. This table will get large because the Account model has auditing enabled with the has_paper_trail method call.

maintenance/account.rb
```
class Account < ActiveRecord::Base
  has_paper_trail
end
```

Since we have auditing in place here, the versions table will get a new row each time an Account is created, updated, or deleted. We can use some of the techniques we've learned in previous chapters to gather metrics around this so we can see the growth trends, but eventually the versions table will become unmanageable.

Having a complete version history in one table seems convenient, but after a while we won't need immediate access to all those version records. For MassiveApp, we feel safe saying that the time interval in which we'll need to retain records is six months. We'll always want to keep older records somewhere in case we need to look something up, but we don't need them in the main versions table. Since we can tolerate a little inconvenience in looking up these older records and since we want to keep the current versions table row count under control, we'll implement *archiving* for this table.

We'll use a simple archiving strategy; specifically, we'll use a nightly cron job and a Rake task to dump records older than six months into a backup SQL file. Once the records are backed up, we'll delete those records from our versions table.

First we dump the records, and then, if no errors occur, we delete them. We'll use a mysqldump to make the record export run quickly; ActiveRecord would just get in the way for this task. For deleting the records, we'll use a simple SQL DELETE to make it run as fast as possible as well. Here's our Rake task:

maintenance/archive.rake
```
namespace :archive do
  task :dump_old_records_to_sql => :environment do
    threshold = 6.months.ago.beginning_of_day
    next if Version.exists("item_type = ? and created_at < ?", "Account", threshold)
    outdir = ENV['OUTDIR'] || Rails.root
    outfile = File.join(outdir, "#{threshold.strftime('%Y%m%d')}.sql")
    where = "created_at < '#{threshold.strftime("%Y-%m-%d")}'"
    config = ActiveRecord::Base.configurations[RAILS_ENV]
    command = "mysqldump "
    command << " -u#{config['username']} "
    command << " -p#{config['password']} " if config['password'].present?
    command << " --single-transaction "
    command << " --quick "
    command << " --tables "
    command << " --where \"#{where}\" "
    command << " #{config['database']} "
```

```
    command << " versions "
    command << " > #{outfile} "
    # Dump the records
    `#{command}`
    # Delete the records
    Version.delete_all(["created_at < ?", threshold])
  end
end
```

To run this nightly, we'll add another cron resource to our massiveapp module.

maintenance/archive_cron/modules/massiveapp/manifests/init.pp
```
cron {
  "massiveapp_archive":
    command => "RAILS_ENV=production \
      /usr/local/bin/rake archive:dump_old_records_to_sql",
    user    => "vagrant",
    hour    => "0",
    minute  => "10"
}
```

We'll deploy massiveapp to get this new task on the server. Then we'll run Puppet to provision the cron job, and that will begin to create new SQL files each night whenever older version table rows are ready to be harvested.

As activity increases, we'll need to change this simple archiving strategy to something more scalable. For MySQL, this might mean partitioning the versions table or perhaps even moving it to a different database server. But the important thing is to be aware of high-volume fills and ensure that we have corresponding empties.

Clearing out logs and old version records protects the system from being burdened with old data, but there's a lot of data in MassiveApp that we never want to lose. To ensure we're keeping our long-term data safe, thus letting us sleep well at night, in the next section we'll set up a process for reliable backups.

8.3   Organizing Backups and Configuring MySQL Failover

MassiveApp is accumulating a lot of data, and losing that data would make our users unhappy. We need to ensure that the data that we're storing doesn't get lost through either hardware failures or programmer errors. So, we need a way to restore data if it's accidentally lost, and we can't restore data unless we back it up first. As the old saw goes, "No one cares about backing up data. Everyone cares about restoring data."

We can zero in on what data we need to back up by thinking about what we don't need to back up.

- We don't need to back up MassiveApp's source code that's deployed on our servers; if a server fails, we'll just redeploy the code to another server.

- We don't need to back up our configuration files such as my.cnf, httpd.conf, and so on. That's all generated by Puppet, and if we lose a server, we'll just use Puppet to build out a new server.

- We probably don't need to back up system or application log files. Any useful data there will be captured and summarized in our Ganglia charts.

- We don't need to back up the data that's held in memcached. The MySQL database is the authoritative source for that data, and if a memcached process goes down, we'll restart it, and it'll get repopulated.

Now we're seeing what really needs to be backed up; it's the data stored in MySQL. This contains the data that MassiveApp's users create, and we can't regenerate it with Puppet or any other piece of automation wizardry. Let's work through how we can protect this data both from hardware failure and from human errors.

Recovering from Hardware Failure

We can lose our MySQL data because of a hardware failure: a motherboard can short out, a few hard drives can die simultaneously, or the server could be physically stolen from a data center. There's not one "set in stone" way to recover from a MySQL master server failure; there's a continuum of responses based on how quickly you need to recover. At one end of the spectrum (the bad end), we have no backup MySQL server. In this situation, a master server failure means we need to provision a new server, restore from offline backups, and repoint applications manually. All that could take quite a while, and MassiveApp would be offline during that time. At the other end of the spectrum is a fully automated, seamless failover built around a network monitoring tool such as Pacemaker,[2] or maybe even failing over between different data centers.

For the purposes of this chapter, we'll pick a middle ground, where we've set up a MySQL slave to be constantly replicating, but we need to manually intervene to make MassiveApp fail over. If the replication slave is not lagging behind the master, our replication master can be destroyed, and we can get MassiveApp back into action without any data loss by repointing it to the

---

2.   http://www.linux-ha.org/wiki/Pacemaker

replication slave. This is a good system to get into place immediately, and we can then iterate toward a more automated failover system.

Let's set up a MySQL replication master and slave on several VMs to make sure we understand what's required to fail over. We'll need three virtual machines.

- A MySQL replication master server that we'll mercilessly kill at the appropriate moment

- A MySQL replication slave server that MassiveApp will fail over to

- An application server that we'll switch from the master to the slave upon failure

Let's set up these VMs. First we'll create a new directory, mysql_replication_test, and create this Vagrantfile in that directory.

```
maintenance/mysql_replication/Vagrantfile
Vagrant::Config.run do |config|
  config.vm.define :mysql_master do |m|
    m.vm.box = "lucid32"
    m.vm.host_name = 'mysql_master'
    m.vm.forward_port 3306, 3406
    m.vm.network :hostonly, "33.33.13.37"
  end
  config.vm.define :mysql_slave do |s|
    s.vm.box = "lucid32"
    s.vm.host_name = 'mysql_slave'
    s.vm.forward_port 3306, 3407
    s.vm.network :hostonly, "33.33.13.38"
  end
  config.vm.define :app do |a|
    a.vm.box = "lucid32"
    a.vm.host_name = 'app'
    a.vm.forward_port 80, 4568
    a.vm.network :hostonly, "33.33.13.39"
  end
end
```

With that Vagrantfile in place, let's start the VMs with vagrant up. This will run for about ten minutes, and we'll have a complete set of VMs to work with.

Since the point of this section is to discuss MySQL failover, we'll just set up MySQL for replication without building out a complete set of Puppet manifests. Let's start by connecting to both VMs. We'll open two separate terminal windows and in one connect into the MySQL master.

```
$ vagrant ssh mysql_master
master $
```

In the other we'll connect into the slave.

```
$ vagrant ssh mysql_slave
slave $
```

Let's get the operating system package lists updated by running the following command on both VMs:

```
master $ sudo apt-get update -y
slave $ sudo apt-get update -y
```

That should take only a few seconds. Once it's done, we can install MySQL by running apt-get on both VMs. When prompted for the MySQL password, we'll just enter root for both master and slave.

```
master $ sudo apt-get install mysql-server -y
# Lots of output, including a password prompt
slave $ sudo apt-get install mysql-server -y
# Lots of output, including a password prompt
```

After the packages are downloaded and installed, we'll have MySQL running on both boxes. Next we'll configure replication. On the mysql_master VM, let's edit the /etc/mysql/my.cnf file and uncomment the following two lines. The server-id gives this MySQL server a unique identifier that is required internally for replication, and the log_bin setting tells MySQL where to put the log files.

```
server-id    = 1
log_bin      = /var/log/mysql/mysql-bin.log
```

In the same file we also need to tell MySQL to bind to an IP address that the slave server can see, so we'll change the bind-address setting so that MySQL binds to all of mysql_master's network interfaces.

```
bind-address = 0.0.0.0
```

Now we'll restart MySQL to get these changes to take effect.

```
master $ sudo service mysql restart
mysql start/running, process 14565
```

Next let's open the permissions to allow the slave machine to connect to the master.

```
master $ mysql -uroot -proot -e "grant all on *.* to root@'%' identified by 'root'"
```

We've configured the master to allow access; now we can gather the information we'll need to set up the slave. We need to block any attempted writes and get the "master log position," which we'll use when configuring the slave so that it will know when to start receiving replication updates.

```
master $ mysql -uroot -proot -e "flush tables with read lock; show master status;"
+------------------+----------+--------------+------------------+
| File             | Position | Binlog_Do_DB | Binlog_Ignore_DB |
+------------------+----------+--------------+------------------+
| mysql-bin.000001 |      230 |              |                  |
+------------------+----------+--------------+------------------+
```

With this information, we can configure the replication slave. Moving over to our connection into mysql_slave, let's do a sanity check to ensure that the slave can communicate with the master. We're using the root user to connect along with the network information that we set up in the Vagrantfile.

```
slave $ mysql -uroot -proot -h33.33.13.37 --port 3306 -e "show databases"
+--------------------+
| Database           |
+--------------------+
| information_schema |
| mysql              |
+--------------------+
```

So, the communication lines are open. Now let's edit the slave VM's /etc/mysql/my.cnf and give it a unique server ID and a binary log. We'll also have it bind to all interfaces; we want to fail over to this machine, and thus we'll need to communicate with it from the app VM.

```
server-id = 2
log_bin      = /var/log/mysql/mysql-bin.log
bind-address = 0.0.0.0
```

And we'll restart the slave MySQL process for those changes to take effect.

```
slave $ sudo service mysql restart
mysql start/running, process 14565
```

Now we need to tell the slave where the master is located, what user account to use when connecting, and what position in the master log to use as a replication starting point. Thus, on the slave machine, we set all this in one fell swoop.

```
slave $ mysql -uroot -proot -e "change master to \
  master_host='33.33.13.37',\
  master_port=3306,\
  master_user='root',\
  master_password ='root',\
  master_log_file='mysql-bin.000001',\
  master_log_pos=230"
```

And then we actually start replicating data.

```
slave $ mysql -uroot -proot -e "start slave"
```

We can verify that data is being moved over by going to our mysql_master VM and creating a database with a table and a row or two.

```
master $ mysql -uroot -proot -e "create database repltest;\
 use repltest;\
 create table tt(id int);\
 insert into tt values (42);"
```

And over on mysql_slave we can see that the new repltest database has appeared along with its data.

```
slave $ mysql -uroot -proot repltest -e "select * from tt\G"
*************************** 1. row ***************************
id: 42
```

All is well and good; we have replication working. Now we need to get an instance of MassiveApp running on our app server and talking to our MySQL database. We went through the procedure to set up a complete Rails stack in Chapter 3, *Rails on Puppet*, on page 27, and the Puppet manifests for that are available, so we won't repeat all that here. If you went through that setup process and still have the app VM available, you can use that VM; if not, just fire up a new VM and run through that basic Rails setup again.

Welcome back. On the other end of that setup process, we have an app server that's running MassiveApp and talking to the MySQL master database server, and the MySQL master is continuing to replicate data over to the slave. So, now we can proceed with our primary goal; we want MassiveApp to fail over from the MySQL master to the slave.

We're going to kill off our master server and switch MassiveApp to read from the slave. Let's look into how exactly that "switch MassiveApp" is going to work. MassiveApp's only knowledge of the database server is encapsulated in config/database.yml. So, to make MassiveApp use a new database server, we need to modify database.yml and restart the application. Rather than changing database.yml, though, we'll add a new standby.database.yml file, which we can use to overwrite the standard database.yml. Our standby file needs to contain the network information for the slave server.

```
production:
  adapter: mysql2
  encoding: utf8
  database: massiveapp_production
  username: root
  password: root
  host: 33.33.13.38
  port: 3306
```

We also need something to get this file into place when the master fails. That sounds like a perfect job for a Capistrano task.

```
maintenance/lib/deploy/switch_to_slave.rb
namespace :deploy do
  desc "Switch application to slave server"
  task :switch_to_slave do
    standby_file = "#{current_path}/config/standby.database.yml"
    run "cp #{standby_file} #{current_path}/config/database.yml"
    deploy.restart
  end
end
```

We're ready to start our failover exercise now. We'll kill off the master just by running vagrant halt to shut down the entire VM.

```
$ vagrant halt mysql_master
[mysql_master] Attempting graceful shutdown of linux...
```

It's dead. Now we would normally receive monitoring alerts, and upon noticing that we no longer have a master database server, we'll switch to our standby. We can do this by running our Capistrano task, which copies standby.database.yml into place and restarts MassiveApp.

```
$ cap deploy:switch_to_slave
  * executing `deploy:switch_to_slave'
  * executing "cp /var/massiveapp/current/config/standby.database.yml\
 /var/massiveapp/current/config/database.yml"
    servers: ["33.33.13.39"]
    [33.33.13.39] executing command
    command finished in 161ms
  * executing `deploy:restart'
  * executing "touch /var/massiveapp/current/tmp/restart.txt"
    servers: ["33.33.13.39"]
    [33.33.13.39] executing command
    command finished in 146ms
```

With this Capistrano task execution, the application is back online, and the downtime was limited to the time between when the server was halted and when the application was restarted with the standby database.yml file.

Of course, once that cutover happened, we were placed in a precarious position since we now have no machine to fail back to. On the bright side, though, our data is still safe, and we can now begin the process of figuring out what happened to our MySQL master and how we can get back to a good place in terms of having a failover.

While going through this failover scenario, we've seen that we can use VMs to practice for when our real machines drop offline. We've also seen that a failover situation has many components that can be automated, and we can look forward to making small improvements to these procedures to reduce our downtime window by doing things faster and reducing the opportunities for human error. Thinking through executing and automating a database failover is a good exercise for your peace of mind. A few changes here and there can make the environment more resilient and prepare you for the inevitable day when hardware fails.

Recovering Deleted Data

A more exciting way to lose MySQL data is by programmer or administrator error. If we're working in the MySQL console, we're always one errant DROP TABLE away from losing data. If someone deploys a migration that deletes a few rows, it takes only a few absent-minded typos to accidentally clear out a critical table.

This situation differs from hardware failure in that a data deletion will quickly propagate to the replication slaves, thus ensuring that all our databases will be equally corrupted. Replication doesn't help here; instead, we need to have a set of offline backups that we can restore. Let's set that up now.

We'll run the backup on a replication slave. This will keep disk load off the master, which is busy keeping our MassiveApp users happy. Here's an invocation of the mysqldump utility that will safely dump a MySQL database:

```
$ mysqldump -uroot -proot --master-data \
  --quick --single-transaction \
  --triggers massiveapp | gzip > massiveapp.sql.gz
```

- The --master-data option ensures that the binary log position information is included in the dump file.

- The --quick option fetches one row at a time; this avoids problems with large tables.

- The --single-transaction option allows us to get consistent dumps of InnoDB tables without locking them.

- The --triggers option includes any database triggers in the dump file. This avoids the unpleasant surprise of restoring a database and things not working because triggers are missing.

- The | gzip part of the command pipes the output to gzip. This compresses the output and greatly reduces disk usage (albeit at the cost of CPU usage).

Running this mysqldump command hourly will give us an offline backup that's reasonably up-to-date. We can write Nagios monitors that will alert us if the database dump is taking more than a few minutes; when the time to dump the database gets to about half an hour, we can then reevaluate backup strategies. Some of the options at that point are upgrading the replication slaves to faster hardware, reducing the database dump frequency, or using filesystem snapshots to avoid needing to dump the database altogether.

Restoring data after an accidental data loss is a complicated business. There are a few scenarios to consider.

- If the data loss involves a table that doesn't change often (for example, a countries table), we can simply restore that table. The primary keys will be restored with the same values as before, so any references from other tables will be reestablished. This is a side benefit of declaring foreign keys; we can't drop a table if there are foreign keys referring to rows in that table.

- In the case of data corruption (for example, some subset of the columns in a table were nulled out or set to an incorrect value), we can reconstruct that table manually. We can restore the backed-up table to a temporary table name (for example, accounts_from_backup) and then write a SQL script (or a Rake task) to reset values in the original table. Writing such a task is a delicate procedure since we don't want to overwrite values that have been updated by the user since the errant update was made. The site may be down at this point, though, and we need to make a business decision as to whether it's more important to ensure that all data is per-fectly restored or to get the site back online. Either way, as soon as things are sorted out, we'll have another good argument for always test-running migrations on a staging server.

- The trickiest case is when we delete a swath of records from a table that has many relationships to other tables and all the dependent records have been deleted as well. In this case, we've lost an entire object graph, and restoring that manually is no small task. Depending on how far-reaching the damage is, we may want to take the main database offline for later analysis, restore the most recent backup to another server, and turn the site back on. Then we're back up and running, and we can ded-icate resources to rebuilding the lost data.

These scenarios are unpleasant to contemplate, but they're worth thinking about in advance. Reacting calmly and professionally to such a situation will pull the team closer together as well; consider that a year later, after

MassiveApp gets acquired by LargeCompany, we'll all enjoy reminiscing about the time that Tom dropped the accounts table.

Next we'll look at the dark and gloomy topic of downtime. But we'll shine the lights of automation and procedures on it and turn it into a more pleasant subject.

8.4 Making Downtime Better

As much as we do to keep MassiveApp running 24/7, there may come times when it will be unavailable. We can partition these sad times into two categories. Planned downtime happens when we explicitly take MassiveApp offline according to a prearranged schedule. Unplanned downtime is when unexpected things happen and MassiveApp goes down regardless of our wishes to the contrary.

Planned Downtime

In a perfect world, with infinitely fast servers and flawless technology, we'd never need to schedule downtime. However, the real world intrudes, and we may need to take MassiveApp offline for a variety of reasons: a data center move, an upgrade to a core service or piece of hardware, or a time-consuming database migration can all introduce outages. The goal, then, is making these planned outages cause a minimum of disturbance to our customers by a combination of planning and communicating.

Part of planning an outage is picking a time period for the outage to occur; this is called a *downtime window*. Generally, we want to schedule downtime at a time when the minimum number of people are actively using MassiveApp. The metrics that we've so painstakingly gathered will help us find that moment, and we can then set the window so it's bisected by that point. If the downtime window is in the middle of the night, we'll set two alarm clocks and get up an hour early so we'll be properly caffeinated at the start of the window. We want at least two people online during this time; having an open phone line and a second brain thinking about the procedure can avoid many an early-morning bad decision. We'll also make the downtime window an hour longer than we expect it to take; that way, we'll be happy when we beat the clock.

A second facet of planning an outage is to script out every necessary step and practice it on a nonproduction setup. This nonproduction setup may be as simple as a few Vagrant VMs running on our laptop, but the more it looks like our production setup, the better. We want the script to list all the steps at a fairly technical level of detail. For example, the script for an outage due to a long database schema change might read something like this:

1. Shut down the cron daemon on all servers (sudo /sbin/service crond stop).

2. Shut down the background workers (sudo /sbin/service workers stop).

3. Deploy the new code with the database change (cap production deploy).

4. In an after_deploy hook, publish the maintenance page *MassiveApp is now offline*.

5. Run the database schema change (RAILS_ENV=production rake db:migrate).

6. Check for schema change success by examining the output of SHOW CREATE TABLE accounts.

7. Remove the maintenance page *MassiveApp is now back online*.

8. Restart the cron daemon on all servers (sudo /sbin/service crond start).

9. Restart the background workers (sudo /sbin/service workers start).

Such a script can undergo a few iterations, and the actual MassiveApp outage time can be reduced to a minimum. This is a valuable document to keep; after a certain number of downtime windows, we may be able to use the constant need for downtime windows as part of a justification for moving part of MassiveApp to a different technology platform. At the very least, we'll have a good understanding of what a particular technology choice is costing us.

We'll communicate the downtime to MassiveApp's user base by posting to status.massiveapp.com, by presenting logged-in users with a message describing the approaching downtime, and by posting a banner on massiveapp.com during the hours leading up to the downtime. Our users won't like MassiveApp's absence, but at least it won't be unexpected. Finally, we'll want a cheery maintenance page for our customers to see when they hit the site during the downtime window. We want something that emphasizes the fact that the site is getting better, and when it comes back online, they'll see improved performance and more features.

Unplanned Downtime

Planned downtime is something we want to avoid, but we can schedule and plan and communicate and generally make it a good experience. Unplanned downtime is a different story. We can't communicate about it in advance, we can't have a script showing how to recover, and it usually happens at the most inconvenient times for our users. But all is not lost. To lessen the impact of unplanned downtime, there are a few actions we can take in advance.

First we need an escalation plan. If MassiveApp goes offline unexpectedly, our monitoring solution should notify someone. That person should have access to a list of phone numbers so that key developers can be contacted. If we have enough people on the team, we'll rotate "on-call" duty so that some folks can sleep soundly. But whoever gets the initial alert will be empowered to call in other folks to help with recovery.

Once the right people are in place, we want to get the site back online as soon as possible. There's a parallel goal of figuring out what went wrong, but we can keep digging through logs and checking metric histories after MassiveApp is back in action. This is where having several people on a conference call becomes useful again; someone can say, "Give me thirty seconds to copy over these logs," and then they can capture the data needed to pinpoint the outage issue.

Communicating with users is key in this situation. A post to the effect of "Site is down…we're working on it" on the status page can at least let the users know that you're aware of the problem. For an extended outage (that is, more than five minutes), updating the status page every fifteen minutes is a good idea. We don't want to say "We'll be back in five minutes" unless we're sure that's the case, but a post like "Recovering from backups now…75 percent done" can let the users know that we're making progress.

Finally, as with planned downtime, remaining calm, honest, and professional is important. No one wanted the downtime to happen, and everyone wants the site back online and to know the cause, so focus on those shared goals. If you made a recent change, even one that "couldn't possibly have caused a problem," then own up; someone else may connect the dots with the data that you supply. Let the scramble of an outage be one of the ties that binds the team together.

In this chapter, we've covered several important areas for keeping an application running once it's in production. We've learned more about archiving old data, managing log files, running backups, handling failures, and coordinating downtime.

## CHAPTER 9

Running Rubies with RVM

In our travels as consultants, we've seen numerous production environments where the Ruby version was not allowed to vary. The standard was set (to Ruby 1.8.7, for example), and if an application was to be deployed, it was required to work with the standard version. However, that's not always the case. A university, a research server, or even just a shared virtual machine might easily have several teams deploying Rails applications with a variety of Ruby versions.

A solution that we like for this situation is the Ruby enVironment Manager (RVM). Per that project's excellent website,[1] RVM enables us to "easily install, manage and work with multiple ruby environments, from interpreters to sets of gems." This means that one team can have a Ruby 1.9.3 application, another team can use Ruby 1.8.7, and another team can use JRuby on the same machine.

RVM is already in widespread use as a development tool for people who are working on several different Ruby applications simultaneously. In this chapter, though, we'll explore using RVM on a server, and we think you'll probably learn some techniques that will be useful in development as well.

To get acquainted with RVM on the server, let's set up a VM with two RVM-controlled Ruby installations—one of Ruby 1.8.7 and one of Ruby 1.9.3. Then we'll get a few applications running under these different Ruby versions while diving into the intricacies of RVM management.

---

1. http://rvm.beginrescueend.com/

9.1   Installing RVM

Let's start by firing up a new VM. In this case, we won't use our lucid64_with_
ruby193 base box since we want to experiment with the Ruby installation; we'll
just use the plain lucid64 base box.

```
$ mkdir ~/deployingrails/vagrant_rvm && cd ~/deployingrails/vagrant_rvm/
$ vagrant init lucid64
$ vagrant up
«lots of output»
```

Now that our VM is running, we'll ensure we're using the latest package lists,
install some development libraries, and remove the default Ruby version.

```
$ vagrant ssh
vm $ sudo apt-get update -y
vm $ sudo apt-get install build-essential zlib1g-dev libssl-dev libreadline-dev \
      git-core curl libyaml-dev libcurl4-dev libsqlite3-dev -y
«lots of output»
vm $ sudo rm -rf /opt/vagrant_ruby
```

With those libraries in place, we can install RVM. The standard method for
installing RVM is to fetch and execute a shell script that uses git to clone the
RVM source code repository.

Another option is to download the installation script and run it with various
command-line arguments (for example, ./rvm_installer.sh --version 1.8.0), but for
this demonstration, we'll just use the shortcut method and install the latest
stable version.

```
vm $ curl -L get.rvm.io | bash -s stable
«lots of output»
```

RVM is in place, but we need to enable it for this login session by reloading
our shell environment.

```
vm $ source .profile
```

Like many other Ruby utilities, RVM is primarily driven through a command-
line interface. We can verify that RVM is installed and also see detailed usage
notes by running rvm with the -h flag.

```
vm $ rvm -h
[![Build Status]\
  (https://secure.travis-ci.org/mpapis/rvm.png)](http://travis-ci.org/mpapis/rvm)

= rvm

* http://github.com/wayneeseguin/rvm
```

```
== DESCRIPTION:
```

```
RVM is the Ruby enVironment Manager (rvm).
«and more output»
```

And we can get more detailed help on any of RVM's commands by specifying
a command name.

```
vm $ rvm help install
```

```
Usage
```

```
  rvm install [ruby-string]
```

```
  For a partial list of valid ruby strings please run
```

```
    rvm list known
«and much more»
```

RVM is useful for running multiple Ruby versions, so let's install a few different
interpreters. First we'll install 1.9.3. RVM will fetch a few utilities and then
download and compile Ruby.

```
vm $ rvm install 1.9.3
Fetching yaml-0.1.4.tar.gz to /home/vagrant/.rvm/archives
Extracting yaml-0.1.4.tar.gz to /home/vagrant/.rvm/src
Configuring yaml in /home/vagrant/.rvm/src/yaml-0.1.4.
Compiling yaml in /home/vagrant/.rvm/src/yaml-0.1.4.
Installing yaml to /home/vagrant/.rvm/usr
Installing Ruby from source to: \
  /home/vagrant/.rvm/rubies/ruby-1.9.3-p194, \
  this may take a while depending on your cpu(s)...
ruby-1.9.3-p194 - #fetching
ruby-1.9.3-p194 - #downloading ruby-1.9.3-p194, \
  this may take a while depending on your connection...
«and much more»
```

Next let's install Ruby 1.8.7.

```
vm $ rvm install 1.8.7
Installing Ruby from source to: \
  /home/vagrant/.rvm/rubies/ruby-1.8.7-p358, \
  this may take a while depending on your cpu(s)...
ruby-1.8.7-p358 - #fetching
ruby-1.8.7-p358 - #downloading ruby-1.8.7-p358, \
  this may take a while depending on your connection...
«lots of output»
```

The rvm list command shows us that RVM knows about both versions.

```
vm $ rvm list

rvm rubies
   ruby-1.8.7-p358 [ x86_64 ]
   ruby-1.9.3-p194 [ x86_64 ]
```

We can easily move back and forth between the two different versions via the rvm use command.

```
vm $ rvm use 1.9.3
Using /usr/local/rvm/gems/ruby-1.9.3-p194
vm $ ruby -v
ruby 1.9.3p194 (2012-04-20 revision 35410) [x86_64-linux]
vm $ rvm use 1.8.7
Using /usr/local/rvm/gems/ruby-1.8.7-p358
vm $ ruby -v
ruby 1.8.7 (2012-02-08 patchlevel 358) [x86_64-linux]
```

This is the beauty of RVM. It uses simple commands to manage the executable path so that working with multiple Ruby interpreter versions is a breeze. It has a variety of other interesting features, but this is the heart of it.

Let's take care of a few more installation details. RVM uses .rvmrc files to determine which Ruby interpreter should be loaded. These files are shell scripts that are executed when a shell session enters a directory containing a file with that name. To manage these files, RVM includes the concept of "trusted" and "untrusted" .rvmrc files; trusted .rvmrc files are loaded automatically, whereas untrusted files need to be manually loaded. For example, if you clone a project from GitHub, you may not want to automatically trust the .rvmrc file since there's no telling what's in there. For the purposes of this overview, however, we can assume all our .rvmrc files are trusted, so we'll set that option in the vagrant user's $HOME/.rvmrc file and reload RVM's configuration.

```
vm $ echo 'export rvm_trust_rvmrcs_flag=1' >> $HOME/.rvmrc
vm $ rvm reload
RVM reloaded!
```

With that background information, let's set up a directory to hold a prospective Ruby 1.9.3 application and configure it to use RVM by creating and loading an .rvmrc file in that directory.

```
vm $ mkdir app193
vm $ echo "rvm use 1.9.3" > app193/.rvmrc
vm $ cd app193/
Using /home/vagrant/.rvm/gems/ruby-1.9.3-p194
```

And we'll set up our Ruby 1.8.7 application the same way.

Creating an .rvmrc File

In this example, we're showing how to create an .rvmrc manually. RVM also includes a command-line interface to generate an .rvmrc; we can use that by executing rvm --create --rvmrc ruby-1.9.3-p194 from a terminal. This generates a file that loads more quickly than the manually created ones, but those .rvmrc files are a bit complicated and hard to read. We usually stick with the manually created files, but the generated files can save a few seconds if there's a lot of switching between projects in your workflow.

```
vm $ cd ~/
vm $ mkdir app187
vm $ echo "rvm use 1.8.7" > app187/.rvmrc
vm $ cd app187/
Using /home/vagrant/.rvm/gems/ruby-1.8.7-p358
```

We have our two Ruby versions installed and loading in separate application directories. Now we need to set up Passenger so it can use the RVM-installed Ruby interpreters to serve applications.

9.2   Serving Applications with Passenger Standalone

In previous chapters we've configured Passenger so all the applications that it runs will use the same Ruby version. This time, though, we want to run two different applications with two different Ruby versions, and we can't put two PassengerRuby directives into our httpd.conf file. So, we'll use Passenger Standalone[2] instead.

Architecturally, Passenger Standalone runs its own web server—an nginx instance. That nginx instance listens on a port and proxies requests through to the designated Rails application. This means that Passenger Standalone can listen on an external port and serve the application by itself, or we can set it up behind a front-end web server that proxies requests back to Passenger Standalone.

In this case, we'll do the former, so let's forward several ports so that once we have Passenger Standalone running, we can do a quick check to see both applications in action.

Let's log out of the VM, edit the Vagrantfile, and configure port forwarding for ports 4000 and 4001.

---

2.   http://www.modrails.com/documentation/Users%20guide%20Standalone.html

```
rvm/with_forwarding/Vagrantfile
Vagrant::Config.run do |config|
  config.vm.box = "lucid64"
  config.vm.forward_port 3000, 4000
  config.vm.forward_port 3001, 4001
end
```

Then we'll reload the VM to enable the forwarding of those ports.

```
vm $ exit
$ vagrant reload
[default] Attempting graceful shutdown of VM...
[default] VM already created. Booting if it's not already running...
[default] Clearing any previously set forwarded ports...
«and more»
```

Next we'll connect back into the VM and set up a small Rails application for Passenger Standalone to serve.

```
$ vagrant ssh
vm $ cd app193/
Using /home/vagrant/.rvm/gems/ruby-1.9.3-p194
vm $ gem install rails -v=3.2.1 --no-rdoc --no-ri
«lots of output»
vm $ rails new .
«lots of output»
vm $ echo "gem 'therubyracer'" >> Gemfile
vm $ bundle
«lots of output»
vm $ rails generate scaffold post content:string && rake db:migrate
«lots of output»
```

A solid little Rails application is in place; now we'll install the Passenger gem.

```
vm $ gem install passenger -v=3.0.11 --no-rdoc --no-ri
Fetching: fastthread-1.0.7.gem (100%)
Building native extensions.  This could take a while...
Fetching: daemon_controller-1.0.0.gem (100%)
Fetching: passenger-3.0.11.gem (100%)
Successfully installed fastthread-1.0.7
Successfully installed daemon_controller-1.0.0
Successfully installed passenger-3.0.11
3 gems installed
```

With the gem in place, we can start Passenger Standalone and tell it to run in the background.

```
vm $ passenger start --daemonize
Nginx core 1.0.10 isn't installed

Phusion Passenger Standalone will automatically install it into:
```

```
/home/vagrant/.passenger/standalone/\
   3.0.11-x86_64-ruby1.9.3-linux-gcc4.4.3-1002/nginx-1.0.10
```

```
This will only be done once. Please sit back and relax while installation is
in progress.
«and more»
```

That was quite a flood of output. And it's doing a lot; when Passenger Standalone starts for the first time, it downloads and builds nginx and then compiles in support for Passenger. At the end of all that, we see this message:

```
=============== Phusion Passenger Standalone web server started ===============
PID file: /home/vagrant/app193/tmp/pids/passenger.3000.pid
Log file: /home/vagrant/app193/log/passenger.3000.log
Environment: development
Accessible via: http://0.0.0.0:3000/

Serving in the background as a daemon.
===============================================================================
```

Now going to http://localhost:4000/posts/ in a web browser displays our humble test application. Go ahead, create a post or two; the data will be stored in a SQLite database in the db directory. The default Rails environment is development, but we could easily start the app in production mode with Passenger's --environment flag.

We've set up one Passenger Standalone instance to run under Ruby 1.9.3; now let's set up one for Ruby 1.8.7. This is more or less the same as our 1.9.3 setup; we need to reinstall the Passenger gem since we're using a different Ruby interpreter. We also need to start Passenger Standalone on a different port, so we'll use the --port argument to start this instance on port 3001.

```
vm $ cd ~/app187/
Using /home/vagrant/.rvm/gems/ruby-1.8.7-p358
vm $ gem install rails -v=3.2.1 --no-rdoc --no-ri
«lots of output»
vm $ rails new .
«lots of output»
vm $ echo "gem 'therubyracer'" >> Gemfile
vm $ bundle
«lots of output»
vm $ rails generate scaffold game name:string && rake db:migrate
«lots of output»
vm $ gem install passenger -v=3.0.11 --no-rdoc --no-ri
«lots of output»
vm $ passenger start --port 3001 --daemonize
«lots of output»
```

We've already set up port forwarding for this second application, so we can open another browser tab to http://localhost:4001/games, and there's our Ruby 1.8.7 application, up and running. Create a few games, and feel the power of multiple Rubies.

9.3 Using Systemwide RVM

We've successfully gotten a single user account to use two different Ruby versions via RVM. If there are numerous users who need access to RVM on a single machine, though, we need to use a technique called a *systemwide* RVM installation. With a systemwide RVM installation, each user can run existing Ruby interpreters and install new interpreters as needed. Now those Rubinious users can get the latest version without waiting for a system administrator to take action.

Let's set this up. First we'll need a new VM with a simple Vagrantfile.

```
$ mkdir ~/deployingrails/vagrant_rvm2 && cd ~/deployingrails/vagrant_rvm2/
$ vagrant init lucid64
$ vagrant up
$ vagrant ssh
```

Now we're in our new VM, so let's follow the same procedures as in Section 9.1, *Installing RVM*, on page 174. We'll install the usual development packages via apt-get, uninstall the system Ruby, and so forth.

```
vm $ sudo apt-get update -y
vm $ sudo apt-get install build-essential zlib1g-dev libssl-dev libreadline-dev \
        git-core curl libcurl4-dev libsqlite3-dev bison -y
«lots of output»
vm $ sudo rm -rf /opt/vagrant_ruby
```

Next we'll install RVM. We're installing as root via sudo, so RVM will be placed into /usr/local/rvm. RVM's installation script will also put a script in /etc/profile.d/rvm.sh so that every user will have access to RVM.

```
vm $ curl -L get.rvm.io | sudo bash -s stable
«lots of output»
```

The RVM installation also creates an rvm group, and any user who needs access to install new Ruby interpreters will need to be in that group. Let's create a new user, hobo, and then we'll add both vagrant and hobo to the rvm group. We're creating the hobo user with a Bash shell; without this shell, that user account won't be able to access RVM because the proper setup scripts won't be executed.

```
vm $ sudo useradd --create-home --shell /bin/bash hobo
vm $ sudo usermod --append --groups rvm vagrant
vm $ sudo usermod --append --groups rvm hobo
```

Now let's log out of the VM entirely to ensure that the vagrant user's profile is reloaded. Then we'll log back in and install a Ruby interpreter as vagrant.

```
vm $ exit
$ vagrant ssh
vm $ rvm install 1.9.3
«lots of output, hit 'q' when prompted»
```

We didn't have to add anything to vagrant's .bash_profile or .bashrc to use RVM. This is a systemwide RVM installation, so the path management settings are contained in the global profile configuration.

So, vagrant can install a Ruby interpreter, but can the hobo account see and use that interpreter? Let's verify that.

```
vm $ sudo su -l hobo
vm $ rvm list

rvm rubies

=* ruby-1.9.3-p194 [ x86_64 ]

vm $ rvm use 1.9.3
Using /usr/local/rvm/gems/ruby-1.9.3-p194
vm $ ruby -v
ruby 1.9.3p194 (2012-04-20 revision 35410) [x86_64-linux]
```

How about the other way around? Let's install another Ruby interpreter as hobo. We'll try Rubinius; this will give your CPU a good workout as RVM builds and installs the new interpreter.

```
vm $ rvm install rbx
rbx-head installing #dependencies
Cloning git://github.com/rubinius/rubinius.git
«lots of output»
vm $ rvm use rbx
Using /usr/local/rvm/gems/rbx-head
vm $ ruby -v
rubinius 2.0.0dev (1.8.7 25e11819 yyyy-mm-dd JI) [x86_64-unknown-linux-gnu]
```

Let's go back to the vagrant user account to ensure Rubinius is available there.

```
vm $ exit
vm $ rvm list

rvm rubies
```

```
    rbx-head [ x86_64 ]
=* ruby-1.9.3-p194 [ x86_64 ]

vm $ rvm use rbx
Using /usr/local/rvm/gems/rbx-head
vm $ ruby -v
rubinius 2.0.0dev (1.8.7 25e11819 yyyy-mm-dd JI) [x86_64-unknown-linux-gnu]
```

At this point, setting up a new application to run under Passenger Standalone
with one of the installed Ruby interpreters is the same as in previous sections:
add an .rvmrc, install the appropriate gems, start Passenger Standalone, forward
ports as appropriate, and so on. And we have the added advantage of having
applications separated by the Unix filesystem permissions, so users can't
interfere with each other's applications.

The combination of RVM and Passenger Standalone makes running multiple
Ruby interpreters simultaneously reasonably straightforward. If you're in a
situation where you can't standardize on a single Ruby version, it's a big
improvement over alternatives like Mongrel.

When setting up a separate Passenger Standalone instance for each application, we introduced a new moving part for each application. If the server gets
rebooted, we need all these instances to be started. If one of them crashes,
we'd like for them to be revived without manual intervention. In the next
section, we'll look at a tool that will handle those situations for us.

9.4 Watching Passenger Standalone with Monit

Passenger Standalone is a fairly solid piece of software, but on the off-chance
that it crashes, it'd be nice to have it restarted automatically. A good tool for
monitoring local processes (and restarting them if they crash) is Monit.[3] Using
Monit with RVM introduces a few wrinkles, so let's set that up now.

First we need to install Monit; this is just a quick apt-get.

```
vm $ sudo apt-get install monit -y
```

Now we need to configure Monit to watch our Ruby 1.9.3 Passenger Standalone
instance. Monit is fairly paranoid about environment variable settings, so
we'll need to use a little RVM utility, rvm wrapper, to set up a script that Monit
will use to start Passenger Standalone. Let's generate this wrapper script.

---

3. http://mmonit.com/

```
vm $ cd app193/
Using /home/vagrant/.rvm/gems/ruby-1.9.3-p194
vm $ rvm wrapper 1.9.3 app193 passenger
```

This places a symlink to a small shell script in /home/vagrant/.rvm/bin/app193_passenger; this script will set up all the environment variables, paths, and so forth, so that Passenger Standalone can be started using the proper RVM settings.

Back to Monit. We'll store the configuration file in /etc/monit/conf.d/passenger_standalone. It's mostly self-explanatory; it needs to know how to start and stop our Passenger Standalone instance, and it can monitor the process for too much CPU or memory usage. We're using the script that we just generated with rvm wrapper, and we run our start script as the vagrant user since that's the account that owns the application directories.

rvm/monit_passenger_standalone
```
check process passenger_standalone
  with pidfile /home/vagrant/app193/tmp/pids/passenger.3000.pid
  start program = "/bin/su - vagrant -c \
    '/home/vagrant/.rvm/bin/app193_passenger start \
    --daemonize --pid-file \
    /home/vagrant/app193/tmp/pids/passenger.3000.pid'"  with timeout 5 seconds
  stop program = "/bin/su - vagrant -c \
    '/home/vagrant/.rvm/bin/app193_passenger stop \
    --pid-file \
    /home/vagrant/app193/tmp/pids/passenger.3000.pid'" with timeout 5 seconds
  if cpu > 60% for 2 cycles then alert
  if cpu > 80% for 5 cycles then restart
  if totalmem > 400.0 MB for 5 cycles then restart
```

Passenger Standalone is configured, but there are a few Monit configuration changes we need to add. Let's ensure Monit picks up our Passenger Standalone configuration file by adding a line to the main Monit configuration file.

```
vm $ sudo sh -c "echo 'include /etc/monit/conf.d/*' >> /etc/monit/monitrc"
```

And we need to tell Monit that it's configured and can start, so let's edit /etc/default/monit and modify the startup directive. We'll just change it from a 0 to a 1.

```
# You must set this variable to for monit to start
startup=1
```

Now we can use Monit to start our Passenger Standalone instance.

```
vm $ sudo monit start passenger_standalone
'passenger_standalone' process is not running
'passenger_standalone' trying to restart
'passenger_standalone' start: /bin/su
```

And we can start Monit so it'll watch Passenger Standalone moving forward.

```
vm $ sudo monit
Starting monit daemon
```

Now we can kill off Passenger Standalone, and Monit will restart it. We have another useful tool in the quest to keep applications up and running.

9.5 Contrasting Gemsets and Bundler

RVM helps manage multiple Ruby interpreters, but an application's Ruby environment is more than just the interpreter. There's also the application's gems to consider. RVM includes yet another useful feature, *gemsets*, to manage those resources. Gemsets allow an application to install its own gems into a dedicated directory. Each application can define a separate gemset, so there's no danger of mixing versions. That's been the benefit of gemsets in the pre–Rails 3 days and for non-Rails applications as well.

These days, however, Rails applications don't have as many problems with gem versions from one application conflicting with versions from another application. That's because most recently written Rails applications are using Bundler to manage gems. With Bundler, an application's gems are held in the shared/bundle directory tree within the application's deployment directory, and Bundler is configured to load gems from that path. Thus, gems are already kept separate on an application-by-application basis. With this in mind, we generally don't find that gemsets are necessary in production Rails deployments. If we're deploying an older Rails application, they are sometimes useful, but for newer applications, things just work thanks to Bundler.

9.6 Conclusion

In this chapter, we've looked at a variety of scenarios where the standard "one Ruby and Passenger per server" model didn't quite fit, and we've built good solutions for those cases using RVM and Passenger Standalone. We've also seen some of the intricacies of setting up RVM in several ways, including the configuration necessary to monitor Passenger Standalone with Monit. At this point, we're able to confidently deploy several Rails applications running different versions of Ruby to the same server, and we know how to enable developers to add and configure new Ruby versions as needed.

In the next chapter, we'll survey a few more server-side technologies that we've encountered in our Rails deployment efforts.

## CHAPTER 10

Special Topics

Thus far, we've focused largely on specific aspects of getting MassiveApp deployed and keeping it running; we've spent chapters exploring deployment, monitoring, metrics, and other major application environment areas. In this chapter, we're going to take a different approach. Rather than limiting ourselves to a particular section of MassiveApp's infrastructure, we're going to take a vertical slice through MassiveApp and its environment. We'll start at the top level by looking at the application code, and we'll move down to the bottom of the stack, that is, the operating system. As we move down the stack, we'll call out tools and techniques that we've found useful at each level.

We'll start in the MassiveApp codebase and show how to achieve better system integration by managing certain cron jobs within MassiveApp's code. Then we'll move downward to look at a general backup utility. Next we'll continue moving away from the MassiveApp code proper and toward the system by examining a popular Ruby runtime environment alternative, and finally we'll conclude at the system administration level by discussing a key security setting.

10.1 Managing Crontab with Whenever

A *cron job* is a program that a Unix system utility, cron, runs according to a schedule to accomplish some task. We've seen some examples in previous chapters, such as the metrics-gathering job in Section 7.3, *Using Ganglia Plugins*, on page 140. Cron jobs live in a gray area between the world of system resources like syslog and ntpd and the more familiar Rails application world of models and controllers. For example, as we saw in Chapter 8, *Maintaining the Application*, on page 153, a cron job to restart a system service would be straightforward to manage via Puppet. On the other hand, a cron job that sends a periodic email based on application events is more of an application resource and thus is more likely to change when the application code changes. We've found that these application-specific cron jobs are more convenient to manage from within our application's code using a handy utility named Whenever.[1]

The Whenever utility lets us define our cron jobs using a small, simple DSL within our application's codebase. It registers Capistrano hooks so that when the application is deployed, the server's cron tab is updated based on those definitions. It even registers a Capistrano rollback hook so that the cron tab is returned to its original state if anything goes wrong during deployment.

The utility is restricted by design in that the Capistrano tasks will invoke whenever on the server that we're deploying to. This means that in order for Whenever to work, the application containing the Whenever configuration must already be deployed to the target server. That's a reasonable restriction, though, given that the point of Whenever is to store cron job definitions within the application. But it's another reason why we usually separate our crons into two sets: one set that requires the application code to be deployed to the server where the cron job runs and another set that doesn't.

Let's walk through an example of Whenever in action. The first step is to add it to MassiveApp's Gemfile. We'll do this with :require => false since Whenever is a deploy-time, not a runtime, dependency of the application.

```
gem 'whenever', :require => false
```

Next we bootstrap the configuration file by running Whenever's helpful generator, wheneverize.

```
$ wheneverize
[add] writing `./config/schedule.rb'
[done] wheneverized!
```

The config/schedule.rb file that Whenever created contains a few commented-out usage examples of the Whenever DSL. Let's replace the contents of that file with the code necessary to generate a cron job that runs once each day at 6 a.m. Whenever's cron job declarations are in the format of a time specifier followed by a block containing what's supposed to happen when the cron job runs.

```
topics/config/schedule.rb
every 1.day, :at => '6:00 am' do
  runner 'Account.send_daily_activity_report'
end
```

---

1. https://github.com/javan/whenever

Our Account model needs to define the method that our cron job is calling, so we'll add that. We'll leave the actual implementation of this method for later since for now we're just getting Whenever in place.

```
topics/app/models/account.rb
def self.send_daily_activity_report
  # Collect activity for yesterday and send an email
end
```

We'll tell Whenever that we're using Bundler by setting the whenever_command variable in our config/deploy.rb. We'll also make the Whenever tasks available to Capistrano by requiring the library.

```
topics/deploy_with_whenever.rb
set :whenever_command, "bundle exec whenever"
require "whenever/capistrano"
```

Let's take a quick look at the vagrant user's existing cron tab; it should be empty.

```
vm $ crontab -l
no crontab for vagrant
```

So, this new cron job will be the first one owned by the vagrant user. Let's deploy MassiveApp and watch Whenever create the cron job.

```
$ cap deploy
«lots of output»
triggering after callbacks for `deploy:symlink'
* executing `whenever:update_crontab'
* executing "cd /var/massiveapp/current && \
  bundle exec whenever --update-crontab massiveapp --set environment=production"
servers: ["localhost"]
[localhost] executing command
** [out :: localhost] [write] crontab file updated
command finished in 822ms
«lots more output»
```

That's the deploy output; now let's check the cron tab.

```
vm $ crontab -l
# Begin Whenever generated tasks for: massiveapp
0 6 * * * /bin/bash -l -c 'cd /var/massiveapp/\
  releases/20111027035345 && \
  script/rails runner -e production \
  '\''Account.send_daily_activity_report'\'''
# End Whenever generated tasks for: massiveapp
```

Our cron job is in place, and it's invoking MassiveApp with the production environment so that all the proper configuration settings will be loaded. We can also see that Whenever wraps the cron jobs that it manages with header and footer comments, so if there are other cron jobs for a user, they won't be removed by Whenever or mixed up with the Whenever-managed jobs.

The Whenever website has copious details on Whenever configuration and customization, including notes on Rake tasks, redirecting output to an alternate file, and using Whenever with RVM. It's a great tool that's being actively developed, and we've found that it makes crons much easier to manage.

Next we'll continue our journey from the application code to the application environment; we'll look at a great utility for backing up MassiveApp's data.

10.2 Backing Up Everything

In Chapter 8, *Maintaining the Application*, on page 153, we looked at database backups. More generally, any time we need to back up data, we need to make a few choices. How much needs to be backed up? Do we back up everything or just changes since we last backed up? Should we encrypt the data, and if so, how?

Some of these questions are further complicated by command-line interfaces of the standard tools. For example, when we discussed backing up our MySQL database, we invoked mysqldump with a few flags and piped it through gzip.

```
$ mysqldump -uroot -proot --master-data \
  --quick --single-transaction \
   --triggers massiveapp | gzip > massiveapp.sql.gz
```

That's quite a flurry of options, and it's easy to lose track of what's happening, especially when several commands are piped together.

This is where the aptly named Backup[2] utility makes its entrance. Backup, to quote the website, "allows you to easily perform backup operations on both your remote and local environments. It provides you with an elegant DSL in Ruby for modeling your backups." With Backup we can set up a variety of useful backup schemes, and, as with the Whenever utility, the Backup DSL may enable us to understand what's going on when we revisit the configuration a month after setting it up.

Backing Up MySQL with Backup

Let's rework our MySQL backup script using Backup. The Backup utility is packaged as a gem, so to install it, we can just use gem install.

---

2.   https://github.com/meskyanichi/backup/#readme

```
vm $ gem install backup
```

We want to dump a MySQL database and compress the result, and Backup supports both running mysqldump and compressing the result with gzip. Backup uses a configuration file to describe the backup operations, and we can use Backup's built-in generator to create most of the contents of that file. Let's run the generator and have it create a configuration file that contains the basic ingredients to dump a MySQL database, compress the result, and store the compressed file locally.

```
$ backup generate --databases=mysql --path . --compressors=gzip --storages=local
```

And here's what we've generated in config.rb. The actual file is a bit longer, but we've removed comments and blank lines to save a little space.

```
Backup::Model.new(:my_backup, 'My Backup') do
  database MySQL do |db|
    db.name               = "my_database_name"
    db.username           = "my_username"
    db.password           = "my_password"
    db.host               = "localhost"
    db.port               = 3306
    db.socket             = "/tmp/mysql.sock"
    db.skip_tables        = ['skip', 'these', 'tables']
    db.only_tables        = ['only', 'these' 'tables']
    db.additional_options = ['--quick', '--single-transaction']
  end
  store_with Local do |local|
    local.path = '~/backups/'
    local.keep = 5
  end
  compress_with Gzip do |compression|
    compression.best = true
    compression.fast = false
  end
end
```

Clearly some parameters (username, password, and so on) need to be replaced with our settings, and only_tables is just an example of how to set that option. Let's add the MassiveApp settings and remove the example lines.

```
topics/with_compression/config.rb
Backup::Model.new(:massiveapp, 'MassiveApp Backup') do
  database MySQL do |db|
    db.name               = "massiveapp"
    db.username           = "root"
    db.password           = "root"
    db.host               = "localhost"
    db.port               = 3306
    db.socket             = "/tmp/mysql.sock"
```

```
    db.additional_options = ['--quick', '--single-transaction', '--triggers']
  end
  store_with Local do |local|
    local.path = '~/backups/'
    local.keep = 5
  end
  compress_with Gzip do |compression|
    compression.best = true
    compression.fast = false
  end
end
```

Now we can run this using Backup's perform command. Each line will be prefixed with a timestamp; we've removed that from all but the first line here for brevity.

```
$ backup perform --trigger massiveapp -d . -c config.rb
[2011/12/10 23:34:18][message] Performing backup for MassiveApp Backup!
Backup::Database::MySQL started dumping and archiving "massiveapp_development".
Backup started packaging everything to a single archive file.
Backup::Compressor::Gzip started compressing the archive.
Backup::Storage::Local started transferring \
  "2011.12.10.23.34.18.massiveapp.tar.gz".
Backup started cleaning up the temporary files.
```

Once this is done, we can see a nicely timestamped backup file in a backups directory in our home directory. We can also see that the file contains a SQL dump.

```
$ ls ~/backups/massiveapp/
2011.12.10.23.34.18.massiveapp.tar.gz
$ tar -ztf ~/backups/massiveapp/2011.12.10.23.34.18.massiveapp.tar.gz
massiveapp/
massiveapp/MySQL/
massiveapp/MySQL/massiveapp_development.sql
```

Copying a Backup to a Remote Server

Backup provides a number of mechanisms for getting the backup file off the local machine, including the ability to synchronize with Amazon's S3, the Rackspace Cloud, and Dropbox. A more prosaic option is to use scp to copy the file to a remote server. To accomplish this, let's edit config.rb and replace the store_with Local invocation with a remote storage option pointing to one of our VMs.

```
topics/with_scp/config.rb
Backup::Model.new(:massiveapp, 'MassiveApp Backup') do
  database MySQL do |db|
    db.name         = "massiveapp"
    db.username     = "root"
```

```
      db.password        = "root"
      db.host            = "localhost"
      db.port            = 3306
      db.socket          = "/tmp/mysql.sock"
      db.additional_options = ['--quick', '--single-transaction', '--triggers']
    end
    store_with SCP do |server|
      server.username = 'vagrant'
      server.password = 'vagrant'
      server.ip       = '33.33.13.38'
      server.port     = 22
      server.path     = '~/backups/'
      server.keep     = 5
    end
    compress_with Gzip do |compression|
      compression.best = true
      compression.fast = false
    end
  end
end
```

Here's a backup run with that configuration file:

```
$ backup perform --trigger massiveapp -d . -c config.rb
[2011/12/10 23:40:57][message] Performing backup for MassiveApp Backup!
Backup::Database::MySQL started dumping and archiving "massiveapp_development".
Backup started packaging everything to a single archive file.
Backup::Compressor::Gzip started compressing the archive.
Backup::Storage::SCP started transferring \
  "2011.12.10.23.40.56.massiveapp.tar.gz".
Backup started cleaning up the temporary files.
```

Now our compressed SQL file is safely on another server.

Encrypting a Backup

We can also use Backup to encrypt the file before transferring it. Let's use a symmetric key to protect our data by adding an encrypt_with block to our configuration file.

topics/with_encryption/config.rb
```
Backup::Model.new(:massiveapp, 'MassiveApp Backup') do
  database MySQL do |db|
    db.name            = "massiveapp"
    db.username         = "root"
    db.password         = "root"
    db.host            = "localhost"
    db.port            = 3306
    db.socket          = "/tmp/mysql.sock"
    db.additional_options = ['--quick', '--single-transaction', '--triggers']
  end
  store_with SCP do |server|
```

```
      server.username = 'vagrant'
      server.password = 'vagrant'
      server.ip       = '33.33.13.38'
      server.port     = 22
      server.path     = '~/backups/'
      server.keep     = 5
    end
    compress_with Gzip do |compression|
      compression.best = true
      compression.fast = false
    end
    encrypt_with OpenSSL do |encryption|
      encryption.password = 'frobnicate'
    end
  end
end
```

Now we see an encryption step being performed as part of the backup process.

```
$ backup perform --trigger massiveapp -d . -c config.rb
[2011/12/10 23:45:34][message] Performing backup for MassiveApp Backup!
Backup::Database::MySQL started dumping and archiving "massiveapp_development".
Backup started packaging everything to a single archive file.
Backup::Compressor::Gzip started compressing the archive.
Backup::Encryptor::OpenSSL started encrypting the archive.
Backup::Storage::SCP started transferring \
  "2011.12.10.23.45.33.massiveapp.tar.gz.enc".
Backup started cleaning up the temporary files.
```

Backup supports several other options including a salt setting that provides for stronger encryption.

Automating Backup with Whenever

Earlier we discussed using the whenever gem to automate cronjobs. Between whenever and backup, we can have a regular backup solution that's driven by Ruby DSLs. For example, to run our backup once a day, we'd add this to our whenever's config/schedule.rb:

```
every 1.day do
  command "backup perform --trigger massiveapp -d . -c config.rb"
end
```

Now we have both a readable backup configuration and a readable cron job definition.

Backup has a variety of other useful features including the ability to synchronize directory trees using rsync, send an email or a tweet on backup job success or failure, and break up large files into chunks. It's an excellent way to get the comfortable night's sleep that good backups can provide.

Next we'll continue our trek down to the lower levels of the stack and look at an alternative Ruby interpreter.

10.3 Using Ruby Enterprise Edition

Ruby Enterprise Edition (REE) is, per the README file, "a server-oriented distribution of the official Ruby interpreter." It's more or less the standard C Ruby 1.8.7 interpreter with improvements in the garbage collection, memory allocation, debugging, and threading subsystems. The net effect of using REE is that an application uses less memory when compared to running with the standard Ruby interpreter. For the curious, there's much more information available on the REE website.[3]

Installing and Configuring

Let's give REE a test run by installing it and setting up Passenger to use it. First let's provision a new VM without Ruby.

```
$ cd ~/deployingrails/ && mkdir vagrant_ree
$ cd vagrant_ree/
$ vagrant init lucid64
$ vagrant up
«box building output»
$ vagrant ssh
vm $ sudo apt-get update
«lots of output»
vm $ sudo apt-get install build-essential zlib1g-dev libssl-dev libreadline-dev \
        git-core curl libyaml-dev libcurl4-dev libsqlite3-dev -y
«lots of output»
vm $ sudo rm -rf /opt/vagrant_ruby
```

We'll also need Apache since we'll want to build Passenger.

```
vm $ sudo apt-get install apache2 apache2-dev -y
«lots of output»
```

Now we can fetch the most recent release of REE using curl.

```
vm $ curl --remote-name \
http://rubyenterpriseedition.googlecode.com/\
/files/ruby-enterprise-1.8.7-2012.02.tar.gz
«download progress output»
```

The REE installer is written in Ruby, but we don't need to install Ruby to run it. REE's distribution is conveniently packaged with several Ruby binaries, including a binary for the x86_64 architecture on the VM that we're using.

---

3. http://www.rubyenterpriseedition.com/

So, we'll unpack the release and run the installer, accepting the various defaults as the installer prompts for input.

```
vm $ tar -zxf ruby-enterprise-1.8.7-2012.02.tar.gz
vm $ cd ruby-enterprise-1.8.7-2012.02
vm $ sudo ./installer
«installation output»
```

And away it goes! After a good deal of CPU burn, we have REE installed in the default location, /opt/ruby-enterprise-1.8.7-2012.02. Here's a version check to ensure things are working:

```
vm $ /opt/ruby-enterprise-1.8.7-2012.02/bin/ruby -v
ruby 1.8.7 (2012-02-08 MBARI 8/0x6770 on patchlevel 358) \
[x86_64-linux], MBARI 0x6770, Ruby Enterprise Edition 2012.02
```

With a fresh installation of Ruby, one would expect to have to install RubyGems and perhaps a few gems to get moving, such as Rake, Passenger, MySQL, and so on. But no, the REE installer also downloads and installs a variety of gems. We can see the list of installed gems here:

```
vm $ /opt/ruby-enterprise-1.8.7-2012.02/bin/gem list

*** LOCAL GEMS ***

actionmailer (3.2.2)
actionpack (3.2.2)
activemodel (3.2.2)
activerecord (3.2.2)
«and many more»
```

Among those conveniently installed gems is Passenger. The gem is installed, but the Apache module isn't compiled yet, so let's take care of that now.

```
vm $ sudo \
  /opt/ruby-enterprise-1.8.7-2012.02/bin/passenger-install-apache2-module \
  --auto
«lots of output»
```

At the end of the script output we see the usual Passenger directives for pasting into our Apache configuration files; these point back to the REE installation in /opt.

REE is now installed, and it can be used exactly the same way as we'd use any other Ruby interpreter. We've done a manual installation here to show the steps involved, but a Puppet module for REE is readily available.[4]

---

4.   https://github.com/dguerri/puppet-ruby_enterprise_edition

Tuning

REE allows its garbage collector to be tuned via environment variables. This is covered in great detail in the Passenger documentation, but as a summary, here are some interesting settings and what they do:

- RUBY_HEAP_MIN_SLOTS: REE's memory manager needs a "heap slot" for each object that's instantiated as a program runs. When all the heap slots are filled, REE will create another batch of heap slots, so if there are enough to start with, Ruby doesn't have to perform this housekeeping task. The correct value for this setting will depend on how much memory is available; the setting for a server with 64GB of RAM will be much higher than the setting for a 1GB VM. For example, setting RUBY_HEAP_MIN_SLOTS to 5,000,000 immediately consumes 200MB of memory on a test VM. The default value is only 10,000, so you could easily set it to be 50 times larger on a machine containing a reasonable amount of memory.

- RUBY_GC_MALLOC_LIMIT: This is the number of C structures that REE will create before starting a garbage collection run. It defaults to 8,000,000. If it's set too low, REE will start a garbage collection run while there are still heap slots available. When you increase the heap size, you need to increase this value as well.

- RUBY_HEAP_FREE_MIN: This defines the minimum number of heap slots that should be available after a garbage collection run completes. The default value is 4,096. This is far too low as well; once started, we want a garbage collection run to free up a good deal of space so it won't have to start again for a while.

For a point of comparison, the documentation states that the engineering team at 37signals uses these settings.

```
RUBY_HEAP_MIN_SLOTS=600000
RUBY_GC_MALLOC_LIMIT=59000000
RUBY_HEAP_FREE_MIN=100000
```

You can add these environment variable settings to any place where the interpreter will pick them up. When we're running REE with Passenger, we like to add them to the Apache configuration file. For example, to set RUBY_HEAP_MIN_SLOTS to 500000 in this way, we would add the following entry to our passenger.conf:

```
SetEnv RUBY_HEAP_MIN_SLOTS 500000
```

We also put these in /etc/profile or ~/.bash_profile so that cron jobs will get the benefit of these settings.

You'll notice that there's no Ruby 1.9.3 version of REE on the site's downloads page. That's because Ruby 1.9.3 includes the GC performance enhancements that REE brings to 1.8.7. Thus, as 1.8.7 fades into the sunset, REE will as well. In the meantime, though, Ruby 1.8.7 is still in widespread use, and for those applications using 1.8.7, REE can provide a performance boost with just a little more installation complexity.

We're almost at the bottom of the technology stack. Next we'll look at one of the few security changes that we recommend for almost every production environment.

10.4 Securing sshd

A newly provisioned host that's accessible via the public Internet can be a nice target for hackers. We've seen servers be subjected almost immediately to thousands of password guesses an hour as bots from around the world attempt to log in. To gain immunity from these password-guessing (or *dictionary*) attacks, one of the first things we do when firing up a new server is to disable ssh password authentication and require public key authentication.

There are a variety of good descriptions of generating a key pair and uploading a public key, so we won't rehash that here. On the server, though, once the public key is in place, we'll shut down password authentication by editing /etc/ssh/sshd_config and changing the following line:

```
#PasswordAuthentication yes
```

to this:

```
PasswordAuthentication no
```

Then we'll signal sshd to reload its configuration file with the following:

```
$ sudo /sbin/service reload sshd
```

Just to be extra safe, while we have this ssh session open, we'll open another terminal window and establish a new ssh connection into the server. That way, we know that things are working before we log out.

We'll capture this configuration in a Puppet manifest by setting up a simple package-file-service relationship.

topics/modules/sshd/manifests/init.pp
```
class ssh {
  package {
    "ssh":
      ensure => present,
```

```
        before => File["/etc/ssh/sshd_config"]
  }
  file {
    "/etc/ssh/sshd_config":
      owner   => root,
      group   => root,
      mode    => 644,
      source  => "puppet:///modules/ssh/sshd_config"
  }
  service {
    "ssh":
      ensure    => true,
      enable    => true,
      subscribe => File["/etc/ssh/sshd_config"]
  }
}
```

We've found this approach to be superior to other dictionary attack prevention mechanisms such as scripts that watch /var/log/secure for failed ssh logins. Those can inadvertently block legitimate users who mistype their passwords a few times, and the constant scanning wastes system resources. Disabling password authentication accomplishes the same ends far more effectively.

10.5 Conclusion

There's our roundup of useful system integration tools and system administration tactics. With those in the bag, we'd like to wrap up with a couple of overall strategies for keeping your Rails infrastructure in a good position.

We've found that we should always be on the lookout for new tools and techniques. There are a variety of weekly email newsletters (for example, DevOps Weekly[5]) that report on the latest developments in the system administration and Rails development worlds. A few moments a week of skimming these newsletters will uncover suggestions that save hours of time or hundreds of lines of code. If you happen to write open source tools or have useful techniques, you can also get your ideas published by one of these newsletters, and you'll get feedback from other folks interested in the same topics. What better way to learn than from other people running large Rails applications?

Another great way to pick up new ideas is to attend local conferences and users' groups. This lets you meet others who are working on similar problems. And once you have a small network established, try to maintain that network

---

5.   http://devopsweekly.com

by meeting folks for lunch occasionally. A casual conversation with another practitioner can spark a great improvement in your setup, and being able to describe your latest problems and successes to a sympathetic and knowledgeable ear is encouraging and motivating.

Throughout this book we've stressed an incremental approach to improving your Rails application infrastructure. A large part of the work involved is not glamorous new feature development; instead, it's one-by-one additions to the monitoring system so that it informs you any time there's an anomaly. Or it's gradually collecting new pieces of data in the metrics system so you can justify the need for hardware upgrades and then demonstrate the performance benefits of those upgrades. Or it's a small change to the deployment scripts so that code is syntax-checked before it's deployed. None of these is an earth-shattering improvement, but when added up over the course of a year or so, they result in a Rails infrastructure that's a pleasure to manage and a pleasure to use.

With that, now is the time to make your Rails infrastructure a little better. Good luck!

A Capistrano Case Study

We've discussed a variety of Capistrano details in this book's two Capistrano chapters. For this appendix, we'll look at a complete Capistrano configuration example. This example was provided by Joe Kutner from his book *Deploying with JRuby*.[1] Since it's for deploying a JRuby application, it's a little different than the usual Capistrano scripts, so that opens up room for exploration.

Let's dive right in and look at the details of this deployment script.

A1.1 Requires and Variables

The file starts with the usual require statement to bring in Bundler's Capistrano scripts.

capistrano_case_study/config/deploy.rb
```
require 'bundler/capistrano'
```

We'll see a few variable declarations related to Bundler a bit later. The most important bit for now, though, is that requiring Bundler brings in the bundle:install hook that runs after deploy:finalize_update so the application's gems will be installed.

Next up is a server declaration. This uses the shorthand notation to declare that localhost is serving in both the app and db roles.

capistrano_case_study/config/deploy.rb
```
server "localhost", :app, :db, :primary => true
```

A longer version of this would be the role-centric usage.

```
role :app, 'localhost'
role :db, 'localhost', :primary => true
```

---

1. http://pragprog.com/book/jkdepj/deploying-with-jruby

But for simple deployments, the one-liner is sufficient. As we discussed in Section 5.3, *Restricting Tasks with Roles*, on page 85, the server list can also be loaded from an external file, so there's a lot of flexibility available here.

Next up are the connection options; in this case, we have a port specification for our VM and a reference to the Vagrant insecure private key.

capistrano_case_study/config/deploy.rb
```
ssh_options[:port] = 2222
ssh_options[:keys] = "~/.vagrant.d/insecure_private_key"
```

Capistrano's ssh_options variable is passed to the Net::SSH library after being merged with any host-specific settings in the ~/.ssh/config file. For example, placing the following settings in ~/.ssh/config would make these ssh_options variables unnecessary:

```
Host localhost
  Identity /your/home/directory/.vagrant.d/insecure_private_key
  Port 2222
```

If you're having problems getting Capistrano to connect to a server, it's worth checking your ~/.ssh/config for any conflicting settings.

Next we have several user-related variables.

capistrano_case_study/config/deploy.rb
```
set :user, "vagrant"
set :group, "vagrant"
set :use_sudo, false
```

The user setting can also be supplied by ~/.ssh/config. It overrides ssh_options[:username] if that setting is also specified. The group variable is not actually used by any of the default tasks; instead, it's just available to be used by any custom tasks. use_sudo tells Capistrano whether to use sudo when attempting to run various commands on the host to which it's connecting.

The next two variables contain application-related data:

capistrano_case_study/config/deploy.rb
```
set :deploy_to, "/opt/trinidad"
set :application, "twitalytics"
```

The application setting is used by the default deploy tasks as part of the directory path to which the application is being deployed. For example, a setting of twitalytics results in the application being deployed to /u/apps/twitalytics. In this case, we're setting a deploy_to directory explicitly, so that's where the application will be deployed.

Next up are several source code management (SCM) settings.

```
capistrano_case_study/config/deploy.rb
set :repository, "."
set :scm, :none
set :deploy_via, :copy
set :copy_strategy, :export
set :copy_exclude, [".git","log","tmp","*.box","*.war",".idea",".DS_Store"]
```

This deployment script is a little out of the ordinary in that it's not pulling the source code from a repository. Instead, per the repository variable, it's using the code in the current directory. This is a useful technique when you want to be able to deploy code without it necessarily being committed to a remote repository. In this case, we need to use the copy deploy strategy since once Capistrano establishes an SSH connection into the remote server, the code won't be available. Specifying the export strategy here is not strictly necessary since the Capistrano SCM class for the repository option none aliases checkout to export. The copy_exclude setting is useful for removing files that are in the repository but don't need to be deployed; as demonstrated here, it accepts file glob patterns like *.war.

The next settings are for Bundler and for setting certain environment variables.

```
capistrano_case_study/config/deploy.rb
set :default_environment,
  'PATH' => "/opt/jruby/bin:$PATH",
  'JSVC_ARGS_EXTRA' => "-user vagrant"
set :bundle_dir, ""
set :bundle_flags, "--system --quiet"
```

The Bundler directory would normally go in the shared directory, but because of the way the application server (Trinidad) handles RubyGem paths, it's set to the root of the deployed application. The default_environment setting ensures the specified environment variables are available to all commands.

A1.2 Hooks and Tasks

Next we have a before hook and a task for managing Bundler installation.

```
capistrano_case_study/config/deploy.rb
before "deploy:setup", "deploy:install_bundler"

namespace :deploy do
  task :install_bundler, :roles => :app do
    run "sudo gem install bundler"
  end
end
```

This ensures that Bundler is installed on all the app servers before the application is deployed. This is an alternative to the method that we discussed in Section 3.5, *Creating the MassiveApp Rails Directory Tree*, on page 47 where we install Bundler with Puppet. One minor improvement here might be to use the Capistrano sudo method, which overrides the use_sudo variable and forces the command to be run using sudo.

```
sudo "gem install bundler"
```

Then we have several life-cycle hooks for the Trinidad server, which runs Rails applications inside Apache Tomcat.[2] These override the default deploy:stop, deploy:start, and deploy:restart tasks.

capistrano_case_study/config/deploy.rb
```
namespace :deploy do
  task :start, :roles => :app do
    run "/etc/init.d/trinidad start"
  end

  task :stop, :roles => :app do end

  task :restart, :roles => :app do
    run "touch #{current_release}/tmp/restart.txt"
  end
end
```

Like Passenger, Trinidad watches the tmp/restart.txt file and reloads the application's code when that file's modification time changes.

Finally, here's the entire file:

capistrano_case_study/config/deploy.rb
```
require 'bundler/capistrano'

server "localhost", :app, :db, :primary => true

ssh_options[:port] = 2222
ssh_options[:keys] = "~/.vagrant.d/insecure_private_key"

set :user, "vagrant"
set :group, "vagrant"
set :use_sudo, false

set :deploy_to, "/opt/trinidad"
set :application, "twitalytics"

set :repository, "."
```

---

2.   http://tomcat.apache.org/

```
set :scm, :none
set :deploy_via, :copy
set :copy_strategy, :export
set :copy_exclude, [".git","log","tmp","*.box","*.war",".idea",".DS_Store"]

set :default_environment,
  'PATH' => "/opt/jruby/bin:$PATH",
  'JSVC_ARGS_EXTRA' => "-user vagrant"
set :bundle_dir, ""
set :bundle_flags, "--system --quiet"

before "deploy:setup", "deploy:install_bundler"

namespace :deploy do
  task :install_bundler, :roles => :app do
    run "sudo gem install bundler"
  end

  task :start, :roles => :app do
    run "/etc/init.d/trinidad start"
  end

  task :stop, :roles => :app do end

  task :restart, :roles => :app do
    run "touch #{current_release}/tmp/restart.txt"
  end
end
```

If you find other useful Capistrano tactics, let us know.[3] We're always interested in hearing about novel Rails deployment ideas!

---

3.   http://forums.pragprog.com/forums/197

Running on Unicorn and nginx

In this book, we've focused on Apache and Passenger because we feel it's a high-quality technology stack that can be set up quickly and can scale to handle a tremendous load. However, an alternative stack is rapidly gaining in popularity, and it deserves a mention.

This alternative consists of two high-quality open source components. The first is nginx,[1] an HTTP server. A major advantage of nginx is its nonblocking architecture, which allows it to handle vast numbers of clients without creating a thread or process for each connection. For example, a mobile (in other words, smartphone) client application may request an HTML page that the server application can generate in only a few milliseconds, but the mobile client may have limited bandwidth and thus take five or ten seconds to download the page. At scale, maintaining a thread or process for each such request can cause a server to run out of available socket connections while still having plenty of CPU capacity to spare.

The other component is Unicorn,[2] which, per its website, is "an HTTP server for Rack applications designed to only serve fast clients on low-latency, high-bandwidth connections and take advantage of features in Unix/Unix-like kernels." Unicorn is very effective when paired with a front-end HTTP server such as nginx. Clients make HTTP requests to nginx, nginx then forwards to Unicorn, Unicorn builds and returns the response, and nginx takes care of feeding data to the client as quickly as the bandwidth allows. Like Passenger, Unicorn runs each Rails application instance in its own process, so there are no thread-safety concerns. Also like Passenger, Unicorn manages a pool of workers, so there's no need to allocate a block of ports as needed with Mongrel.

---

1. http://nginx.org
2. http://unicorn.bogomips.org/

Now let's jump in to getting MassiveApp running using these technologies.

A2.1 Installing and Configuring nginx

First let's install nginx on a new VM; we'll need a working directory.

```
$ mkdir ~/deployingrails/nginx
$ cd ~/deployingrails/nginx
```

We'll use our standard lucid64_with_ruby193 base box. We also want to access an HTTP service on this VM, so we'll forward a host port to port 80 on the guest. Here's our Vagrantfile:

unicornnginx/Vagrantfile
```
Vagrant::Config.run do |config|
  config.vm.box = "lucid64_with_ruby193"
  config.vm.forward_port 80, 4567
end
```

Now we can start the VM and connect.

```
$ vagrant up
«lots of output»
$ vagrant ssh
vm $
```

We'll install nginx using apt-get and then start a new nginx process.

```
vm $ sudo apt-get install nginx -y
Reading package lists... Done
Building dependency tree
«and more»
vm $ sudo /etc/init.d/nginx start
Starting nginx: the configuration file /etc/nginx/nginx.conf syntax is ok
configuration file /etc/nginx/nginx.conf test is successful
nginx.
```

Now when we point a browser to port 4567 on our host, we see a cheery "Welcome to nginx!" greeting, so that verifies we have nginx installed and running.

We can trace the path nginx took to display this greeting by starting with the main nginx configuration file, /etc/nginx/nginx.conf. That file contains an http block that has serverwide configuration settings; one of them is an include directive that loads all the configuration files in /etc/nginx/sites-enabled/.

```
include /etc/nginx/sites-enabled/*;
```

The /etc/nginx/sites-enabled/ directory contains one symlink, default, which links to /etc/nginx/sites-available/default. In that file we see a server block that defines the configuration for the default virtual host, one part of which is a location block specifying the root directory.

```
location / {
  root   /var/www/nginx-default;
  index  index.html index.htm;
}
```

And if we look in /var/www/nginx-default/index.html, we see the default server message in a trivial HTML page.

```
$ cat /var/www/nginx-default/index.html
<html>
<head>
<title>Welcome to nginx!</title>
</head>
<body bgcolor="white" text="black">
<center><h1>Welcome to nginx!</h1></center>
</body>
</html>
```

So, we have nginx up; now we need to hook it to MassiveApp. To do this, we'll define an nginx *upstream* to point to where we'll be running MassiveApp. We will make this change in /etc/nginx/sites-available/default at the top of the file. We're naming the upstream after the application that it'll be serving, and we're specifying a fail_timeout value of 0 since that forces nginx to retry a request in case the Unicorn worker times out.

```
upstream massiveapp {
  server unix:/tmp/.sock fail_timeout=0;
}
```

Now we'll modify the server block so that it proxies requests through to MassiveApp. The Unicorn documentation has copious notes[3] on this configuration, but to summarize, nginx is serving static files, is setting forwarding-related headers, and is proxying all nonstatic requests through to MassiveApp.

```
server {
  listen   80 default;
  server_name  localhost;
  root   /var/massiveapp/current/public/;
  access_log  /var/log/nginx/localhost.access.log;
  try_files $uri/index.html $uri.html $uri @app;
  location @app {
    proxy_set_header X-Forwarded-For $proxy_add_x_forwarded_for;
    proxy_set_header Host $http_host;
    proxy_redirect off;
```

---

3. http://unicorn.bogomips.org/examples/nginx.conf

```
    proxy_pass http://massiveapp;
  }
}
```

That's our nginx configuration. A quick sudo /etc/init.d/nginx restart, and nginx is ready to go. Now we'll look at the changes necessary to run MassiveApp on Unicorn.

A2.2 Running MassiveApp on Unicorn

Getting Unicorn running requires that we make a few changes to the MassiveApp codebase to accommodate it; to summarize, we'll be referencing Unicorn in the Gemfile, adding a Unicorn configuration file, and modifying the Capistrano configuration. We cloned the MassiveApp Git repository in Section 1.3, *Learning with MassiveApp*, on page 7, so we'll move into that directory.

$ **cd ~/deployingrails/massiveapp/**

We've built a with_unicorn branch containing all the changes in this chapter. If you'd like to use that branch, just check it out with git checkout --track with_unicorn; if not, just add the changes as we describe them.

Unicorn is delivered as a RubyGem, so we'll add an entry to the Gemfile.

```
gem 'unicorn'
```

We'll need to run bundle to get that gem installed, of course. Next, we need to tell Unicorn how to run MassiveApp; that configuration goes in config/unicorn.rb. The Unicorn project has excellent notes[4] on this configuration file, but most of the settings are just telling Unicorn where MassiveApp lives, where to log, and so forth. One interesting part is the before_fork hook, which is called for each worker and allows new workers to shut down old workers.

unicornnginx/config/unicorn.rb
```
worker_processes 4
working_directory "/var/massiveapp/current" # available in 0.94.0+
listen "/tmp/.sock", :backlog => 64
timeout 30
pid "/var/massiveapp/shared/pids/unicorn.pid"
stderr_path "/var/massiveapp/shared/log/unicorn.stderr.log"
stdout_path "/var/massiveapp/shared/log/unicorn.stdout.log"
preload_app true
GC.respond_to?(:copy_on_write_friendly=) and GC.copy_on_write_friendly = true

before_fork do |server, worker|
  defined?(ActiveRecord::Base) and ActiveRecord::Base.connection.disconnect!
```

---

4.   https://github.com/defunkt/unicorn/blob/master/examples/unicorn.conf.rb

```
    old_pid = "#{server.config[:pid]}.oldbin"
    if old_pid != server.pid
      begin
        sig = (worker.nr + 1) >= server.worker_processes ? :QUIT : :TTOU
        Process.kill(sig, File.read(old_pid).to_i)
      rescue Errno::ENOENT, Errno::ESRCH
      end
    end
  end
end

after_fork do |server, worker|
  defined?(ActiveRecord::Base) and ActiveRecord::Base.establish_connection
end
```

That's it for application-specific configuration. Now we'll configure Capistrano to deploy Unicorn.

A2.3 Deploying to nginx and Unicorn

We've set up nginx to pass requests to MassiveApp, and we've configured MassiveApp to run inside Unicorn. Now we'll modify our Capistrano configuration to deploy MassiveApp to Unicorn rather than Passenger.

We'll add just one line to config/deploy.rb.

```
set :bundle_cmd, "/usr/local/bin/bundle"
```

More significantly, we'll delete the Passenger-related task definitions; deploy:start, deploy:stop, and deploy:restart can all be removed. With those gone, we can add replacement tasks in lib/deploy/unicorn.rb. The new deploy:start task runs Unicorn in the context of MassiveApp and ensures it uses the configuration we added in the previous section. The deploy:stop task uses the process ID to kill the Unicorn master process. Lastly, the deploy:restart task sends a USR2 signal to Unicorn; when combined with the before_fork that we added to config/unicorn.rb, this enables a zero downtime deployment.

unicornnginx/lib/deploy/unicorn.rb
```
set :unicorn_config, "#{current_path}/config/unicorn.rb"
set :unicorn_pid, "#{current_path}/tmp/pids/unicorn.pid"

namespace :deploy do
  task :start, :roles => :app, :except => { :no_release => true } do
    run "cd #{current_path} \
      && #{bundle_cmd} exec unicorn -c #{unicorn_config} -E #{rails_env} -D"
  end
  task :stop, :roles => :app, :except => { :no_release => true } do
    run "#{try_sudo} kill `cat #{unicorn_pid}`"
  end
end
```

```
task :restart, :roles => :app, :except => { :no_release => true } do
  run "#{try_sudo} kill -s USR2 `cat #{unicorn_pid}`"
end
end
```

With those changes in place, we can plunge ahead and deploy MassiveApp.
We'll assume that the VM has been provisioned with the Puppet scripts that
we've prepped in previous chapters, so we can get MassiveApps in place by
running the usual tasks.

```
$ cap deploy:setup
«lots of output»
$ cap deploy:cold
«lots of output»
  * executing `deploy:start'
  * executing "cd /var/massiveapp/current
    && /usr/local/bin/bundle exec
    unicorn -c /var/massiveapp/current/config/unicorn.rb -E production -D"
    servers: ["localhost"]
    [localhost] executing command
    [localhost] sh -c 'cd /var/massiveapp/current
    && /usr/local/bin/bundle exec
    unicorn -c /var/massiveapp/current/config/unicorn.rb -E production -D'
    command finished in 1954ms
```

Now we can browse to localhost:4567 and see MassiveApp up and running.
Subsequent deploys will have slightly different output because they'll use our
deploy:restart task.

```
$ cap deploy
«lots of output»
  * executing "kill -s USR2 `cat /var/massiveapp/current/tmp/pids/unicorn.pid`"
    servers: ["localhost"]
    [localhost] executing command
    [localhost] sh -c
    'kill -s USR2 `cat /var/massiveapp/current/tmp/pids/unicorn.pid`'
    command finished in 5ms
```

And there we have it—an end-to-end deployment using Unicorn and nginx.

A2.4 Where to Go Next

In Section 9.2, *Serving Applications with Passenger Standalone*, on page 177,
we discussed Passenger Standalone and how it uses a combination of nginx
and Passenger to serve applications. We applied it in the context of running
multiple Ruby versions on a server, but using nginx as a front-end server for
any Rails application is a useful option. Even a somewhat old-school cluster

of Mongrel instances could be placed behind an nginx process to improve performance and scalability.

Once a team has some collective knowledge of how to operate and tune nginx, it's worth a look around to see whether there are other places where it can be employed. For example, we've seen nginx used effectively as a front-end server in place of a more traditional HTTP load balancer like haproxy.[5] In this scenario, an nginx upstream can be pointed to any number of back-end application servers. Each back-end server can be configured with a weight to send more traffic to the more capable servers, a maximum number of failures can be set before a server is taken out of the loop, and various other useful load-balancing parameters are available. nginx can even serve as an SSL decryption layer to offload the SSL handshake computations from application servers.

The combination of nginx and Unicorn is an interesting alternative to Apache and Passenger. It's certainly worth a look if you don't have a lot of experience with Apache or if you're running into any Apache/Passenger-related problems.

5.   http://haproxy.1wt.eu/

Bibliography

[Bar08]   Wolfgang Barth. *Nagios: System and Network Monitoring.* No Starch Press, San Francisco, CA, 2nd, 2008.

[Koc08]   Wojciech Kocjan. *Learning Nagios 3.0.* Packt Publishing, Birmingham, UK, 2008.

Index

A

Amazon EC2, 3, 9

Apache
configuration files, 36–38, 41–43
configuring for Ganglia, 133
configuring for Nagios, 100–101
configuring for Passenger, 51–53, 60
configuring for REE, 194
htpasswd, 100
installing with Puppet, 33–44, 59
log rotation, 154–155
piped log rotation, 155–156

Apache Tomcat, 202

application failover, 161, 165–166

application hosting, 1–5

application maintenance
data archiving, 158–160
data backups, 160–161, 167–168, 188–192
data loss, 168–169
database migrations, 74
downtime, 169–171
log management, 153–158
release deployment, 75, 210

application metrics, 143–148

application monitoring, 121–124, 128

automation philosophy, 6–7

B

Backup utility
automating backups, 192
copying to remote server, 190–191
encrypting backups, 191–192
installing, 188
MySQL database backups, 188–190

base boxes (Vagrant), 16–18

Bundler
installing Capistrano, 63
installing with Puppet, 49
and mysql2 gem, 64
vs. RVM gemsets, 184

C

Capfile, 64

capify, 64

Capistrano
application failover, 166
Capistrano shell, 90–93
Capistrano::CLI, 78
$CAPISTRANO:HOST$, 84
capture method, 89
command-line utility, 63
copy strategy, 66–67
creating deployment configurations, 65–67
database migrations, 74
deployment hooks, 77–79
file uploads/downloads, 83–85
hooks from Whenever utility, 186
JRuby case study, 199–203
multistage deployment, 87–88
pushing a release, 69–75
put method, 84
recipes, 64
remote commands, 88–93
roles, 66, 77, 79–80, 85–86
setting up, 62–65
ssh key pairs, 62, 200
ssh port forwarding, 66
stream method, 90
subdirectory setup, 68–69
symlinks in bulk, 81–83
tasks, 67, 76–77
timestamped filenames, 71
Unicorn deployment, 209
variables, 65–67
wiki, 77

Chef, 29

cloud hosting, 3–4

config.vm.customize, 19, 25

config/deploy.rb, 65–67

copy_exclude, 201

cron jobs
data archiving, 159–160
log rotation, 158
managing with Whenever, 185–188
metrics gathering, 142–143

D

data archiving, 158–160

data backups, 160–161, 167–168, 188–192

data loss, 168–169

database, *see* MySQL

deploy, 75

deploy:cold, 69–75
deploy:setup, 68–69
deploy:symlink override, 81–83
DevOps, 5–7
downtime planning, 169–171

E

Engine Yard, 4

F

facter utility, 30
failover, 161, 165–166

G

Ganglia
    Apache configuration, 133
    clusters, 134, 139
    configuration files, 134–137
    custom metrics with Ruby, 146–148
    integration with Nagios, 148
    plugins, 140–146
    Puppet module for, 131–140
    reasons for selecting, 129
    remote host monitoring, 138–143
    Vagrant setup for, 130–131
    web interface, 137–138
Ganglia plugin repository, 140
gmetad daemon, 132–133, 135, 151
gmetric scripts, 140–146, 151
gmond daemon, 131, 133, 135, 139, 150

H

Heroku, 2–3
hooks (Capistrano), 77–79, 201–202
hosting alternatives
    buying servers, 4
    cloud hosting, 3–4
    outsourcing, 1–3
    renting servers, 4

J

JRuby application deployment, 199–203

L

load balancing, 211
log management, 153–158

M

manifests (Puppet), 27
    Apache example, 33–44, 59
    MySQL example, 44–47
MassiveApp, *see also* application maintenance; application metrics; application monitoring
    deploying with Capistrano, 64–67, 69–75
    Git repositories, 8
    setup, 47–50
metaparameters, 42
modules (Puppet), 38–41
Mongrel, 205, 211
Monit, 182–184
monitoring concepts, 95, 105–106
monitoring *vs.* metrics, 129
multistage deployment, 87–88
Murder deployment tool, 80
MySQL
    archiving records, 159–160
    configuring with Puppet, 44–47
    database backups, 167–168, 188–192
    failover setup, 162–165
    gmetric scripts for, 141
    native extension and Bundler, 64
    replication slaves, 162–165
    restoring data, 168–169
mysqldump, 167–168

N

Nagios
    Apache configuration, 100–101
    browser interface, 102, 125
    checking Passenger, 117–121
    checking Rails, 128
    checks, 100
    concepts and terminology, 105–106
    configuration files, 107–108
    defining new commands, 121
    file management with Puppet, 108–109
    immediate checks, 102–105
    inheritance, 107
    integration with Ganglia, 148
    monitoring applications, 121–124, 128
    monitoring database backups, 168
    monitoring local resources, 106–110
    monitoring Nagios server, 107
    monitoring remote services, 110–121
    notification strategies, 125
    NRPE plugin, 112–115
    object definitions, 107–108, 127–128
    Puppet module for, 98–105
    reasons for choosing, 95–96
    Vagrant setup for, 96–97
Nagios Exchange, 126
nginx, 205–211
    configuring, 206–208
    installing, 206
    for load balancing, 211
    nonblocking architecture, 205
    and Passenger Standalone, 177, 179
nodes (Puppet), 54
NRPE
    installing, 112–115
    monitoring application servers, 115–116
    monitoring memcached, 116–117
    monitoring Passenger, 117–121

O

Oracle VirtualBox, *see* VirtualBox

P

Pacemaker, 161
Passenger
    installing with Puppet, 50–54

monitoring with Nagios, 117–121
Standalone monitoring and restarting, 182–184
Standalone setup, 177–180
performance
    Capistrano overhead, 82
    load balancing, 211
    nginx nonblocking architecture, 205
    Ruby Enterprise Edition, 193–196
    server metrics, 129, 131–138
    shared hosting, 2
    Unicorn *vs.* Passenger, 205
    VM, 3
Pingdom, 107
port forwarding, 15, 20, 43, 177
public key authentication, 15, 62, 196–197
Puppet
    apply subcommand, 32
    vs. Chef, 29
    classes, 39
    command-line utility, 32
    configuration language, 57
    dependencies, 41
    describe subcommand, 34, 42
    environments, 57
    file management, 36–38
    flow control, 57
    help, 32
    installing, 30–32
    manifests, 27
    --meta option, 42
    metaparameters, 42
    modules, 38–41
    multiple hosts, 54
    nodes, 54
    --noop option, 37
    package management, 34–35
    pre-install setup, 28
    resource declarations, 34–36
    Ruby gems, 49
    stages, 57
    subcommands, 32
    --verbose option, 33
Puppet Dashboard, 57

PuppetForge, 58
PuppetMaster, 57

R

Rackspace Cloud, 3, 9
Rails
    application log rotation, 156–158
    building directory tree in Puppet, 47–49
    checking, with Nagios, 128
    precompiling static assets, 73
Rake
    db:create *vs.* Puppet, 45
    monitoring application data thresholds, 122–123, 128
Redis, 85
release deployment, 75, 210
rmc wrapper, 182
roles (Capistrano)
    defining, 79, 85–86
    predefined, 66, 80
    ROLES environment variable, 80, 86
    in tasks, 77, 80, 85–86, 199
Rubinius, 181
Ruby
    custom metrics for Ganglia, 146–148
    installing gems in Puppet, 49
    multiple versions, 175–177
    multiple versions in Passenger, 177–180
    updating in Vagrant base box, 16–18
Ruby Enterprise Edition (REE)
    installing, 193–194
    tuning, 195–196
RVM (Ruby enVironment Manager), 173
    installing, 174
    systemwide installation, 180–182
    usage, 174–177
.rvmrc files, 176–177

S

server metrics, 129, 131–138
server monitoring, 95–121

shared hosting, 1–2
ssh
    and Capistrano overhead, 82
    key pairs, 15, 62, 196–197
    monitoring, 110–112
    port forwarding, 66
    securing sshd, 196–197
    ssh_options, 200

T

Trinidad, 202

U

Ubuntu, 12
Unicorn, 205–211
    configuring, 208–209
    installing, 208

V

Vagrant
    box index, 12
    bridged networking, 24
    configuring networks, 19–20
    creating a VM, 12–15
    customizing VMs, 16–19, 25
    Ganglia setup, 130–131
    installing, 11
    managing VMs, 15
    multiple VMs, 21–24
    MySQL failover setup, 162
    Nagios setup, 96–97
    port forwarding, 15, 20, 43
    including Puppet, 55–56
    setting VirtualBox options, 19
    sharing folders, 20
    ssh key pairs, 15
virtual private servers, 3
VirtualBox
    guest additions, 14
    installing, 10
    setting options in Vagrant, 19
    VM naming, 22
VM outsourcing, 3–4, 9
VM tools, 10–24

W

Whenever, 185–188
    automating backups, 192

Go Beyond with Rails and JRuby

There's so much new to learn with Rails 3 and deploying on the Java VM. These titles will get you up to speed on the latest.

Thousands of developers have used the first edition of *Rails Recipes* to solve the hard problems. Now, five years later, it's time for the Rails 3.1 edition of this trusted collection of solutions, completely revised by Rails master Chad Fowler.

Chad Fowler
(350 pages) ISBN: 9781934356777. $35
http://pragprog.com/titles/rr2

Deploy using the JVM's high performance while building your apps in the language you love. JRuby is a fast, scalable, and powerful JVM language with all the benefits of a traditional Ruby environment. See how to consolidate the many moving parts of an MRI-based Ruby deployment onto a single JVM process. You'll learn how to port a Rails application to JRuby, get it into production, and keep it running.

Joe Kutner
(224 pages) ISBN: 9781934356975. $33
http://pragprog.com/titles/jkdepj

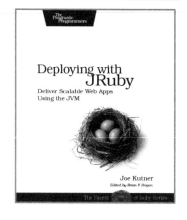

Welcome to the New Web

You need a better JavaScript and more expressive CSS and HTML today. Start here.

CoffeeScript is JavaScript done right. It provides all of JavaScript's functionality wrapped in a cleaner, more succinct syntax. In the first book on this exciting new language, CoffeeScript guru Trevor Burnham shows you how to hold onto all the power and flexibility of JavaScript while writing clearer, cleaner, and safer code.

Trevor Burnham
(160 pages) ISBN: 9781934356784. $29
http://pragprog.com/titles/tbcoffee

CSS is fundamental to the web, but it's a basic language and lacks many features. Sass is just like CSS, but with a whole lot of extra power so you can get more done, more quickly. Build better web pages today with *Pragmatic Guide to Sass*. These concise, easy-to-digest tips and techniques are the shortcuts experienced CSS developers need to start developing in Sass today.

Hampton Catlin and Michael Lintorn Catlin
(128 pages) ISBN: 9781934356845. $25
http://pragprog.com/titles/pg_sass

Pragmatic Guide Series

Get started quickly, with a minimum of fuss and hand-holding. The Pragmatic Guide Series features convenient, task-oriented two-page spreads. You'll find what you need fast, and get on with your work.

Need to learn how to wrap your head around Git, but don't need a lot of hand holding? Grab this book if you're new to Git, not to the world of programming. Git tasks displayed on two-page spreads provide all the context you need, without the extra fluff.

NEW: Part of the new *Pragmatic Guide* series

Travis Swicegood
(160 pages) ISBN: 9781934356722. $25
http://pragprog.com/titles/pg_git

JavaScript is everywhere. It's a key component of today's Web—a powerful, dynamic language with a rich ecosystem of professional-grade development tools, infrastructures, frameworks, and toolkits. This book will get you up to speed quickly and painlessly with the 35 key JavaScript tasks you need to know.

NEW: Part of the new *Pragmatic Guide* series

Christophe Porteneuve
(160 pages) ISBN: 9781934356678. $25
http://pragprog.com/titles/pg_js

Testing is only the beginning

Start with Test Driven Development, Domain Driven Design, and Acceptance Test Driven Planning in Ruby. Then add Cucumber and friends for the ultimate in Ruby and Rails development.

Behaviour-Driven Development (BDD) gives you the best of Test Driven Development, Domain Driven Design, and Acceptance Test Driven Planning techniques, so you can create better software with self-documenting, executable tests that bring users and developers together with a common language.

Get the most out of BDD in Ruby with *The RSpec Book*, written by the lead developer of RSpec, David Chelimsky.

David Chelimsky, Dave Astels, Zach Dennis, Aslak Hellesøy, Bryan Helmkamp, Dan North
(448 pages) ISBN: 9781934356371. $38.95
http://pragprog.com/titles/achbd

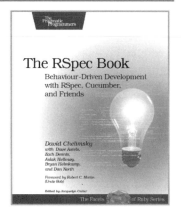

Your customers want rock-solid, bug-free software that does exactly what they expect it to do. Yet they can't always articulate their ideas clearly enough for you to turn them into code. *The Cucumber Book* dives straight into the core of the problem: communication between people. Cucumber saves the day; it's a testing, communication, and requirements tool – all rolled into one.

Matt Wynne and Aslak Hellesøy
(250 pages) ISBN: 9781934356807. $30
http://pragprog.com/titles/hwcuc

Advanced Ruby and Rails

What used to be the realm of experts is fast becoming the stuff of day-to-day development. Jump to the head of the class in Ruby and Rails.

Rails 3 is a huge step forward. You can now easily extend the framework, change its behavior, and replace whole components to bend it to your will, all without messy hacks. This pioneering book is the first resource that deep dives into the new Rails 3 APIs and shows you how to use them to write better web applications and make your day-to-day work with Rails more productive.

José Valim
(184 pages) ISBN: 9781934356739. $33
http://pragprog.com/titles/jvrails

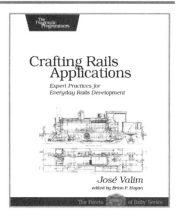

As a Ruby programmer, you already know how much fun it is. Now see how to unleash its power, digging under the surface and exploring the language's most advanced features: a collection of techniques and tricks known as *metaprogramming*. Once the domain of expert Rubyists, metaprogramming is now accessible to programmers of all levels—from beginner to expert. *Metaprogramming Ruby* explains metaprogramming concepts in a down-to-earth style and arms you with a practical toolbox that will help you write great Ruby code.

Paolo Perrotta
(296 pages) ISBN: 9781934356470. $32.95
http://pragprog.com/titles/ppmetr

Learn a New Language This Year

Want to be a better programmer? Each new programming language you learn teaches you something new about computing. Come see what you're missing in new languages and the latest crop of NoSQL databases.

You should learn a programming language every year, as recommended by *The Pragmatic Programmer*. But if one per year is good, how about *Seven Languages in Seven Weeks*? In this book you'll get a hands-on tour of Clojure, Haskell, Io, Prolog, Scala, Erlang, and Ruby. Whether or not your favorite language is on that list, you'll broaden your perspective of programming by examining these languages side-by-side. You'll learn something new from each, and best of all, you'll learn how to learn a language quickly.

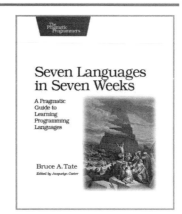

Bruce A. Tate
(328 pages) ISBN: 9781934356593. $34.95
http://pragprog.com/titles/btlang

Data is getting bigger and more complex by the day, and so are your choices in handling it. From traditional RDBMS to newer NoSQL approaches, *Seven Databases in Seven Weeks* takes you on a tour of some of the hottest open source databases today. In the tradition of Bruce A. Tate's *Seven Languages in Seven Weeks*, this book goes beyond a basic tutorial to explore the essential concepts at the core of each technology.

Eric Redmond and Jim Wilson
(330 pages) ISBN: 9781934356920. $35
http://pragprog.com/titles/rwdata

The Pragmatic Bookshelf

The Pragmatic Bookshelf features books written by developers for developers. The titles continue the well-known Pragmatic Programmer style and continue to garner awards and rave reviews. As development gets more and more difficult, the Pragmatic Programmers will be there with more titles and products to help you stay on top of your game.

Visit Us Online

This Book's Home Page
http://pragprog.com/titles/cbdepra
Source code from this book, errata, and other resources. Come give us feedback, too!

Register for Updates
http://pragprog.com/updates
Be notified when updates and new books become available.

Join the Community
http://pragprog.com/community
Read our weblogs, join our online discussions, participate in our mailing list, interact with our wiki, and benefit from the experience of other Pragmatic Programmers.

New and Noteworthy
http://pragprog.com/news
Check out the latest pragmatic developments, new titles and other offerings.

Save on the eBook

Save on the eBook versions of this title. Owning the paper version of this book entitles you to purchase the electronic versions at a terrific discount.

PDFs are great for carrying around on your laptop—they are hyperlinked, have color, and are fully searchable. Most titles are also available for the iPhone and iPod touch, Amazon Kindle, and other popular e-book readers.

Buy now at *http://pragprog.com/coupon*

Contact Us

Online Orders:	*http://pragprog.com/catalog*
Customer Service:	*support@pragprog.com*
International Rights:	*translations@pragprog.com*
Academic Use:	*academic@pragprog.com*
Write for Us:	*http://pragprog.com/write-for-us*
Or Call:	+1 800-699-7764